The ONE YEAR®
BOOK OF

DEVOTIONS
FOR
WOMEN
ON THE GO

The ONE YEAR®
BOOK OF

DEVOTIONS
FOR Women
on the Go

STEPHEN
ARTERBURN
AND
PAM FARREL

TYNDALE HOUSE PUBLISHERS, INC.
WHEATON, ILLINOIS

Visit Tyndale's exciting Web site at www.tyndale.com

TYNDALE is a registered trademark of Tyndale House Publishers, Inc.

Tyndale's quill logo is a trademark of Tyndale House Publishers, Inc.

The One Year Book of Devotions for Women on the Go

Copyright © 2004 by Stephen Arterburn. All rights reserved.

The One Year is a registered trademark of Tyndale House Publishers, Inc.

Cover photograph by Amber Burger. Copyright © 2004 by Tyndale House Publishers, Inc. All rights reserved.

Author photograph of Stephen Arterburn copyright © by David Riley & Associates. All rights reserved.

Author photograph of Pam Farrel copyright © 2004 by Ken Hansen/Hansenphoto.com. All rights reserved.

Designed by Beth Sparkman

Edited by Susan Taylor and Cheryl Crews

Published in association with the literary agency of Alive Communications, Inc., 7680 Goddard Street, Suite 200, Colorado Springs, CO 80920.

Where noted, some devotions contain excerpts from Pam Farrel, *Woman of Influence: Ten Traits of Those Who Want to Make a Difference* (Downers Grove, Ill.: InterVarsity Press, 1996).

Unless otherwise indicated, all Scripture quotations are taken from the *Holy Bible,* New Living Translation, copyright © 1996. Used by permission of Tyndale House Publishers, Inc., Wheaton, Illinois 60189. All rights reserved.

Scripture quotations marked NIV are taken from the *Holy Bible,* New International Version®. NIV®. Copyright © 1973, 1978, 1984 by International Bible Society. Used by permission of Zondervan Publishing House. All rights reserved.

Scripture quotations marked KJV are taken from the *Holy Bible,* King James Version.

Scripture quotations marked "NKJV" are taken from the New King James Version. Copyright © 1979, 1980, 1982, 1991 by Thomas Nelson, Inc. Used by permission. All rights reserved.

Scripture quotations marked NASB are taken from the *New American Standard Bible,* copyright © 1960, 1962, 1963, 1968, 1971, 1972, 1973, 1975, 1977, 1995 by The Lockman Foundation. Used by permission.

Scripture quotations marked AMP are taken from *The Amplified Bible.* Old Testament copyright © 1965, 1987 by The Zondervan Corporation. *The Amplified New Testament* copyright © 1958, 1987 by The Lockman Foundation. Used by permission.

Scripture quotations marked CEV are taken from the Contemporary English Version, copyright © 1991, 1992, 1995 by American Bible Society. Used by permission.

Scripture quotations marked *The Message* are taken from *THE MESSAGE.* Copyright © 1993, 1994, 1995, 1996, 2000, 2001, 2002. Used by permission of NavPress Publishing Group.

Library of Congress Cataloging-in-Publication Data

Arterburn, Stephen, date.
   The one year book of devotions for women on the go / Stephen Arterburn with Pam Farrel.
      p. cm.
Includes bibliographical references and index.
ISBN 0-8423-5757-2 (pbk.)
1. Christian women—Prayer-books and devotions—English.   2. Devotional calendars.   I. Farrel, Pam, date.
II. Title.
BV4844.A78   2004
242′.643—dc22   2004005999

Printed in the United States of America

10   09   08   07   06   05
7   6   5   4   3

❀ ❀ ❀

To Robin, for praying me through.
To my Young Women of Influence group: mentoring you
brings me joy, hope, and the promise that God is passing
the baton of faith securely to the next generation.
To all my fellow "on the go" friends who read this book:
may God meet you as you read it in the same way
he met me while I wrote it!

The Lord God is our light and protector. He gives us
grace and glory. No good thing will the Lord withhold
from those who do what is right.

PSALM 84:11

INTRODUCTION

You look at your watch—no time! You look at your to-do list—no time! Does everyone seem to want a piece of you? Does it seem as if the more you give, the more people want from you? Do you wonder how you can give any more or go any more? Has your "get up and go" gone? If so, this devotional is for you. It is for any woman who wants to grow in a relationship with God and go through her busy, on-the-go days with God.

Within its pages you will discover timeless truths from God's Word that will revive, restore, reenergize, and renew you; principles to help you cope with crushing circumstances and nagging irritations; suggestions to help stabilize your life for success in the long haul. You'll also find ideas for strengthening your intimate relationship with God and with others, as well as ways to cope with emotions and fears common to women. You might think of the devotions as spiritual vitamins or a protein bar for producing character on the run. I know this because I wrote them on the go: my days are filled with speaking schedules, three teenagers, writing projects, responsibilities as a pastor's wife, and our ministry, *Masterful Living.*

God is so personal. He meets us where we are: waiting for kids at soccer or ballet practice; dragging home bone tired at the end of a rugged workday, or rushing out the door for the daily commute. Our full schedule doesn't affect his presence with us. He is right there, just waiting for you to carve out a few minutes so that he can give you a glimmer of hope or a nugget of wisdom from his Word.

Tuck the *One Year Book of Devotions for Women on the Go* in your glove compartment, your briefcase, your purse, in your desk, or in your nightstand. Make a commitment to God that you will give him at least five minutes every day. He longs to give you rest and refreshment, and he promises to meet you wherever you are—even on the go!

Pam Farrel   ❀ ❀ ❀

January

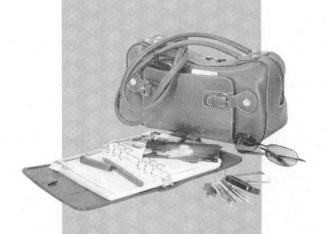

TO READ
Proverbs 2:1-11

Tune your ears to wisdom, and concentrate on understanding. . . . Then you will understand what it means to fear the Lord, and you will gain knowledge of God. PROVERBS 2:2, 5

First Things First

Sometimes on our daily path in our relationship with God, spending time with him can seem like just one more thing on an already long to-do list. With responsibilities that seem to keep us unendingly on the go, it's easy to lose perspective about exactly why we *need* to spend time in God's Word daily. And yet God's Word itself promises wonderful benefits to those who will take the time to pursue wisdom:

> My child, listen to me and treasure my instructions. Tune your ears to wisdom, and concentrate on understanding. Cry out for insight and understanding. Search for them as you would for lost money or hidden treasure. Then you will understand what it means to fear the Lord, and you will gain knowledge of God. For the Lord grants wisdom! From his mouth come knowledge and understanding. He grants a treasure of good sense to the godly. He is their shield, protecting those who walk with integrity. He guards the paths of justice and protects those who are faithful to him.
>
> Then you will understand what is right, just, and fair, and you will know how to find the right course of action every time. For wisdom will enter your heart, and knowledge will fill you with joy. Wise planning will watch over you. Understanding will keep you safe. (Proverbs 2:1-11)

Doesn't this seem like a great deal? If you have spent years second-guessing yourself, the wisdom in God's Word builds confidence in decision making. If you have felt like a victim in some aspect of your life, God's Word is a shield, and God is a protection. If you are depressed, God's Word gives comfort and knowledge that are pleasant to your soul. If you are struggling with the consequences of unwise or foolish choices, God's Word can teach you discretion that will protect and guard you from this point forward. Considering all the benefits of gaining God's wisdom, our busy days will go much more smoothly once we have God's wisdom firmly in our minds and hearts.

TO READ
2 Corinthians 4:16-18

That is why we never give up. Though our bodies are dying, our spirits are being renewed every day.

2 CORINTHIANS 4:16

 ## Can or Can't

"Whether you say you can or you can't, you are probably right." This is one of my son Zach's favorite coaching quotes.

Recently I was attending the All-star National Cheerleading competition, where my son, Zach, was on the team.

Going into stiff competition, Zach's team was favored to win the nationals and had been working hard to prepare for this day. During warm-ups, Andre, one of the team members, dislocated a shoulder. He was one of the key "stunters," and at many points in the routine he needed to lift another cheerleader above his head, a move requiring split-second timing. There was no room for delay or error. Somehow Andre managed to pop his shoulder back into place, but every time he tried to raise his arm over his head, the pain was so excruciating that tears would run down his cheeks. (And strapping young men like Andre don't cry!)

The team was worried about Andre. They knew the pressure he felt—and the pain. Although Andre was new to his faith, he had heard verses such as, "I press on toward the goal" (Philippians 3:14, NIV). But how was he going to do that?

Laying my hand on his shoulder, I prayed that God would give him strength and send Andre someone who could help him. Immediately after I prayed, another coach noticed that Andre was in pain and offered medical help.

We all held our breath and prayed as the team performed with so much responsibility resting on Andre. In spite of his pain, Andre pushed through—and they won the national title.

He could have said, "I can't," but Andre chose to go forward and say, "I can."

I stay awake through the night, thinking about your promise. PSALM 119:148

 ## Promises, Promises

Creating your own Bible promise book can help you navigate through the pain of grief, divorce, illness, or job loss. God knows what your pain is, and his Word can be a healing balm.

You might decide to use three-by-five-inch cards, a small journal, or a perpetual calendar. To make a calendar, simply have 365 index cards or similar-sized paper bound together at your local printer.

One of these calendars was given to me a year ahead by a group that had scheduled me to speak. A small group committed to use a calendar with my name in it to pray for me each day! What a gift!

Inscribe in the front of your book the promises about the promises:

"Deep in your hearts you know that every promise of the Lord your God has come true. Not a single one has failed!" (Joshua 23:14).

"Your promises have been thoroughly tested; that is why I love them so much" (Psalm 119:140).

Devotionals can also be a way to keep hearts of friends and family connected over the miles. One Christmas my mother gave every daughter and daughter-in-law in our family the same quiet-time book and journal. When we saw each other throughout the year, we shared promises that we had gleaned from God for our own lives and one another's lives.

Share a precious promise today.

TO READ
Romans 15:1-7

May God, who gives this patience and encouragement, help you live in complete harmony with each other—each with the attitude of Christ Jesus toward the other. ROMANS 15:5

 ## Circle of Support

Friends, family, and colleagues: As you live out your calling, you will need a circle of support. The Bible calls this *koinonia,* or partnership. How can you cultivate those relationships with others so that they understand and can share in your vision?

Be honest: Share your story. Let them see how God brought you to the point of change or calling. The more personal the time is when you share your experience, the more likely the sharing will go well. When you share one-on-one, you give people the opportunity to ask questions, which helps with clarity.

Be in contact: When you have a vision, it is easy to run ahead of the pack. Be selective about what you share. Break down the change or calling into bite-size pieces. When I was in my first month as director of women's ministries, I saw a plan for personal and leadership development clearly in my mind. I invited the women of our church over to hear my vision; I laid out a time-consuming challenge, then called for a huge commitment. I look back now at the time and energy those first team members invested, and I am amazed that seven hung in there with me that first year.

I soon realized that God had given me an ability to see the full picture all at once. When others couldn't see the full me picture, the path ahead, they could stay with me in the vision only if I broke the plan down a bit. So I adjusted my expectations, and then more of my support team could run with me.

Make it easier for people to want to run with you as you live out your vision.

TO READ
Luke 12:42-48

And the Lord replied, "I'm talking to any faithful, sensible servant to whom the master gives the responsibility of managing his household and feeding his family." LUKE 12:42

 ## Faithful in All Things

The number one trait that workers say they desire in a boss or leader is integrity. Integrity will help you build a team, it may help you secure financing for the dream, and it will be the honey that draws people to you and the plan to make a difference. When you step out to make a difference, what builds your integrity with others?

Integrity Is Built By

Consistent work ethic: A proven track record is vital. Matthew 25:23 says, "You have been faithful with a few things; I will put you in charge of many things" (NIV). Do the small things well—no matter how mundane. If you have been assigned small things, do them with excellence, and more and greater things will be given to your charge.

Consistent behavior: When I have spoken with the children of highly visible Christian leaders, I always ask, "What did your parents do right?" The number one answer is, "My parents had integrity. They were the same at home as in the pulpit." Be dependable; have self-restraint, self-control, and self-respect! Before you make a decision, ask, "Does this build my reputation or tear it down?"

Florence Littauer says, "Do what you do better than anyone else doing it, and you'll always be a success."

TO READ
1 Peter 5:6-11

Be careful! Watch out for attacks from the Devil, your great enemy. He prowls around like a roaring lion, looking for some victim to devour. 1 PETER 5:8

 Off the Sideline!

Sometimes when we're challenged, it's easier to step off to the sideline. While writing *Woman of Influence*, a book to encourage and equip women to be all God designed them to be, I sent the book out for outside critique. When it was returned with notes from the critics and the editor, I was to take out one hundred pages. Although the criticisms were helpful, some hurt. Like the one that said, "I'm not sure English is her first language." But the one that really stung was, "Not sure I'd want to be her friend." After building my whole ministry on relationships, I felt as if I'd failed God.

I had only a few weeks to get the manuscript in shape and return it to the publisher—and now I wasn't sure I had anything to say! I went to a conference begging God to work, but I felt no one should follow me anytime, any place, for any reason! At the end of the conference, I finally asked for prayer—I got off the sideline. I went home the following day, and it was as if the text were highlighted. I knew exactly what to take out and save for the next book. *Woman of Influence* has gone into multiple printings and helped women launch businesses, ministries, and careers.

Satan knew influence for God might happen, so he tried to sideline me. The Bible warns of this in 2 Corinthians 11:3: "I am afraid that just as Eve was deceived by the serpent's cunning, your minds may somehow be led astray from your sincere and pure devotion to Christ" (NIV). So if you doubt, go back to a sincere and devoted commitment to Christ. Be honest, seek help, and ask for prayer! Get off the sideline!

TO READ
Philippians 3:12-14

I strain to reach the end of the race and receive the prize for which God, through Christ Jesus, is calling us up to heaven. PHILIPPIANS 3:14

 ## *Eye on the Goal*

I was a competitive gymnast growing up. To perform a medal-winning beam routine, I had to keep my eyes on a fixed point ahead to keep my balance. To look down or look away would mean a fall. The writer of the book of Hebrews understood this, so he encouraged those in the persecuted church to "fix [their] eyes not on what is seen, but on what is unseen (2 Corinthians 4:18, NIV). "Fix your thoughts on Jesus" (Hebrews 3:1, NIV). "Let us fix our eyes on Jesus" (Hebrews 12:2, NIV).

In these verses the word *fix* means "to reach a goal, fix, or look attentively at the goal in front of you:

Picture it! Cut out pictures of the goal. If you are raising funds for a project, keep the renderings in front of your desk. If you have a goal of writing, tear the best-seller list from the newspaper and hang it on the refrigerator. If you are losing weight, place pictures of the outfit you'll wear when you reach your goal.

Chart it! Plan out step-by-step how you will attain the goal. I use a chart that looks like a set of stairs. I put the long-term goal at the top of the stairs; then I break it into smaller steps with due dates for each step. If you are trying to get out of debt, make a graph so you can see your progress.

Write it! Place motivational, inspirational quotes all over your mirror, on your desk, or on your file cabinet. Choose your favorite verses, those that give you emotional and physical strength.

Think it! Create your own motivational tape, or listen to speeches and sermons from the leaders who inspire you to excel.

As you focus on your goal, you will see your success as well.

TO READ
Psalm 23:1-6

He lets me rest in green meadows; he leads me
beside peaceful streams. PSALM 23:2

 Cultivating the Quiet

First Peter 3:4 explains that a gentle and quiet spirit is of great worth in
God's sight. With less and less "white space," or margin, in our lives, it is
hard to find a moment's silence. A quieted heart is a receptive heart—so
how can you find or create a quiet place?

Look along the path: Find a table in the corner of a quiet coffee shop, a
comfy chair in a hotel lobby, or a bench in a park or by the water. There are
quiet places all along our everyday path, but we fail to see them most days.

Look away from the crowd: Grab a backpack and head to the hills, to a lake,
to the beach, or to a rooftop. Go away from the crowd—walk on a cloudy
day, go to the zoo in the rain, or rise earlier than the norm.

Look in your home: What robs the quiet? Turn off the TV, the radio, and
the stereo. Fold up the newspaper, and walk into your own backyard. Sit
under a tree—or up in one. Hang a hammock or a front porch swing.
Create a quiet place.

Look at your schedule: Is everyone always talking to you or talking at you?
Is every waking moment full? Take an eraser, and remove 30 percent of
your obligations for a week—you'll find some quiet space.

Cultivate the quiet spirit in a quiet place.

TO READ
James 4:7-10

Draw close to God, and God will draw close to you.

JAMES 4:8

 ## *Alone with God*

Spending time with God is crucial for us in order to change and move ahead. Apart from God we're stuck in old lies, old habits, old unhealthy relationships, etc.

But how can you spend quality and quantity time with God? In my book *Woman of Influence*, I list thirty ways to wake up a quiet time. You can look up those ideas later if you like, but what is most important is your desire to build into the relationship. Can you say, like David: "I wait for the Lord, my soul waits, and in his word I put my hope" (Psalm 130:5, NIV).

Splurge on your relationship with God. Get some tools to help you hear his voice louder than other voices. Since the Bible is God's love letter to humankind, collect some tools to help you get more out of the letter.

A concordance: My favorite is Wordsearch, a computer software program to find verses by looking up words, phrases, or references. There are many software options, and there are also many hardback versions, including *Strong's Exhaustive Concordance*. Find a concordance that can help you locate verses to answer the questions on your heart.

A Bible dictionary and encyclopedia: There are words, people, and customs in the Bible that are new or different from your everyday life. You'll gain more from a passage of Scripture if you understand its historical and cultural relevance too. Again, computer software, such as iLumina, can be a great tool for expanding your knowledge and understanding of what the Bible says.

A journal: Write out your questions, your impressions, your feelings— write back to God!

TO READ
Luke 6:27-36

Love your enemies! Do good to them! Lend to them! And don't be concerned that they might not repay. LUKE 6:35

 ## EGR: Extra Grace Required

One of my friends describes those hard-to-love people in our lives as EGRs: Extra Grace Required. Often, EGR people can be naysayers. When you feel you need to convince them of your point of view, instead, make it a priority to love them by faith. The Bible puts it simply: "We who are strong ought to bear with the failings of the weak" (Romans 15:1, NIV). How can you bear with someone you can barely bear?

Try to identify one positive trait in him or her, focusing all your attention there. One woman came to me wanting to leave her spouse because she had no romantic feelings for him anymore. "He never does anything romantic! He just sits there!" I said, "Before you leave, let's pray and see if God can show you one positive trait in him." So she prayed and came back saying, "I thought of one—he's still here!"

We brainstormed a list of positive ways to say, "You're here!" So she would see him sitting in his recliner, then walk by and say kindly, "It's nice having you around." Or she would pat his shoulder and say, "It's nice some things in life remain the same, isn't it?"

Then one day he got up out of that recliner, came in, and started asking her spiritual questions. The next Sunday he was in church, where he's been ever since.

Sometimes the grace we give can be God's vehicle into the heart of the one we can't "bear."

TO READ
Mark 9:17-29

This kind can be cast out only by prayer. MARK 9:29

 ## I've Been Praying for You!

Around the lunch table we shared our personal testimonies. Mark began, "My girlfriend in high school came to me and said, "I can't keep dating you. I can't be unequally yoked."

"What do I have to do with an egg?"

"No, not that kind of yolk. Never mind, just come to church with me this week."

"Sure," Mark said.

At church that week Mark heard a clear presentation of the gospel. Later that night he prayed, "God, I don't know everything. I don't know much of anything, but I do know that if all the stuff I heard today is true, and I think it is, I need you."

Then Mark called his girlfriend and said, "Hey, I'm one of you."

"What? What do you mean?"

"You know that prayer, I prayed it."

"You mean you asked Jesus into your heart?"

"Yes."

Then Mark went to youth group. When he walked in, his girlfriend told everyone that Mark had received Christ.

"Hey, Mark! I've been praying for you! What took you so long?"

Mark thought, *Took me so long—I just heard this God stuff a few days ago.* Later in the evening he learned his friends from school who were in the youth group had been fasting one day a week and praying for months that he would come to faith. They could see his heart and his pain, and they knew God was the answer. Have you prayed for the passion, plan, and people God has laid on your heart?

TO READ
Mark 16:15-18

Go into all the world and preach the Good News to everyone, everywhere. MARK 16:15

 ## Out of the Pew

My friend Phoebe O'Neal is an amazing woman. Married to a minister, Glenn, who went on to become the dean of Talbot Seminary, Phoebe was active in mentoring young seminary wives, me included. Over the years Phoebe shared many profound things, but one stands out. As a widow in her seventies, Phoebe was worried about one of her younger family members. So she began to spend time with him, share her faith with him, and love him, hoping to get him reconnected to God. What she didn't expect was that her own connection to God would be strengthened.

After one conversation with this young man, he said, "If you really believe all this stuff about Jesus—like if you don't have a relationship with Jesus, you won't be in heaven—you should tell people."

"I am. I am telling you."

"But if you really think people are going to hell, you should be telling everyone, everywhere."

Phoebe took this as a challenge, and she started looking for ways to tell everyone in her world. She held coffees at her home, worked in a crisis pregnancy clinic—she got out of the pew and into the world.

"Pam, his comment was a wake-up call. He said, 'If you believe it, you should tell everyone you meet!' That sounds a lot like Jesus when he said, 'Go into all the world and preach the good news to everyone, everywhere.' So that's what I am going to do."

Have you gotten out of your pew?

TO READ
2 Peter 3:13-18

Grow in the special favor and knowledge of our Lord and Savior Jesus Christ. 2 PETER 3:18

 ## *Progress to Perfection*

Carissa has come a long way. She has overcome being abandoned by her birth mother and stepmother, the drug-overdose death of her father, and abandonment by her first husband. But she still avoids driving mountain roads—too scary!

Skye has experienced life-changing faith that turned her from a former flower child and free spirit into a serious parent and teacher, but she is still afraid to fly.

Sandy is a strong leader, a role model to younger Christian girls, and a Bible teacher, yet she feels weak at the knees if she's asked to speak in front of a large group.

Renee used to be afraid of leaving her home, meeting new people, and making phone calls—people basically freaked her out. Now she is out of the house for work and church, but she still feels her chest tighten when she's forging new relationships. Small talk is fine, but somewhere in each new friendship she has to fight the impulse to run away.

Works in progress. Why do we feel that if we are not perfect, we are a failure or "less than" another in spirituality or emotional health? Romans 8:1 proclaims, "There is no condemnation for those who belong to Christ Jesus." *Condemnation* means there is now no adverse sentence.

Quit overreacting to your shortcomings. Let's give a new definition to emotional well-being: progress. Movement, not perfection, should be our goal. Next time you are feeling guilty that you are afraid to drive in traffic or don't want to fly alone, call one of your less-than-perfect friends, own up to the fear, ask for prayer, refuse the guilt, and walk forward knowing there is a whole team of imperfect people—in fact all of humanity—backing you up.

TO READ
John 21:4-12

When Simon Peter heard that it was the Lord, he put on his tunic (for he had stripped for work), jumped into the water, and swam ashore.

JOHN 21:7

 Take the First Step

Every single day she walked across the street. Renette was living in a white barrio, and hope, to her, seemed just across the street. She would stand for hours and wait until I finished teaching a class of children. I would always walk over and say the simplest thing, "How are you today?"

That's all it would take for her to peek from behind her long disheveled bangs and answer. At first with just a shrug, then with a word or two, like "Okay, I guess." She'd walk with me to my car, often carrying files or boxes—anything to delay reentry into her house.

I knew I'd broken through when one day she said, "I don't want to go home." Then came the story: an alcoholic mother and an abusive stepfather. Mom's anger would be sparked by the slightest offense, and Renette would get hit with the nearest object: an iron, a TV cord, a catalog, or a pan.

"Honey, call the police, they will help."

"No, they won't," she replied. "I am eighteen. They say I don't have to live there. But where will I go?"

"Anywhere, somewhere—I'll help you find somewhere!"

Are you feeling like Renette? There is a somewhere. There's always somewhere when you reach out for help from a stable person who cares. It may feel like a leap, a jump into the unknown, but the smartest step Renette made was that first step to cross the street to meet a woman who seemed kind to children. Take a step.

TO READ
Ephesians 2:1-10

It wasn't so long ago that you were mired in that old stagnant life of sin. You let the world, which doesn't know the first thing about living, tell you how to live. . . . We all did it, all of us doing what we felt like doing, when we felt like doing it.

EPHESIANS 2:1-3, *The Message*

Drama Queen

She was delightful. She was kind, stable, friendly, sweet, and a quiet joy. But she once commented, "As my kids got older, like all teens, they were out with friends more and more. Sometimes I wondered if it was because we weren't very exciting."

Excitement is way overrated, especially the excitement that comes from living in danger. Drama, trauma, conflict, and crisis—that is a usual day for many women. Is that how you define being "alive"? Are you bored if the day is simply full of responsibility and duty? It's easy to become addicted to the adrenaline of conflict and chaos. We exchange stability for scenes straight from the soaps.

In the path to wellness, there will be many boring days. Many days will be full of nothing but responsibility, self-discipline, and hard work. But the life of stability builds the potential for excitement minus the drama or trauma! I think that's why Jesus used this example: "Therefore everyone who hears these words of mine and puts them into practice is like a wise man who built his house on the rock. The rain came down, the streams rose, and the winds blew and beat against that house; yet it did not fall, because it had its foundation on the rock" (Matthew 7:24-25, NIV).

How can you move away from desiring unhealthy excitement that puts you in danger or continual drama and move toward the kind of healthy excitement that develops from newfound opportunity when you reach out to your God-given potential? The key to hope is self-control, plain and simple—doing what's right no matter what you *feel* like doing.

TO READ
James 5:13-20

Confess your sins to each other and pray for each other so that you may be healed. JAMES 5:16

 Bad Coffee

Karin ruled her family with her explosive, irrational anger. Her children and grandchildren never knew what would set her off. It felt like being air-dropped into the minefields of Afghanistan—everyone knew they had to get out, but everyone was too afraid to take a step.

Out of the blue, on a family trip to an amusement park, Karin stopped in the middle of the crowded cobblestone pathway and screamed at her children and grandchildren. They were in "the happiest place on earth," but Mama wasn't happy—again. All the daughters-in-law quickly escorted the grandchildren out of earshot while Karin unleashed her venom. Even strangers passing with their children gave Karin a wide birth. Finally, her two sons were able to get Karin to lower her voice as she continued to rant and rave. Her answer was to leave the family, abandoning the family event, and she pursued her own plan.

No one in the family knew where she went, until her husband called a few days later. While dad conversed with his adult children, Karin got on the phone and said, "Oh dear, wasn't the park just awful? I got ahold of some bad coffee and just wasn't myself."

From then on, any time Karin had an outburst, she blamed it on "bad coffee." Do you have some "bad coffee"?—some excuse you are using for out-of-line behaviors? Are you still rationalizing choices because you say you are "tired," "under a lot of stress," or some other unique yet unbelievable excuse?

Call it what it is: a behavior, a choice, or an overstated reaction is really a sin that is holding you back in life. James 5:16 explains, "Confess your sins to each other and pray for each other so that you may be healed." Confess your sin—everyone knows it isn't the coffee.

TO READ
2 Timothy 2:1-10

You have heard me teach many things that have been confirmed by many reliable witnesses. Teach these great truths to trustworthy people who are able to pass them on to others. 2 TIMOTHY 2:2

 Keep Going! You Can Do This!

When a young mother, Ariel, called needing some advice and encouragement, part of my advice was to reconnect her to Michelle, an older woman who had discipled her when she was a high schooler and college student. The strand of faith was passed from one to another to another, generation to generation.

Many times when you are trying to walk the straight and narrow, the road seems hard and the mountain steep, and you need to hear the reassuring voices of those who have made it to the top. You need to hear, "Keep going! You can do this! It's worth it!"

A few moments after I hung up the phone from my conversation with Ariel, the phone rang again. It was Michelle, calling to thank me for being like a spiritual mom to her. When Ariel told her I recommended she call Michelle, Michelle had been reminded of the benefit of connecting one generation to another and passing on the baton of faith. I had mentored Michelle, and Michelle had mentored Ariel, so I had a connection to Ariel, too! The connection has remained intact over years and miles. We all need connections. To those who are older, Psalm 145:4 directs us: "One generation will commend your works to another; they will tell of your mighty acts" (NIV).

Conversely, those younger in the faith need to find someone who will tell them of the mighty acts of God. Make a list of five to seven women you would trust with your heart: women who will encourage, strengthen, and tell you God's truth. If you can't think of seven women to call, then call one and ask her to connect you to someone who will disciple you. Create a success net by learning from those who have gone before and then passing the baton of belief forward.

TO READ
1 Thessalonians 5:5-11

Encourage each other and build each other up, just as you are already doing. 1 THESSALONIANS 5:11

 Connections

The young mother of four was in tears as she talked on the phone with me. Her Christian husband was in crisis and was now struggling.

"Pam, I—we—have always wanted a strong Christian marriage and family. We try so hard; I don't want our marriage to be one that fails. How come Christian marriages fall apart?"

My answer was simple: "Often Christian couples don't do what you just did. They don't call for help. They isolate. They quit going to church. They quit socializing with strong Christian couples because they feel inadequate. Or they keep thinking somehow it will magically get better, but they pull away from God, from each other, from family, and from friends who could help.

When you pull away, the lies grow, and the truth fades into a whisper. Isolation kills love. Fight to stay connected, and fight to help your husband stay connected." Luke 6:19 gives a picture: "The people all tried to touch him, because power was coming from him and healing them all" (NIV). People long for connection that heals.

I worked with this young mom to create an emergency connection plan, one for her and one for her husband. "As you look back on your life, who are the older godly Christian women from whom you have learned, who strengthen you? Call them and ask if you can call once a day for at least two weeks. Then ask your husband if he'll contact some Christian men and do the same thing. You need a support net under you since life has you both feeling like you are on the high wire. With more connections in the net, you'll be more likely to travel across the wire well, and even if you or your husband falls, plenty of people will be there to catch you."

Are you walking on an emotional tightrope? Then give an old trusted friend a call and have her pray for you.

TO READ
Matthew 26:36-41

Keep alert and pray. Otherwise temptation will overpower you. For though the spirit is willing enough, the body is weak! MATTHEW 26:41

 ## Keep Alert and Pray

Sometimes forward movement in life needs to come by supernatural intervention. However, as women, we feel a need to maintain control—kind of help God out—when what he wants us to do is release our prayer requests, hopes, and dreams to his care. We women often carry heavy burdens for our husbands, our children, our extended family, our future, and the future of all those we love. How can we learn to let go? Jesus told his disciples in the garden to "keep alert and pray" (Matthew 26:41). He gave them an assignment while they waited and prayed.

One summer a group of women and I gathered with our photo scrapbooks as part of a women's prayer project. We created prayer pages for each person we cared about. We listed requests we were praying for each person and then found verses to pray for each request. We left plenty of space for a photo and a place to write the answers to our prayer requests.

By creating a tangible prayer reminder, each day we could commit the people we loved to God's care. We saw some amazing results: we became less controlling and less pushy with our families. We felt more peace and calm. And we became more aware of small answers to prayers—movement in the lives of those we love. And creating a photo album gave us an assignment to do while we waited and prayed for the work God would do in the lives of our loved ones.

Return, O Lord, and rescue me. Save me because of your unfailing love. PSALM 6:4

 Stripped Bare

Claire had practically raised herself.

"I had a mother who was an alcoholic and drug user. She'd drink and pass out; then my older brothers would beat me and my sister. Or worse, they'd try to touch us, so we'd run and lock ourselves in the bathroom for hours. As we got older, my sister and I would do anything not to go home. Then my mom died when I was fifteen. I didn't want to live with my brothers, so I set off on my own. I worked all kinds of jobs—waitress, fast food, and a maid. Then I heard there was real money working in a club downtown— a strip club.

"I felt like men had used me my whole life, so why not get paid for it? The money could pay for college, or at least that's how I rationalized it. I went into the club. I batted my eyes a few times, and the job was mine. I went into the back dressing room and began to strip down. Then I heard a song playing on the radio. The song was 'Mary, Mary.' It was a Christian song. At that moment I felt ashamed that I had allowed my life to get this out of control.

"When I was little, a neighbor had taken me to church, where I heard that Jesus loved me. I had responded to that love, prayed a prayer, and asked him to come into my life—but I guess growing up in the home I grew up in, I never felt loved—until that moment, standing in the back of a strip club. It was as if God said, 'I see you, the real you, and I love you and died for you.' I ran out of that club—and I've never been back. What I did go back to was those friends from the neighborhood who took me to church, and I got reintroduced to Christ. His love is enough to change a life. I know—he changed mine."

A dramatic example of God's love? Sure. But that's just what Jesus did.

TO READ
Philippians 4:10-14

You have done well to share with me in my present difficulty. PHILIPPIANS 4:14

 ## Killer Cool Whip

Many of us are "functioning" dysfunctionals—or at least it seems like we are functioning, for a little while anyway. At one lunch several of us in ministry were sharing the dysfunctions found on our particular family tree. One of us had a great grandmother who was agoraphobic. Grandma just didn't like to leave her home—for any reason. When friends, neighbors, or relatives would come to visit, they would give Grandma a hug, and she would say, "Oh, and if you stop by the store, could you pick up some Cool Whip for me?"

The kindhearted person would then pick up some Cool Whip and drop it by Grandma's. When Grandma died, the family went in to clean out her home. There in the garage were hundreds and hundreds of washed and neatly stacked Cool Whip containers! It seems Grandmother had nothing in her refrigerator but Cool Whip. She had been "living" on Cool Whip for years.

Hiding a fear, the way Grandma hid her agoraphobia, could be a deadly decision. To live longer, Grandma needed to ask for help. Even asking someone to do her grocery shopping would have shown the people closest to her that she was living in terror.

A caring friend or family member might have brought up the topic of Grandma's fear, or someone might have researched some real help for her so she could once again go through the front door of her own home.

Luke 8:50 gives Christ's invitation: "Don't be afraid. Just trust me, and she will be all right." If you're afraid, tell someone!

TO READ
Matthew 5:21-26

If you are standing before the altar in the Temple, offering a sacrifice to God, and you suddenly remember that someone has something against you, leave your sacrifice there beside the altar. Go and be reconciled to that person. MATTHEW 5:23-24

 ## Close the Gate behind You

I grew up on a family farm. I was often assigned the job of helping move either the cattle or sheep from one pasture to another. My whole job was to close the gate behind the herd so they couldn't backtrack and get into a field of alfalfa. All I had to do was close the gate behind me. Sounds simple enough, right?

But gate closing is boring work. Gate closing is a whole lot of waiting until something happens. Gate closing isn't prestigious or exciting, but it is vitally important.

On the path to wellness, wholeness, and emotional health, there are many gates to close. There are groups to attend, homework to complete, and amends to make. Closing the gates means not leaving loose ends hanging. Are there some people with whom you have some loose ends? Is there a phone call you need to make to say, "I'm sorry"? Do you need to return something that you "borrowed"? Is there restitution that might renew a relationship?

My mama used to tell me, "Close the gates behind you." And most often she wasn't talking about the field gate, but rather making amends to repair or restore a relationship. Jesus was so serious about the need to make things right that he told people not to give a gift to God unless they first made things right with others (Matthew 5:23-24).

Pray and ask God to remind you of open gates in relationships that may need to be closed so you or another can gain freedom to move forward.

TO READ
Luke 17:1-4

It would be better to be thrown into the sea with a large millstone tied around the neck than to face the punishment in store for harming one of these little ones. LUKE 17:2

 ## *But I'm in Pain*

The e-mail read: "My marriage is the pits. He is a jerk. I'm in so much pain. I just want out."

My reply in abbreviated form was something like this: "I know you are in pain. I know this is a real issue. Here are some options for help. Remember your four kids. They need you. If things get worse, put his bags on the doorstep while he's at work, and if necessary, call the police if he creates any kind of a scene. Or if you really don't feel safe, you take the kids and head to your friends, family, or a shelter. Remember, the kids are depending on you. Choose well."

Then I got an e-mail a few weeks later: "I left. It was too much."

My reply was sympathy, then a question: "How are the children?"

Her answer broke my heart. "I don't know. I was in too much pain to deal with them, too, so I left them." She left her kids with a man she had just told me was unkind, uncaring, and unhealthy. Her decision didn't make sense.

So I asked a question I already knew the answer to: "Is there another man?"

Her predictable reply was yes. She rationalized the decision until I got an e-mail saying the court was not looking with favor on a mom who abandoned her children.

"I was just in so much pain. I felt I deserved better."

Then I asked another question, "Who's in pain now?"

"I am. My kids are. I pushed my pain off onto them, didn't I?"

What are you doing with your pain? Are you pushing it onto someone else?

TO READ
Jeremiah 24:6-7

I will give them hearts that will recognize me as the Lord. They will be my people, and I will be their God, for they will return to me wholeheartedly.

JEREMIAH 24:7

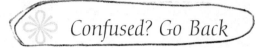

Confused? Go Back

Now that I can see what direction God is leading, where do I go from here? Whom do I talk to? Where can I go for help? How do I handle roadblocks? obstacles? opposition? How can I move the dream further? How can I move myself forward?

When I am confused in any way, I go back to the people, places, and passages of Scripture that first helped me understand the truth about God and myself.

People: Go back to the people who best explained the plan of God to you. Some of our best friends and mentors were first our professors or disciplers. When I feel unsure, I may even reread books that were pivotal in my growth.

Places: When we have a big decision ahead or need some clarity, we go back to the same comforting places, such as Christian conference centers or favorite vacation spots to seek God again. God can speak anywhere, but we have noticed we "hear" better in some places! There's something reassuring about going back to the same chapel where you first heard the call, to listen again.

Passages: When I am seeking God, I often go back to the verses I have underlined or highlighted in my Bible. Hezekiah, a good king of Israel, sent a letter throughout all Israel that is good advice today: "People of Israel, return to the Lord, the God of Abraham, Isaac and Israel, that he may return to you who are left" (2 Chronicles 30:6, NIV).

Remembering how God has led in the past brings a sense of security. By going back, I often get what I need to go forward.

TO READ
Romans 13:1-7

Give to everyone what you owe them: Pay your taxes and import duties, and give respect and honor to all to whom it is due. ROMANS 13:7

 ## *Take Responsibility*

On occasion people come into our office who just can't see why everyone in their family and friendship circle is upset with them. Their side of the story usually sounds like this: "Everyone picks on me." "My mom [or dad] is so unreasonable [or crazy or abusive, etc.]." "They just don't know what my life is like." "They are power hungry! They want to take my kids away from me and rule their lives too!"

Then the friends and relatives come in and we hear: "She won't get a job—she's twenty-seven!" "He expects we'll bail him out every time he gets in trouble." "She acts so deprived, but we paid for her college, her car, and even got her into an apartment. All we ask is that she keep a job and keep the apartment so she doesn't have to move back home." "We are old. We thought we'd be on our second honeymoon or at least able to retire, but we are afraid of what will happen to our grandkids if we don't step in."

Can you say irresponsible? Romans 14:12 says, "Each of us will have to give a personal account to God." We're all accountable for *ourselves*. Life is not a free ride. Life doesn't owe you anything. It is a healthy day in a teen's life when he or she realizes no one ever has to do anything for you—any help you are given is a gift. It is tragic when that day of realization hits people in their twenties, thirties, forties, or later.

Are you carrying an attitude that someone owes you? Take off the blinders and see that the only way to feel good about yourself is to take responsibility for yourself.

TO READ
Psalm 145:1-7

Let each generation tell its children of your mighty acts. PSALM 145:4

 ## I Made It, You Can Too

Childbirth is a glimpse of what we as women can do when circumstances call for courage. My first labor was more than twenty-four-hours long and was followed by an emergency C-section.

I had just read the story of women who traveled the Oregon Trail in covered wagons. They would stop the caravan for only a moment for the delivery; then if there were any problems, like a child dying during birth, they would dig a grave between the wagon wheels and place the baby in it so wild animals wouldn't be able to dig up the body. The wagon wheels traveling over the grave would pack down the dirt. A woman could never return to that place of pain—she was forced to go forward.

Even at times when God shows us change would be beneficial, it can still seem too hard, the burden too heavy. But I think back to the women who have gone before.

In the Bible the young widow Ruth looked to her mother-in-law for a plan to go forward. She trusted Naomi so much she moved with her to Israel. She declared, "Don't urge me to leave you or to turn back from you. Where you go I will go, and where you stay I will stay. Your people will be my people and your God my God" (Ruth 1:16, NIV).

Booker T. Washington, the renowned abolitionist, was sold as a child. His mother would finish her labors in the field, walk twelve miles to the farm where he was living, hold and rock him to sleep, and then walk twelve miles back home before sunrise. With an example of courage like that, it is no wonder that he went on to lead the charge against slavery.

When the burden feels great, look to the examples of those who have gone before.

TO READ
Romans 5:14-16

I have written you quite boldly on some points, as if to remind you of them again, because of the grace God gave me. ROMANS 15:15, NIV

 ## *Repeat, Repeat*

When God is trying to cause movement and change in a life, he tends to repeat himself.

I grew up in a home with an alcoholic father who was constantly criticizing, yelling, and at times throwing things. When he raged, my mom would first try to calm him down, but sometimes she would get pulled into the shouting match herself. When they wanted to correct our behavior as children, they often yelled at us. I didn't want to be a screaming mother, but at times of high stress, I would feel anger welling up inside me. Most of the time I control my desire to raise my voice; however, one day God repeated himself to get down to the core of my issue.

I went to the mailbox and pulled out a Christian women's magazine with a lead article about handling anger. Then I walked into the house and flipped on the radio. The preacher's text? "Do not let the sun go down on your anger." Later, in a conversation I had with a friend, she talked about struggling with anger toward her spouse. Then I came home and my older sons began to yell down requests from their upstairs bedroom—breaking a family rule: When you want something from a parent, walk to the parent and ask—do not yell your request.

I then walked to the stair rail and yelled up the stairs, "Guys, you know I hate it when you yell. If you want something, come down here and ask!"

Then my little Caleb, a preschooler, tugged on my pant leg, and when I turned to face him, he said in his sweet little voice, "Mommy, I don't think God likes it when you yell at us." All the reminder roads converged into one intersection with a flashing yellow light. God had my attention.

Is God repeating a message in your life?

TO READ
Matthew 5:33-37

Just say a simple, "Yes, I will," or "No, I won't."
Your word is enough. MATTHEW 5:37

 Keeping Focus

We all need focus to live out God's calling. But how do you maintain focus? Know when to say no. And learn to say no with kindness, grace, and strength.

Learn to identify distractions. For example, your home needs to be cleaned—but you don't have to be the only one cleaning it. (Yes, your family—even your friends—can help. Sometimes our own pride stands in the way of accomplishing a goal. Asking for help is not a sign of weakness!) Before you make the phone call, reorganize the closet, or volunteer on a project, ask, "Am I the only one who can do this?" Try to spend the majority of your time doing what you do best. Try praying this verse (paraphrased): "Teach [me] to number [my] days aright, that [I] may gain a heart of wisdom" (Psalm 90:12, NIV).

Learn what can wait. Remodeling the kitchen, repapering the bedroom, and repainting the bath—wait, wait, wait! Sometimes the adage "If it ain't broke, don't fix it!" does buy you time. People often ask me how I accomplish the amount of work I do and still find time to write. It is simply because I don't do many things: I don't shop much, I don't craft much, I am choosey about social engagements, and I don't need to be entertained.

Ask yourself, *Do I really need to do this now?*

TO READ
Psalm 26:1-12

I am constantly aware of your unfailing love.

PSALM 26:3

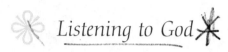

Listening to God

Our relationship with God requires a listening heart. We need to make the same commitment that David did in Psalm 85:8: "I will listen to what God the Lord will say; he promises peace to his people" (NIV). So what can you do while you listen?

Think: Research the issue. Do a topical study. Write down your questions, your dreams, and your ideas. Then take the key words and phrases, look them up in a concordance, and seek to find the heart of God through his Word.

Pray: Talk to God about your dreams, ideas, fears, or habits. Talk to him about your successes and frustrations. Tell him your hopes—and hang-ups. Find a time and place to pray. Start a prayer journal and log your requests, key verses to pray, your impressions, and the thoughts and ideas you sense may be from God. Weigh out your impressions against the truth found in the Word of God. You might listen to the Bible on tape or CD to create a backdrop of truth in your heart.

Walk: Exercise. Creative juices flow after physical activity. Endorphins release ideas, so get out and about. Move, dance, run, ride a horse, cycle, or kickbox out your frustrations—but move! Physical movement makes white space in the mind. For example, when I swim in a pool, I can pray through my life without interruption. When I swim in the ocean, my problems nearly disappear as I concentrate on the rhythm of the waves.

When you fall in love, you make dates that allow for conversation. The same is true with your relationship with God. Make some space in your life to listen to his Word.

TO READ
Matthew 6:25-34

Don't worry about everyday life—whether you have enough food, drink, and clothes. Doesn't life consist of more than food and clothing? . . . He will give you all you need from day to day if you live for him and make the Kingdom of God your primary concern. MATTHEW 6:25, 33

Right on Time

Sometimes you're sure about what God wants you to do, but movement seems slow and hard.

When we were called into the senior pastorate from youth ministry, there were about six months when Bill ran his own business. We didn't have a large savings account, and when clients were late paying their bills, we were between a rock and a hard place. I put a list of "needs" on the refrigerator: grocery items, electric bill, gas for the car, etc. Each day I'd pray, "Give us each day our daily bread" (Luke 11:3, NIV). I realized that I expected God to provide ahead of time, instead of day by day. I was secure only if I could see money in the bank.

While I believe the Proverbs clearly teaches that the wise save for a rainy day, sometimes life's storms last longer than the savings. I began to pray, "Lord, help me not feel the need, until it is a need." And "God, give me faith to believe you will provide right on time." Some days I prayed, "Just let me go one more day and trust your provision." I prayed verses like Psalm 37:25: "I was young and now I am old. Yet I have never seen the godly forsaken, nor seen their children begging for bread." And if things felt really tight, "Lord, help me make it one more hour, with my focus on you, not the need!"

I kept a journal of God's provision. The unexpected job that paid cash, the diaper rebate check that bought milk the day we ran out, etc. God provided what I *needed* right on time.

TO READ	They will fly high on wings like eagles. They
Isaiah 40:27-31	will run and not grow weary. They will walk
	and not faint. ISAIAH 40:31

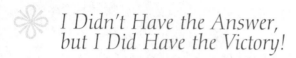

I Didn't Have the Answer, but I Did Have the Victory!

JoAnn was the only woman graduate in her Bible school.

"The leaders said to me, 'We don't know what we're going to do with you—we do have this situation in Memphis. A church closed and we need you to go start a Sunday school. All we can offer you is eighty dollars a month.'"[1] Once in Memphis she stayed with a pastor and his wife, who gave her room and board for forty dollars a month. She spent the other forty dollars on ministry. For six weeks she knocked on doors, cleaned the decaying church building, and cut the grass, but no one came.

"One day I sat on the piano stool and cried, 'I don't know what I am going to do. I can't go home. I feel like you've called me, Lord, but I don't know what to do.'"

Then a promise from Isaiah 40:30-31 came to her mind: "Even youths will faint and be weary, and the young will fall exhausted; but those who wait for the Lord shall renew their strength" (NRSV).

Her hope returned. "I didn't have people, but I had the victory!"

She began to see the neighborhood with new eyes. She saw that people were needy, and she felt that God wanted her to meet their needs. She felt that God was asking her, "Step in, and I'll show you what I can do with five dollars." She decided to go to the thrift shore and buy as much as she could with her five dollars. "I loaded up my car with clothes. I gave the kids things to wear—and they started to come to Sunday school!"

Can you see the victory in your life today?

February

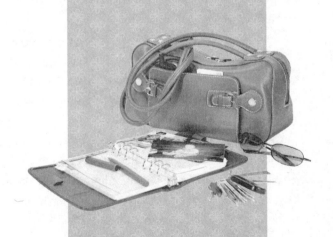

TO READ
Philippians 4:4-9

Fix your thoughts on what is true and honorable and right. Think about things that are pure and lovely and admirable. PHILIPPIANS 4:8

 ## Hide and Seek

Krista had experienced it all: drug and alcohol abuse, promiscuity, and the death of her mother. Her past could have defined her future, except she decided to go on a women's retreat. As Krista entered an empty chapel, God's Holy Spirit swept over her so powerfully that she fell to her knees and wept a host of cleansing tears.

"Satan tried to attack me—but I fought back with obedience: attending church weekly, daily reading of God's Word and prayer, attending a care group, tithing, and serving others. Philippians 4:8 became my stronghold, and I made sure that everything I heard, read, or watched was "worthy of praise."

Are you using obedience to fight back attacks? Are you guarding your heart and life by choosing praiseworthy activities and interests? Why obey? Psalm 103:17-18 says, "The Lord's love is with those who fear him, and his righteousness with their children's children—with those who keep his covenant and remember to obey his precepts" (NIV).

Ask yourself, *If I were introduced to Jesus at a party this week, could I brag about: What I have seen? What I have heard? What I have done?*

One of the early warning signs that your choices may be off is that you feel you can't share your choices with family members, your pastor or other spiritual leaders, or friends who love God. If you can't be excited about your choices around them, check to see if the choice was "worthy of praise." If you feel you have to hide something you have read, watched, or done, then confess your poor choice to God and go immediately to the someone you might be hiding it from and ask for help.

Don't play hide and seek—instead seek help and hide nothing.

TO READ
2 Peter 1:3-11

As we know Jesus better, his divine power gives us everything we need for living a godly life.

2 PETER 1:3

 ## I Gave It to You Already!

Cheryl's statement to me was simple and powerful. "The key to overcoming has been the realization that God created me with all the tools I needed to overcome all things if I rely on him to guide me to them."

Cheryl's words had impact as she relayed all she'd overcome: the death of her mother when she was a teen, the infidelity of her husband, her husband's mistress having his baby, and Cheryl's own diagnosis of multiple sclerosis.

This year she and her husband will celebrate twenty-five years together.

"I know God wants my complete dependence on him. He knows me better than any other and created me with all the strength I need to face these issues and any others the future may hold. With confidence and with him as my champion, I can overcome!"

Did God really create you to overcome? Yes! Consider his gifts:

- A brain to learn new tools
- A heart to feel pain—but also peace, joy, and hope
- An ability to give and receive affection and affirmation
- Power stronger than your own through your relationship with him

The choice is yours: let the gifts sit unwrapped and unused—or use his gifts to go on and go forward.

Pray: "God, show me what you have already given me that will help me move forward."

TO READ
1 Corinthians 15:51-58

When this happens—when our perishable earthly bodies have been transformed into heavenly bodies that will never die—then at last the Scriptures will come true: "Death is swallowed up in victory. O death, where is your victory? O death, where is your sting?" 1 CORINTHIANS 15:54-55

 ## *From Pain to Peace*

Kim couldn't believe where she found herself. This was supposed to be a family vacation, and now she and her family were standing over the lifeless body of their darling daughter, Nicole, who had been killed while riding an ATV over a sand dune.

"Our family went immediately to prayer. My husband prayed God would keep Satan out and that we would be rescued from despair. We went immediately to prayer because we had been in ministry long enough to see that the longer after trauma a person or a family waits to pray, the more quickly their walls go up. We prayed that God would soften our hearts even amidst the pain."

More than seven hundred people came to Nicole's funeral, many of them youth. Eventually, Kim decided that she wanted to grieve by doing things that would emotionally connect her to Nicole. She listened to her music and wore her clothes, but more than anything, she ministered to Nicole's friends. She has launched a mentoring program for young women. Through a place of pain, Kim has found peace as she continues to be a youth leader in her church.

Do you need to pray Kim's prayer in your place of pain?

Pray with the psalmist, "I am in pain and distress; may your salvation, O God, protect me" (Psalm 69:29, NIV). Kim prayed, "God keep me from despair." And God not only rescued her, he also redeemed her pain.

TO READ
Matthew 9:27-31

Because of your faith, it will happen.

MATTHEW 9:29

 Big Things

God has often asked me to trust him for "big things." How about you? <u>What is a "big thing" you are trusting God for?</u>

Recently I was on a committee to organize a stadium outreach event in our community. Here was the catch: there would be no charge. And if the love offerings and donations given at the event didn't cover expenses, then all of our churches had to cover the difference, perhaps hundreds of thousands of dollars.

The first meeting was filled with many women leaders from all size congregations, mine being one of the smaller ones. I would say the word that best described the mood was caution, a blinking yellow light. The leader of the group asked us to go home, pray, fast, ask God to lead us, and come back with a verse.

During this time I was reading a Bible through and marking it up to give to my sixteen-year-old son for a gift. As I read a verse, God began to convict me, "Pam, every day you ask your son to step onto his high school campus and live and speak out for me—he's only been walking with me for about twelve years. Yet all you women in that room have less faith in my ability to work than he does."

I had my answer, <u>"The people who know their God shall be strong, and carry out great exploits"</u> (Daniel 11:32, NKJV). I took the verse back to the group, and—no surprise—the woman there had received a similar verse giving a green light to the event.

Months later, after God had sidelined me from leadership in the event because of my traveling schedule, I walked into the stadium and found it filled to standing room only.

Do you trust God for the <u>"big thing"</u> in your life?

TO READ
Psalm 27:1-14

Wait patiently for the Lord. Be brave and courageous. Yes, wait patiently for the Lord.

PSALM 27:14

 ## Give It Time

Relationships with the opposite sex can be the biggest blessing and the biggest obstacle to our emotional strength and well-being.

Our "feelings" of love can influence our decision about what kind of commitment to make to a man. Often we give ourselves and our bodies away far too easily. We move in, rush an engagement, or plunge into a marriage after knowing someone just a short time.

Give relationships time—time enough to see whether he can set *and reach* goals, time enough to see how he reacts under stress, and time enough not only to meet his family but also to observe how he relates to each person in the family. Give him time to show his true colors. Anyone can wow a girl for a short while—but see how he treats not just you but his friends, his promises, his boss, and yes—children and his mother!

Definitely give him time to see you at your worst. Let him see you without makeup. Let him see you sick. Definitely let enough time transpire to see how he handles a mistake you made that impacts *him!* How does he handle it when something you do isn't what he would have done?

Slow down. Wait and make sure that this is the relationship that God is leading you to.

Let each generation tell its children of your mighty acts. PSALM 145:4

 ## *Watch and Learn*

When Bill and I were newlyweds, we realized we definitely did not have the example of parents in loving marriages to draw on as models for marriage. So we began to look for models, mentors, and mature marriages that we could emulate and learn from.

One sweet couple, married sixty-plus years, always sat in front of us at church. He was so kind to her, an arm around her shoulder or a loving stroke on her wrinkled hand. She always looked at him with adoration. Even the most basic of statements would garner a look from her that read, "You are so profound!"

He'd carry her Bible. She'd straighten his jacket lapel. All the little gestures of care gave a loud and clear message of lasting love. In all the years we attended that church, never—not once—did Bill or I hear either of them say anything unkind or disrespectful about the other. They never even corrected each other in public.

All in all we learned that kindness pays. No surprise, since God's Word recommends, "Be kind and compassionate to one another, forgiving each other, just as in Christ God forgave you" (Ephesians 4:32, NIV).

We now teach marriage seminars, counseling couples who want stronger, more romantic, and more intimate marriages. What we can't package is what we saw week after week, year after year, in our darling mentor couple. But those couples are out there. Those healthy relationships do exist.

Ask God to show you a real couple or a parent-child relationship that models his love. Then just watch and take notes—you will learn volumes by what you see.

TO READ
Isaiah 43:1-7

When you pass through the waters, I will be with you; and when you pass through the rivers, they will not sweep over you. When you walk through the fire, you will not be burned; the flames will not set you ablaze. ISAIAH 43:2, NIV

 ## I Will Survive!

"Pastor, my house is burning to the ground!"

The firemen tried desperately to save her home, but to no avail. Bill had called me en route, and I offered to help in any way I could. Later that evening, about 10 P.M., I got another call from Bill. "Honey, Marjorie only has the clothes on her back, and she wants to know if you'll take her shopping."

I drove Marjorie to our local discount store, and I was so impressed with her frame of mind on such a catastrophic night. As we walked to the checkout, something on our faces must have given a clue to our emotional state. The checker said, "Cheer up! It's almost Christmas! It can't be that bad."

I replied, "It can be. My friend's home burned to the ground today."

In silence he rang up the purchases then reached across and touched Marjorie's hand. "Ma'am, I am so sorry. I will pray for you."

That gesture of care meant so much to my friend, Marjorie. As we stepped out into the cool, crisp Christmas air, Marjorie said, "Pam, in the end, the Bible says everyone's stuff will burn—mine just went up sooner than yours!" Then she smiled.

I was amazed at her courage. Then she added, "It's just stuff. I've survived worse. I'll hang on to God, and I'll survive."

Marjorie, a woman whose husband beat her and then left her for another, whose only son was killed in an automobile accident, and who had poured herself into a successful career only to watch it crumble months before her retirement, instinctively clung to Jesus when her house burned.

Hold on to Jesus—you will survive!

TO READ
Ruth 2–3:11

Now don't worry about a thing, my daughter. I will do what is necessary, for everyone in town knows you are an honorable woman. RUTH 3:11

 ## A Life God Can Reward

How can you live a life God can reward? Let's step into the story of Ruth.

Boaz, a godly, rich landowner, sees Ruth and comments to her, "May the Lord, the God of Israel, under whose wings you have come to take refuge, reward you fully" (Ruth 2:12). What had Ruth done? In the original text this chapter has five paragraphs, so let's see what five things Ruth did to live a life God could (and would) reward.

Be with quality people. It started when Ruth left her pagan ways and joined Naomi on her trek back to Israel. Then once there, they had to find a way to get food, so Naomi directed Ruth to Boaz's fields so she could glean safely. If you are new to a community, or if you want to improve your friendship circle, find quality people at churches, service groups, Bible studies, seminaries, or self-improvement classes.

Be a hard worker. In verse 7 there is a comment on how Ruth had been "hard at work"—doing field labor! This was backbreaking work. When people see your work ethic, they want to help. When God sees it, he is moved to reward you.

Be humble. When Boaz called Ruth over, "she bowed down with her face to the ground" (v. 10, NIV). God promises that if we humble ourselves under his mighty power, he will honor us at the proper time (1 Peter 5:6).

Be yourself. Boaz invited Ruth to lunch, and "she ate all she wanted" (Ruth 2:14, NIV). She didn't put on airs and pretend she wasn't hungry because she was on a date! Ruth was real.

Be generous. Ruth always took food home to Naomi. In fact, Ruth cared for Naomi in such a way that Boaz said to Ruth, "Everyone in town knows you are an honorable woman" (3:11).

TO READ
Romans 13:12-14

Get rid of your evil deeds. Shed them like dirty clothes. Clothe yourselves with the armor of right living, as those who live in the light. ROMANS 13:12

 ## Inside Out

Gabrielle looked in the mirror. Somehow this outfit that she had felt so comfortable in last spring no longer felt appropriate. She felt exposed. The stares of men and the ability to turn their heads used to be something she looked forward to.

But now as she looked in the mirror, her outfit just didn't seem to match the person she was becoming.

"Lord, you have brought me so far this year. I have dealt with the pain of being abused and raped. I feel more confident than ever. So why am I so uncomfortable when I go out?"

Then she felt the Holy Spirit impress on her heart, *Make the outside match the internal change I've made.*

The next morning Gabrielle went through every item in her closet, asking, *God does this reflect the new me you are making me to be? I want people to see my heart, not my body, when I meet them. Lord, I'm learning that I am the temple of your Holy Spirit, so how would you like your temple decorated?*

Gabrielle observed and wrote down what the godliest women wore at different occasions.

"But Lord, I don't want to be a clone! How can I be me—not a clone of others but a reflection of the new me?"

The next morning she read in her quiet time 1 Corinthians 10:23: "'Everything is permissible'—but not everything is beneficial. 'Everything is permissible'—but not everything is constructive" (NIV).

How about you? Does your outward appearance match the inward you?

TO READ
Exodus 15:22-26

I am the Lord who heals you. EXODUS 15:26

 ## Who's Your Counselor?

David was a bright ten-year-old, a brilliant and creative writer, a whiz on the computer. He was outgoing, friendly, and fun—until his parents started having marital problems.

His mother suffered with depression and bipolar disorder in addition to the marital stress. She began to pour out her hatred for his father so much that David refused to live in the same house with his dad. Then she spewed out her anger over work, church, and social situations, systematically poisoning her own son against everyone in his world—even those in helping positions who could have lent aid.

As she continued to go to her son for counsel when she was suicidal, David's grades began to slide as he, too, became more and more depressed. David withdrew from youth group and his friends, started skipping classes, avoided any physical exercise, and found himself seeking solace in food. His mother homeschooled him, blaming the school for her son's problems.

As he gained weight, he became more and more depressed. His mother had such distrust for all authority figures that she refused help from psychological, psychiatric, and pastoral professionals.

Cut off from anyone who tried to reach him, he thought that suicide was a better alternative. One night he tried to kill himself, leaving a note that read, "This world is not worth living in. I want out! Mom, I'm sorry I won't be there for you anymore. Please forgive me."

Mom had used David, her child, as her counselor. That is not a job for our children!

Are you parenting your children, paying the professionals to counsel you, and praying to the One who can truly rescue you from your pain?

Be humble, thinking of others as better than yourself. PHILIPPIANS 2:3

 Kids First

Teresa and Cameron were very young when they married. Neither had a strong relationship with God. Their love train was derailed within a few years, and they had a small daughter to factor in. The divorce was initially hostile, but soon Teresa came to faith, and eventually she remarried a wonderful, godly man.

Then her ex-husband came to faith in Christ, and he made amends with Teresa. With God's view of relationships, he now had the skills to maintain a God-centered marriage, and he remarried too.

One holiday Teresa realized if she didn't rebuild a bridge with her ex-husband, her daughter would have a lifetime of birthdays, holidays, and special school days filled with memories of awkwardness or hostility. Teresa wanted more than that for her daughter, so she prayed for a plan.

With their spiritual transformations, Teresa, her ex-husband, and both their spouses decided to "Put the kids first!" They would work together to overcome any awkwardness so both sets of parents felt comfortable at the big moments of their daughter's life. Then they took a step further: If Christ's love could overcome all and God could redeem anything, why couldn't they celebrate birthdays and holidays together as families for the sake of all the children? So they tried—and it worked!

Are any of your family relationships strained (with a former spouse or an in-law)? What steps would God want you to take to place the children's needs above your own?

Is there a phone call you can make? a dinner meeting you can hold? a person you can forgive or love by faith? A creative plan will help you put your children's needs first.

TO READ
Ruth 1:1-22

So Naomi returned. Ruth 1:22

 ## *The Return*

Naomi was in a downward spiral: Her husband had died. Her sons were dead too. She had been living for years in a foreign land where few worshiped God.

Now she had two daughters-in-law to provide for, and she felt she couldn't even care for herself. She was in an emotional and spiritual famine. Naomi was so depressed she even changed her name. "Instead, call me Mara, for the Almighty has made life very bitter for me" (Ruth 1:20).

She knew if she stayed in this barren place, she would die. And if she didn't make provisions for her daughters-in-law, they might die too.

Naomi made a pivotal decision. She must go back to the place she knew she would hear the voice of God again, to her home in faraway Bethlehem, even if she had to walk each step of the way alone. Naomi knew she needed to return to a place where there was not only food for her body but also food for her soul. The first step out of this depression was to go where she would receive good counsel and care.

When we find ourselves in the deserts of life, we need to go back to the people and places that first helped us hear and learn about God. Going back to those who we know will give us healthy wisdom is not a step backward; rather, going back is often the first step in going forward again.

Who are the people, what are the resources that first gave you healthy teaching about God and emotional wellness? It is not failure to return or retrace the steps that made you well the first time. Going back will move you forward.

TO READ
Luke 5:17-26

Immediately, as everyone watched, the man jumped to his feet, picked up his mat, and went home praising God. LUKE 5:25

The Next Thing

Often when navigating a life change, the array of decisions can seem daunting.

Carol realized that living with her parents, as an adult single mother, wasn't the best choice for her and her two children. Her alcoholic parents kept her in the same role—the family scapegoat. She knew she needed to move, but to move she needed a higher-paying job, and she wasn't sure how she could do that. Then she would need child care. On top of all this, she felt guilty for waiting so long to move her children out of the unhealthy environment. She wasn't sure where to start. And she felt depressed, anxious, and fearful—too paralyzed to even go out of the house. How could she find a job if she couldn't get out the front door?

Do the next thing. When you are not sure where to start, start with the obvious: Get dressed, clean the house, take your children to school. Then while you are out, do the next logical thing—immediately.

Second Corinthians 6:2 explains with emphasis: "I tell you, now is the time of God's favor, now is the day of salvation" (NIV). Do it *now*. Carol got dressed, dropped her two children off at school, and went to the career center at her local community college, where she found a bulletin board of job openings. She copied down a few numbers and went to the nearest pay phone to call and ask if she could stop by. Carol was afraid if she went home, she might be too afraid to go out again. The second place she called, the person said, "Are you available today?"

"Sure, till three, when my children get out of school."

"Then come by—immediately! We can use you today!"

Be very careful to love the Lord your God.

JOSHUA 23:11

 God's Statements of Love to You

A relationship with God is possible. Look at his statements of love to you: I love you and have a plan for you:

- My purpose is to give life in all its fullness. (John 10:10)
- God so loved the world that he gave his only Son, so that everyone who believes in him will not perish but have eternal life. (3:16)

I know you are imperfect, so you are separated from my love; our relationship is broken.

- We've compiled this long and sorry record as sinners . . . and proved that we are utterly incapable of living the glorious lives God wills for us. (Romans 3:23, *The Message*)

I love you so I, who am perfect, paid the price for your imperfection in order to restore our relationship.

- God showed his great love for us by sending Christ to die for us while we were still sinners. And since we have been made right in God's sight by the blood of Christ, he will certainly save us from God's judgment. For since we were restored to friendship with God by the death of his Son while we were still his enemies, we will certainly be delivered from eternal punishment by his life. (Romans 5:8-10)

To initiate this new relationship, all you need to do is to accept my payment for your imperfection. I cannot make you love me; that is your choice.

- For if you confess with your mouth that Jesus is Lord and believe in your heart that God raised him from the dead, you will be saved. (Romans 10:9)

The word is out: God loves you. Want to tell God you love him?

TO READ
Psalm 101:1-8

I will refuse to look at anything vile and vulgar. I hate all crooked dealings; I will have nothing to do with them. PSALM 101:3

 ## *TV Truth*

It was well after 10 P.M. I had nursed the baby, and Brock, then just a little over two, was tucked safely in bed. I was lying with the baby on my chest when the TV show I was watching ended and a movie came on. I could tell from the first few minutes of the movie that it was going to be too sensual and too violent. But it had been a popular R-rated movie in the theaters recently, and I rationalized that since it was on TV, it was edited and should be better. However, after a few moments, I knew it hadn't been edited enough. Then I rationalized that if I changed the channel, I'd wake the baby. So I continued to watch even though verses flew through my head:

"Blessed are the pure in heart" (Matthew 5:8, NIV). . . . "Whatever is pure, whatever is lovely . . . think about such things" (Philippians 4:8, NIV).

Just then, my two-year-old sleepily wandered into the living room. The sound of the violent gun scene must have wakened him. I hastily rushed to turn off the TV so he wouldn't be exposed. I rocked him and the baby back to sleep and tucked them in bed. I was tagged! I felt God had to wake up my son because I wasn't awake to his Spirit's leading.

Going back to the living room, I flipped open the Bible to Psalm 103:3 and resolved to "refuse to look at anything vile or vulgar" again!

God wants you to be holy, so you should keep clear of all sexual sin. 1 THESSALONIANS 4:3

 ## The Gifts

I had been concerned about a new Christian I hadn't seen at church for several weeks. I had been praying for her and e-mailed her to see if I could stop by. I was at her home just a few minutes when she poured out her thoughts.

"Pam, I have been so jealous of your relationship with Bill. I want a man who treats me like Bill treats you. A few years ago you told me that living with a man or having sex with a man before marriage would short-circuit my love life. But honestly, I didn't believe you. I couldn't imagine life without sex, so even though I was learning about God at church, I was still sleeping with men.

"Then a few weeks ago I let Richard move in. Last week it hit me. He was sitting on the sofa, and he said, "So you want to go to the bedroom?" That was the furthest thing from my mind. He wanted me in the bedroom, and I wanted him out of my house! That's when I realized that if I want a man like Bill, I have to become a woman like you. You have Bill in your life because of the person you let God make you. Is that what you were trying to get across to me years ago when you said sex outside marriage would short-circuit my happiness?"

That was exactly what I had meant. I even remember the conversation:

"Kerry, 1 Thessalonians 4:3 says, 'God wants you to be holy, so you should keep clear of all sexual sin.' I know this sounds hard right now, but it is really a gift God wants to give you. It's as if God has hundreds of wonderful, perfect gifts under a Christmas tree, and they all have your name on them. But you'll only be able to receive the gifts if you are in the room where the tree is. Obedience moves you into the room where the gifts are."

TO READ
Proverbs 17:3-24

It is senseless to pay tuition to educate a fool who has no heart for wisdom. PROVERBS 17:16

 ## I Have a Problem

No money, again. Mom had taken the last emergency cash out of her husband's locked desk drawer. Desperate for money to gamble, she had taken a crowbar to the drawer to unleash its precious cargo. She had discovered the children's savings bonds and cashed them in for less than their value and gambled those away too.

When Tom explained to Brian and Kelly that Mom had spent all the money—again, they each ran to their rooms. Kelly was in tears and slammed her door.

Brian simply walked up to his mother and said, "How could you, Mom? How can we eat? How can I play football? How can we pay the bills if you keep doing this? Don't you love us enough to stop? You promised! You promised, you liar!" He turned his back and walked away.

Her husband, Tom, walked into the garage, his escape from the reality of the financial ruin he was facing.

Sara looked at the pile of cut-up charge cards Tom had thrown in the air like confetti. No one in her family wanted to talk to her, and she was running out of creative ways to fund her habit. Her cupboards were as barren as her soul felt. Proverbs 17:16, says, "It is senseless to pay tuition to educate a fool who has no heart for wisdom."

I've been a fool! No more, she thought. Then she did what she knew she should have done years before—she pulled out the telephone book. Tom had circled one number: Gambler's Anonymous. She dialed it, then immediately got into her car and drove to a meeting. She didn't announce it; she just did it.

But she did leave behind a simple note: "I'm sorry. I love you. I have a problem. I went for help. I will be back. I can't do this to you anymore. See you at ten. Love, Mom"

TO READ
Psalm 37:1-7

Be still in the presence of the Lord, and wait patiently for him to act. PSALM 37:7

 Give God Time

On the same day, two women called me. Their names were different, but their stories were nearly the same.

Both had husbands who were inattentive to their needs. Neither husband was helpful in parenting their young children or around the house. Both felt their dreams were being crushed. Both felt devalued. Neither was abused in any way. Both were in a midlife transition of their own, trying to find themselves and blaming their husbands for their own discontent.

My advice was the same: "Focus on your own growth. Don't wait for your husband to be your cheerleader. He might not be able to do that because of issues in his own life. Pray and ask God to meet your needs. Also start praying for your husband. For the sake of your children, don't just abandon the relationship. Pray and give God time to work."

A year later I got an e-mail from one of the women. She had ignored my advice, left her husband and children in the middle of the night, and fled to the arms of a lover. Now she was in a huge custody battle for her children. By her own admission, her children were now unhappy because she had chased a dream for happiness.

A few weeks later the other woman called. She relayed her own journey: "I was looking to my husband to meet a need only God could fill. As I let God redefine me and remake me, I found my husband was really a pretty nice guy after all. My kids are doing so great—probably because I'm not such a control freak anymore!"

This woman now helps other women find contentment in God alone. Statistics say that when couples experiencing great marital discord stay together even if they don't "feel" happy, within five years they rate their marriage as happy or very happy.

Give God time.

TO READ
Proverbs 3:1-8

Trust in the Lord with all your heart; do not depend on your own understanding. Seek his will in all you do, and he will direct your paths. PROVERBS 3:5-6

 Stew on a Verse

Since childhood, I have memorized Scripture. We used to be rewarded with little Bibles, pencils, or my favorite—a cross that glowed in the dark! But as I grew older, I began to see that memorizing is its own reward.

For me, familiarity and need are the two key ways I memorize. Familiarity: I post it, I say it, I sing it, and I use it in conversation. The verse is always handy and in sight. However, to be honest, need is a greater motivator.

Early in my own journey, stewing on Proverbs 3:5-6 kept me going forward. At that time I couldn't trust my own feelings, judgment, or ability to choose wisely. My flesh, the selfish side of me, wanted to give in to old patterns and habits to fill my insecurities.

But by meditating on God's Word, especially trusting in his "understanding" rather than my own, I gained the ability to fight back my flesh and learn new skills that developed new habits and a new, better life. Sure, it felt uncomfortable at first, but I kept reminding myself of the payoff: "He will make your paths straight." I got on the right path—one that has been filled with joy, hope, fulfillment, and blessing.

After twenty-four hours, you may accurately remember 5 percent of what your hear, 15 percent of what you read, 35 percent of what you study, 57 percent of what you see and hear, but 100 percent of what you memorize.[1]

Stew on God's Word for a while today!

TO READ
Colossians 1:9-14

I plan to keep on reminding you of these things—even though you already know them and are standing firm in the truth. 2 PETER 1:12

Then the way you live will always honor and please the Lord, and you will continually do good, kind things for others. All the while, you will learn to know God better and better. COLOSSIANS 1:10

How happy I was to meet some of your children and find them living in the truth, just as we have been commanded by the Father. 2 JOHN 1:4

The Reminder

Every time a "big name" Christian leader hits the headlines because of a moral failure, I am reminded just how much Satan wants to ruin Christ's reputation through human leadership. It is a reminder that we wear a bull's-eye on our life because of our desire to influence others for Christ.

This year, right before Christmas, a friend we had known in ministry since our first year in youth ministry had an article printed about him in a local paper. He had a major morality issue that caused an affair, the breakup of a marriage in his congregation, and the loss of his church and his national ministry. I was praying that he wouldn't lose his own marriage or his children as a result.

In response to the scandal, I gave a gift to our church staff and to a group of young writers and speakers I had been mentoring. It was a simple frame with a set of verses in the front and a note on the back of the frame: "It is my prayer that you will always live a life of integrity, like the verses on the front. I hope to never read about you in the papers, like the article sandwiched inside. Praying protection on you. Always call if you ever need help, before it's too late."

I also had one made for my desk, so every day I would see 2 Peter 1:12, Colossians 1:10, and 2 John 1:4.

TO READ
Matthew 7:7-12

Do for others what you would like them
to do for you. MATTHEW 7:12

 Sharing Your Vision

When God gives you a vision for how to make an impact for Christ, you
need the support and advice of others. As you seek their help, it's essential
that you share with them what God has done in your life. How can you
share your vision with others most effectively?

Prepare ahead of time. Do your homework. Luke 14:28 warns us, "Suppose one of you wants to build a tower. Will he not first sit down and estimate the cost to see if he has enough money to complete it?" (NIV). Think it
out. What is the best way to share the experience so that the hearer catches
your vision? Give the person information, background, heart-tugging stories, but most of all give him or her a well-thought-out presentation. The
more important the person and his or her help are to you, the more vital
this is. You may be all excited about the new adventure, but don't expect
someone to be excited just because you are. It honors the other person to
plan your time with him or her.

Be courteous. When you phone, ask if the person has time to talk. Give a
time estimate. When you e-mail, thank him or her for the response. If he
or she gives time, connections, or advice, show appreciation. Be bold, definitely, as it is a compliment to ask someone for advice. However, be gracious. Don't tell someone God told you they would respond in any given
way to you. Let God guide them just as he guided you. Romans 13:7 gives
some wisdom: "Give everyone what you owe him: . . . if respect, then
respect; if honor, then honor" (NIV).

It will pay off, thoughtfulness always does. Every day people ask for my
help, but those I am most willing to go out of my way to aid are those who
show preparation and courtesy.

TO READ
Revelation 2:2-5

Look how far you have fallen from your first love! Turn back to me again and work as you did at first. If you don't, I will come and remove your lampstand from its place. REVELATION 2:5

 ## What's Wrong?

Wrong? We all hate to admit it, but sometimes we are wrong! Sometimes we rush a decision or miss information that would have shed a different light on the decision. Determine what went wrong.[2] But how? Then what?

Look at how God fixed the problem of sin.

Acknowledge the problem. God makes it clear in his Word: "All have sinned and fall short of the glory of God" (Romans 3:23, NIV).

Admit you are part of the problem. That's what repentance is all about—agreeing with God and turning in a new direction.

Actively pursue all relevant information. Did you gather all the facts? Did you listen to old mental tapes or have any old voices steering your heart? Did you look equally at all choices or jump to quick conclusions? Did you seek outside advice from seasoned godly professionals and trusted friends? Did you fall into pride? competitiveness? a power trip?

Amend relationships. Was anyone else hurt by your poor decision? Tell that person you are sorry.

Accentuate the positive. What did you learn? What new information do you have?

Activate a new process. Look at all the new ideas and options created by the situation.

Act! Decide and put the new plan in motion! Don't replay guilt, shame, or self-doubt; instead, repent and regroup!

<table>
<tr><td>TO READ
Exodus 34:21-24</td><td>Six days are set aside for work, but on the Sabbath day you must rest, even during the seasons of plowing and harvest. Exodus 34:21</td></tr>
</table>

 ## The Best Advice

Elijah killed 450 prophets of Baal, then ran miles to beat the king back to Jezreel. Then, being afraid of the king, he went another day's journey into the desert—and collapsed! He was so tired, he prayed that he would die (1 Kings 18 and 19). Exhaustion does weird things to you.

After seminary we moved to a townhouse for Bill to start a full-time position in youth ministry. We still had boxes in our living room when my extended family came for my brother's wedding. My uncle generously volunteered to hook up our ice maker to the refrigerator while were went to the wedding rehearsal. Arriving home late, we found a flood of water rushing out the door. Needless to say, we were up late!

The next day, Saturday, was the wedding, and then Sunday, with our family there, Bill was officially inducted into ministry, our first baby was dedicated, and we hosted a big family lunch. That night after the evening service, we went to the birthday party of our senior pastor's wife.

When we arrived, the baby was hungry, so I slipped into a quiet room alone—but he wouldn't settle down and nurse. He—I mean "I"—was too agitated. I walked out and handed him to his dad. Then I went to the buffet table, looked at the food, and started to cry. It was just too much activity and emotion in too little time!

The senior pastor's wife came up and asked me, "What's wrong, honey?" I told her about our packed weekend. Then she gave me some great advice: "Sometimes it isn't a spiritual problem; sometimes you just need a nap!"

Howard Hendricks once said, "Eighty-five percent of spirituality is a good night's sleep!"[3]

TO READ
Psalm 34:8-10

Taste and see that the Lord is good. Oh, the joys of those who trust in him! PSALM 34:8

 ## *You Can't Outgive God*

When we were young parents, Bill and I wrote a marriage mission statement to use as a grid for making decisions. It is common for me to have several requests for speaking engagements for the same weekend, so I use our mission statement to help me choose which ones to accept.

One of the repeating themes in our statement is that it is fun to be in God's will. Another is that "memories are more important than material goods." So when a church offered to teach my entire family to snowboard in exchange for my speaking—it matched our mission statement perfectly!

Not only did it match, but the associate pastor's kids taught my three boys to snowboard, and after we arrived, I learned they were on two Christian magazine covers as solid role models who were training to secure a spot on the Olympic team!

That night my thirteen-year-old son blessed the food at dinner and prayed, "God, thanks that Mom speaks well so we can snowboard. Amen!" No honorarium could have matched the thrill my boys experienced that day on the slopes—or the visual picture that God gives more when you give your skills and talents to him.

In God's economy you can't out-give God!

TO READ
Psalm 145:5-7

Your awe-inspiring deeds will be on every tongue;
I will proclaim your greatness. PSALM 145:6

 ## *Tell Someone!*

Sun Mee was young and inexperienced, but she had a passionate call. She believed God wanted her in broadcasting. When she shared her dream with adults, she got reservations, excuses, and rationalizations of why she shouldn't or couldn't expect to succeed in television.

Sun Mee believed that God's spot for her was on television in one of TV's meccas, Chicago. Her peers and adults scoffed, but when she shared her dream with the fourth-grade girls she taught in Sunday school, they were excited! They all wanted to pray. Those little girls were still unjaded and idealistic. Matthew 18:3 tells how Jesus understood this: "I tell you the truth, unless you change and become like little children, you will never enter the kingdom of heaven" (NIV).

Sun Mee knew she had to walk by faith—after all, now she had an audience that was watching what God could do! Sun Mee sent résumés, made phone calls, and visited networks. Within a year she was in front of the camera. Her fourth-grade cheerleaders now believed God could do great things for them, too!

Sun Mee has become an award-winning television producer. As she looks back, one of the most important first steps was to tell her vision to someone who would believe God with her for a miracle!

Have you made your dream public? Choose to tell someone who believes God with childlike faith, who believes in you and in dreams that can come true!

TO READ
1 Corinthians 9:24-27

Remember that in a race everyone runs, but only one person gets the prize. You also must run in such a way that you will win. 1 CORINTHIANS 9:24

 Run for the Prize

America cheered for her as she ran down the track to gold, not once or twice, but three times. Most people wouldn't have given Florence Griffith Joyner any hope. She was one of eleven children raised by a single mother in a Los Angeles housing project.

"I've always had this everlasting faith that has taught me that with faith, with belief in myself, and if I carry God everywhere I go, I'll be able to move mountains. And despite all the obstacles . . . I've never gone alone."

People have commented on seeing her talk to herself at the starting line like she did at the 1988 Olympics, "I wasn't talking to myself; I was asking Jesus, 'Lord, stay right here. Don't make me the winner. Just give me the strength to do what you've given me to do, what I've practiced all my life for. And that's to do the best I can do. I don't care if I win or lose, as long as I give my best. And if my best is a gold medal, then yes, I would like the medal.'"[4]

She attacked life with that same faith. "I read my Bible every day, and I surround myself with positive people, positive books, positive everything as much as I can. . . ." Flo-Jo wanted to teach kids to do the same so she started the Florence Griffith Joyner Youth Foundation.

Flo-Jo encouraged everyone to dream a little: "Set goals and write them down. Doing so will help you know where you want to go. . . . Make sure your goals are your goals. . . . No one else can run the race for you."

TO READ
Psalm 119:25-32

I weep with grief; encourage me by your word.

PSALM 119:28

 Out of Gas!

"Oh no!" I cried as I looked at the gas gauge in disbelief. It was one of those hectic, "terrible, horrible, no-good, very bad days."[5] I had a to-do list the size of a phone book, and now my car was sputtering to an abrupt halt on the freeway. It refused to move despite my pleadings. "We're almost to the off-ramp; you can at least make it there! Please move—just a little farther. Don't be out of gas. Not here. Not now!" I was definitely out of gas.

Out of gas. That phrase rang in my head. *That's how I feel, Lord. I've given and given so much lately. I'm running on empty.*

I longed to be filled up by the Word. The psalmist experienced this as he wrote in Psalm 119: "My soul is weary with sorrow; strengthen me according to your word. . . . My soul faints with longing for your salvation, but I have put my hope in your word. . . . Your word is a lamp to my feet and a light for my path. . . .You are my refuge and my shield; I have put my hope in your word. . . . I rise before dawn and cry for help; I have put my hope in your word" (Psalm 119:28, 81, 105, 114, 147, NIV).

Walking down the freeway to the off-ramp, I had plenty of time to think about how hungry I had become for God. I tried rationalizing. *God, you know I've been very busy—school, kids, work, ministry, the house. . . .* The words seemed so hollow.

I recalled the bookmark in my Bible, a quote from Oswald Chambers: "My worth to God in public is what I am in private."[6]

TO READ
Psalm 84:8-12

The Lord God is our light and protector. He gives us grace and glory. No good thing will the Lord withhold from those who do what is right.

PSALM 84:11

 Honor for Honor

One of the first verses I came across in my quiet time when I first recommitted my life to Christ as an eighteen-year-old college student was the simple principle of Psalm 84:11. The principle seemed clear: Those who honor God, God honors.

Shortly after, I read how I should not be unequally yoked with an unbeliever, so I broke up with my boyfriend. Then I met Bill. I read how God wanted my heart to be pure, so Bill and I decided that all our choices would be above reproach—we decided not to kiss until we were engaged, and we dated so that our hearts could remain pure before God moment by moment. Now I see the fruit of that choice: a marriage that defies all odds. Both Bill and I come from homes that, by statistics, say our relationship should have ended in divorce early on—especially since we married at twenty. Instead, Bill and I lead marriage conferences and have a happy marriage that will mark twenty-five years this anniversary.

As a first-time mother, I cried out to God, "Parent me, so I can parent Brock." In response God through his Word laid out parenting priorities for us. Years later, Brock, our eighteen-year-old, graduated from high school with numerous awards and scholarships. Of course, honoring God is not a formula for gaining what the world considers success. Many parents follow the same biblical priorities and don't see their children choose the right path. But if you honor God, eventually you will be able to look back and see ways in which he has honored you. Honor comes in many forms—some public adulation, some trophies and awards, but mostly in relationships and love, joy, and personal peace.

March

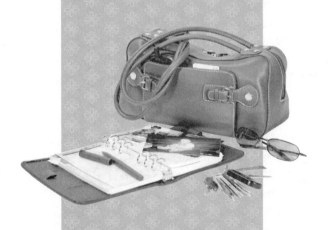

TO READ
Romans 6:9-11

We are sure of this because Christ rose from the dead, and he will never die again. Death no longer has any power over him. ROMANS 6:9

 ## Don't Give Up!

Our son Caleb gave his testimony at his baptism (emphasis added):

My dad is a pastor, so I know a lot about God. But just like others, I fought giving my heart to Jesus. The way I gave my heart to God is all because of my mom. When I went to church Palm Sunday when I was five, I came home and told my mom, "Mom, Jesus rode in on a donkey, and they waved branches. Then he died on the cross."

My mom said, "That's right, then Jesus was placed in a tomb. But death couldn't hold him, and he rose again and he's alive."

I said, *"No, he's dead."*

The next day Mom said, "Caleb, let me show you some verses. She told me that after Christ rose, all his disciples saw him, and even Thomas put his hands in his side and touched the holes in his hand" (1 Corinthians 15:3-8).

I said, *"Mom, Jesus is dead!"*

The next day she told me that over five hundred people saw Jesus after he rose from the dead, and I said, *"No Mom, Jesus is dead."*

The next day Mom pulled out a big book, *Evidence That Demands a Verdict,* and she read me all this stuff this lawyer, Josh McDowell, wrote to prove Jesus rose, and I said, *"Mom, Jesus is dead."*

The next day Mom told me her testimony and said, "Jesus is alive, his Spirit lives in my heart."

I said, "That can't be true—Jesus is dead!" The next day Mom told me Dad's testimony, and I said, *"Jesus is dead!"*

That Sunday was Easter, and I went to church for an Easter play. After the play, Mom and I were rocking together in the rocking chair, and I said, *"Mom, Jesus is alive! I want him in my life."* Then I prayed, and Jesus is alive in my heart now!

Mom, thanks for not giving up on me.

TO READ
Galatians 6:1-5

Carry each other's burdens, and in this way you will fulfill the law of Christ. GALATIANS 6:2, NIV

 Safe Harbor

Jan has a large extended family. She was the first in her family to come to faith in Christ and the first to grow into an emotionally healthy lifestyle. With her family watching, God has restored her marriage and held her together through some very trying times, like job changes, teen crisis, and hospice care for her in-laws.

Members of her extended family want what she has but are at different places in their spiritual journeys. Many are seekers who want to learn more about God but have yet to trust him with their lives. When trouble comes, they call Jan.

Recently Jan confessed, "Pam, I have been observing my life this last year. When I am in my small group, I seem to have the strength and the answers to deal with my family. Each time I think I am too busy and don't have time for it in my schedule, I start feeling like a ship that has taken on water.

"But when I get back to my small group, I feel like my head comes up out of the water. It's like Bible study is my life jacket or a little blow-up dinghy. I need to make it a priority. I'll drown without it."

We all need to make time for Bible study. David writes in Psalm 73:26, "My flesh and my heart may fail, but God is the strength of my heart and my portion forever" (NIV).

The word *strength* means "God is our boulder, a rock to lean on, a foundation to stand on, a refuge." Only as I make God's Word a priority do I have anything to give. A Bible study should be a refuge, a safe harbor.

TO READ
Colossians 3:12-17

You must make allowance for each other's faults and forgive the person who offends you. Remember, the Lord forgave you, so you must forgive others.

COLOSSIANS 3:13

 ## *The Call*

Honestly, I had written her off. I had dedicated numerous hours to helping her achieve her goals, learn to make wiser choices, and heal. I had sacrificed time with my family and friends to make time for her. Then she decided to walk away from me, our church, God, and anything that resembled a good choice. She was in full rebellion.

But she'd drop in on occasion—she'd come to church high on drugs or alcohol. She would come to an event dressed provocatively. Once she put younger believers in a bad place, so I had to gently confront her. I tried to explain how she was hurting herself and others. She responded with one of the most vicious verbal attacks I have ever received. Everything ugly she had ever thought or felt came spewing out at me. All I had ever done was love her—and this was how I was being repaid.

She stormed out. I prayed, asking God for a miracle—because I certainly wasn't able to penetrate her pain.

Years went by. Then the call came.

"Pam, do you have a minute? I'd like to tell you what God has done in my life. I am so sorry. God has revealed to me lately the long string of people he sent my way to help me and how I hurt every one of them. So now I am calling each one of them to say, 'I'm sorry, and please forgive me.'"

Is there someone whose forgiveness you need to ask?

Finally, I confessed all my sins to you and stopped trying to hide them. I said to myself, "I will confess my rebellion to the Lord." And you forgave me! All my guilt is gone. PSALM 32:5

 *Own Up!*

I was running late. The conference where I was speaking had run over. What was once enough time to travel from the conference, drive home, pick up my husband, and catch a plane for a media tour was now uncomfortably tight.

I called Bill's cell phone to see if he could do a couple of things for me ahead of time. I got him on the phone and explained the situation, to which he replied, "Honey, I have some good news and some bad news. The good news is I love you. The bad news is I'm not home. Brock's car broke down in Oceanside [twenty minutes away from home], and I'm waiting for a tow truck. So there are a few things I need you to do for me when you get home."

My list had just doubled, so I was very stressed when I hit the front door. Our middle son was home, so I quickly briefed him on the situation and enlisted his help. Then I hit the pavement running. As I whizzed through the living room, I saw that Zach was sitting down. Something inside me snapped. I felt a rush of anger. Then I stopped myself.

"Pam, this situation is triggering old baggage. You feel like you are going to fail, and when you feel this way, anger is your first response—but it's a wrong response. You cannot verbally explode on Zach. That would be unfair and wrong. He did not cause this problem. You chose to run with a tight margin. This is your issue, not Zach's. Own the issue."

Psalm 32:5 reminds me of this process: "I confessed all my sins to you and stopped trying to hide them."

Don't blame someone else—own up to your sin.

TO READ
Proverbs 11:25-31

The generous prosper and are satisfied; those who refresh others will themselves be refreshed.

PROVERBS 11:25

 Give and Get

My mother lives in Idaho. She is a loving grandmother and wishes she could live closer to give more TLC to her grandchildren, so she began to pray that since she couldn't be here, God would send others to "grandparent" her grandsons.

Rose and Dan are active seniors in our church. They are committed Christians who have raised some wonderful leaders, including a married daughter who is a missionary in Bolivia. Their only grandchildren are on the mission field.

Bill and I travel and speak together at marriage conferences. We began to notice that our youngest seemed to fall behind at school when he stayed with his friend who had very contentious parents. After talking to him, we discerned he needed *one* stable loving couple to befriend him when we had to travel. We asked Rose and Dan to pray about "grandparenting" Caleb. They said they'd try it out and see if Caleb liked it.

At our annual Thanksgiving Eve service, eleven-year-old Caleb stood and shared with the congregation: "What I am thankful for this year is Mr. and Mrs. Senor. They love me and take care of me when my parents have to travel. They are so nice. And Mrs. Senor is a really good cook!"

Instead of feeling sorry for themselves, Rose and Dan have generously loved Caleb, and in return, Caleb loves them. In giving, they receive.

My mom and Rose have formed a friendship. Either woman could have chosen depression, but instead they chose to turn their desire for close relationships into a generous gift that in turn became a boomerang of love.

TO READ
Proverbs 11:1-14

With many counselors, there is safety.

PROVERBS 11:14

 Choir of Advisors

Shelly decided the only way out of the incest was to run. Fortunately, she had met a wonderful family at camp the summer before. She gathered up all her money and took the first bus across the country. The family took her in and helped her get counseling and feel like a normal high school student: flag team, volleyball, church youth group, and e-mailing buddies.

However, one day in an e-mail chat room, Troy logged on, and a relationship formed over the high-tech highway. They decided to meet. When she told her host family and youth leader, they went ballistic. The host mom said, "What do you know about this guy? Who's his family? Where does he work? Where does he live?"

When she explained he was 37 and lived in Chicago, her surrogate mom had more reservations. "You aren't even eighteen. This is like a repeat of what happened with your father. Honey, please don't go meet him. I just don't have a good feeling about this."

When she told her youth leader, she was sure she'd get a sympathetic ear, but it was like a replay of her host mother. When she shared the idea of meeting her new "love" with her friend from summer camp, she thought at least she'd understand, but instead, it was the same echo of questions.

Is there a chorus of voices in your life? Are you surrounded by people who care about you, God, and the truth? If everyone who loves God is questioning your decisions, you might want to check that decision with a few more solid sounding boards, like a trained counselor, a pastor, a Bible study leader, a teacher, or a coach who loves God.

 If all these people who love God are in agreement—it's definitely time to listen!

Guard me as the apple of your eye. Hide me in the shadow of your wings. PSALM 17:8

 ## *Replay*

Teresa felt as if a dark cloud were following her around. But why? From the outside her life seemed wonderful. She had a kind husband and two excelling children.

Each day brought mail with more good news—so why was she feeling a sense of doom? She felt like she was going to collapse with a mix of contrasting emotions: anger, frustration, depression, panic, and hopelessness for herself and her family. She knew she couldn't keep living this way. Her family couldn't deal with her being this way. Something had to change—or someone had to change.

It's not unusual to sense anxiety when your child is approaching the age you were when some traumatic event or abuse may have happened in your own life. Unchecked, your actions and feelings will become more overstated, and you will feel out of control. If those who love you are asking you questions like, "What is up?" "Why are you overreacting?" Those can be signals that the problem isn't with your spouse, your child, or even your life, but with *you.*

If it feels like the black clouds are rolling in, and you're afraid of the coming storm, what's the first step out of the rain? Take shelter from the fear by investing in resources to broaden your view of God. The bigger, stronger, more loving, and more able you see God, the smaller your sense of doom and gloom will become.

Is there something in your past that could be impacting your future? Knowing that fears might be ahead will help you prepare. Step out of the storm and under God's wings of care.

| TO READ
Titus 2:3-5 | Teach the older women. . . . These older women must train the younger women. Titus 2:3-4 |

 Older and Wiser

An angel shows up to tell you that you are going to give birth to the Son of God. How would you react?

"'I am the Lord's servant,' Mary answered" (Luke 1:38, NIV).

She was a fearful teenager but agreed to the plan—reservedly. Then just a few verses later, we witness a transformed Mary, rejoicing:

"My soul glorifies the Lord and my spirit rejoices in God my Savior. . . . From now on all generations will call me blessed, for the Mighty One has done great things for me" (Luke 1:46-49, NIV).

What happened to bring such a change?

Mary went to Zechariah's home to visit her cousin, Elizabeth. This was Mary's older and wiser cousin who had also witnessed an angel explaining she was to bear a special child—John the Baptist. If validation and confirmation were what Mary was looking for—she got them:

> When Elizabeth heard Mary's greeting, the baby leaped in her womb, and Elizabeth was filled with the Holy Spirit. In a loud voice she exclaimed: "Blessed are you among women, and blessed is the child you will bear! But why am I so favored, that the mother of my Lord should come to me? . . . Blessed is she who has believed that what the Lord has said to her will be accomplished!" (Luke 1:41-45, NIV)

This mentoring relationship was exactly what God had planned to encourage Mary's heart. Do you have someone older and wiser to whom you can go for encouragement?

TO READ
Leviticus 25:1-7

During the seventh year the land will enjoy a Sabbath year of rest to the Lord. Do not plant your crops or prune your vineyards during that entire year. LEVITICUS 25:4

Sabbatical

Israel was commanded by God to take a Sabbath rest every seven years. Instead of planting and harvesting, the people were to spend the year in rest, reflection, and restoration.

A Sabbath break can be welcome time off to rest physically, emotionally, and socially. By setting aside time that would have been filled by the regular ebb and flow of our daily life, we can replenish our lives.

Professors often take a semester off to travel or do research. A few fortunate pastors have churches that invest in sabbaticals so they will gain more to give.

After my father passed away, I took a minisabbatical from my ministry responsibilities for several months because I needed time to process my grief and handle other responsibilities with my family. Some of my friends in leadership have planned extended times of rest during career transitions. Some families have built periods of rest and replenishment into their lives yearly, setting up summers off or at least working part-time and planning a change of location: cabins by the lake, a few weeks at summer camp, or a month in the country.

If you are feeling worn out, get out your calendar and budget, and figure out how you can take time for rest and relaxation. However, a true sabbatical isn't just a vacation; rather, it is a plan for restoration and replenishment.

Worship, study in the Word, time with positive people, and quiet moments of reflection, contemplation, and prayer should all be included. A sabbatical isn't dropping out of life; rather, it is dropping into God's presence so you can gain a better, stronger view of your life. By taking time to take care of yourself both physically and spiritually, you will feel stronger for the journey ahead.

TO READ
James 1:12-18

Whatever is good and perfect comes to us from God above, who created all heaven's lights. Unlike them, he never changes or casts shifting shadows.

JAMES 1:17

 ## The Convertible

Candy announced to the married coworker who sat at her kitchen table, "I'm sorry. You came here tonight probably thinking something was going to happen between us, but I need you to leave right now."

She had planned to have an affair, but the Spirit inside her screamed, "No!" Had she drifted so far from God that she'd been willing to have an affair?

"God, I trust you with everything: my heart, my finances, and my future—all of it. If you want me to go to the singles conference with the kids so I can really restart my life with you, I trust you can get me there."

As a single mother of two, she didn't know how she could go. She had no money, and her car was broken down.

That weekend she went to a single-parent day where she won a free car rental in a drawing. Then she got a phone call that said she was the recipient of a scholarship for the conference. But a change in child care was going to take an extra two hundred dollars out of her budget. She wasn't sure she'd have enough money for food, let alone for any activities with her children during the camp's free time.

Then an envelope arrived in the mail. Inside was one hundred dollars and a note that said, "In case you need money for the kids this weekend." So Candy had her friend drop them off at the car rental company. When Candy took her certificate to the counter, the clerk said, "Here you go. It's the black convertible."

Not only was Candy going to the conference—she and the kids were going in style!

God has so much more to give us than what we expect.

TO READ
2 Corinthians 1:3-7

All praise to the God and Father of our Lord Jesus Christ. He is the source of every mercy and the God who comforts us. He comforts us in all our troubles so that we can comfort others. When others are troubled, we will be able to give them the same comfort God has given us. 2 CORINTHIANS 1:3-4

 Never Again!

"Never again will I be beaten. Never again will my children see their mother hit—never again!"

Jeanette got up a different woman: calm, confident, with a clear plan. She had just a few days to move herself and her children to a safe place. Her husband was in jail for domestic violence, but he would be released soon. She had to locate financing, find a home, move, and then figure out how to provide for her two toddlers.

She left with a handful of phone numbers and a heart full of hope. Her support team would meet with Jeanette in a few days to assess her progress and to help her discern the next few steps.

Jeanette brought two notebooks. "This one is for me, and this one is for the women's ministry team. I keep finding more resources that are available to battered women, single moms, and those going through divorce. I want to help other women who might need it."

Jeanette became like an investigative reporter logging the vital information. Each time the support team met, Jeanette was more confident. She gathered evidence that her lawyer used to ensure her husband's maximum jail time.

When time for his release came near, she decided that with full custody of the children, her ex-husband's violations of court orders, and his threatening letters, she and the children would be safer in another state.

She completed her education and went to work for a sheriff's department, where she was named to head a domestic violence task force.

How can God use your pain to provide help for others?

I pray that from his glorious, unlimited resources he will give you mighty inner strength through his Holy Spirit. EPHESIANS 3:16

 Struggles That Define

"It is our struggles that define us," my friend Donnie said to me.

Think of some of the heroes of the faith: Abram was called to move "to the land that I will show you" (Genesis 12:1). This was a struggle to walk by faith not sight. God renamed him Abraham, and he is known as the father of three religions: Judaism, Islam, and Christianity.

Joseph was sold into slavery by his brothers, a struggle of the ultimate betrayal. Yet he forgave his brothers, and God rewarded him with the post of Egypt's second-in-command.

Daniel, a slave, struggled to worship the true God—but he did. He was thrown into a den of lions and lived to tell about it.

Esther, a queen, struggled, knowing that her people were about to be annihilated. Only she could risk walking into the king's presence and asking for mercy. Her statement of courage, "If I perish, I perish," has gone down in history.

Naomi was a widow struggling for survival for herself and two daughters-in-law. She didn't know how they could all live. In the end her decision to return to Bethlehem gained her economic survival, a precious relationship with Ruth, a new son-in-law, and a new grandchild in the messianic line.

What is your struggle? Can you see how God is defining you and his work in your life through it? Cling to him, and he will bring you to the other side.

TO READ
Jeremiah 29:11-14

"I know the plans I have for you," says the Lord. "They are plans for good and not for disaster, to give you a future and a hope." JEREMIAH 29:11

 ## There Is a Plan

"Trish," I said as I pulled up next to the young, shy woman I had met at church, "would you and the kids like a ride home?" Her story quickly tumbled out. She had been sexually molested by a member of her own family, and as a result, she went looking for love. A high school classmate used her in the same way, and she found herself pregnant at fifteen and married to him—thinking he would rescue her.

He moved her and the baby, and then two babies, into a small travel trailer. He would leave her and the children for weeks without food, diapers, heat, or money.

One day an old friend of her husband's came to visit. He saw how Trish was living and said, "You can't live like this. Come live with me." So she did. Trish left her marriage and moved into a live-in arrangement with John, who she thought was her knight in shining armor. He soon took her welfare money and spent it on drugs, alcohol, and gifts for other women. Trish discovered she had a sexually transmitted disease—and then he began to beat her.

That is why Trish had fled to church that night.

"Trish, God loves you, and he has a plan for your life to give you and the kids a future and a hope—and Trish, this isn't God's best for you."

"I really want to know God's plan. I don't want my kids to grow up and have to go through what I've been through. Please tell me how I can know God's plan. I want a fresh start—whatever it takes."

Have you been looking for a rescuer? Look up—God has a plan for your life.

TO READ
Galatians 5:13-18

I advise you to live according to your new life in the Holy Spirit. Then you won't be doing what your sinful nature craves. GALATIANS 5:16

 ## The Destroyer's Fingerprint

The phone call changed my entire day. All of life's priorities were reshuffled with a single call. A friend from my son's football team had called to say a former player's mom had committed suicide. I rallied support for her husband and sons, first by calling Bill, who visited the family, and then by putting in place a series of helping gestures. We just did what we do—help.

But I couldn't shake the picture of a woman I knew feeling so blue and desperate that death seemed a better option than life. I discovered that she had struggled with mental illness and had gone off her medication.

Then I became angry at Satan. In John 10:10 it says "The thief does not come except to steal, and to kill, and to destroy. I [Jesus] have come that they may have life, and that they may have it more abundantly" (NKJV).

That's what had happened: kill, steal, and destroy. A life, a precious mommy, was gone. Dreams were stolen. Hope was destroyed.

We can't turn the clock back, but if we could, we'd probably be able to see the early lies Satan whispered. His lies always kill our confidence; steal our peace, joy, and love; and destroy our hopes, dreams, and relationships. In fact, that's how we can discern his handiwork. If we are thinking thoughts that are destroying our love, joy, peace, patience, kindness, gentleness, faithfulness, or self-control, then Satan, not the Spirit of God, is doing the whispering. If our actions or words are stealing our hope or future, then Satan is in charge. If people are being destroyed by our words or actions, then the Spirit isn't guiding those words or actions.

Look for Satan's fingerprint: kill, steal, and destroy. If you see them, walk 180 degrees in the other direction, and you'll be headed toward God.

TO READ
Hebrews 12:1-4

We do this by keeping our eyes on Jesus, on whom our faith depends from start to finish. He was willing to die a shameful death on the cross because of the joy he knew would be his afterward. Now he is seated in the place of highest honor beside God's throne in heaven. HEBREWS 12:2

 ## It's All about Me

"I never get time for *me*. . . . I thought it was time to spend money on *me*. . . . I deserve something for *me*. . . . I needed to have the plastic surgery for *me*. . . . No, I can't come to Bible study—I need to do more for *me*. . . . It is *my* turn. . . . I need to find *myself*."

Me, myself, and I. When I start hearing those words repeated in every conversation I have with a woman, I fear she is headed for disaster. It is interesting that *selfishness* is translated "strife" in the KJV, and in Greek it means "contention." Nothing good comes to mind with those words!

While it is important and necessary that a woman discover her gifts, use her talents, and understand who she is, too many women turn to self-centered pursuits on their journey of discovery. The danger in making life "all about you" is that you will often succeed. A life that is egocentric—centered on fulfilling your hopes, dreams, and goals regardless of the price—becomes an empty life.

Your husband may patiently endure, but his heart will detach emotionally. Your children, no matter their age, will pick up on the vibes that you and your needs are a higher priority than they are and their needs. Soon they, too, will look for others to meet their emotional needs.

A woman who thinks she can solve her emotional pain by turning inward is a woman on a lonely journey. Friends, family, and coworkers will get your message loud and clear: "Leave me alone. Let me live my life!" They will let you, and your world will shrink down to *one*.

Take your pain, questions, and need for personal space or identity and look up, not in. God will answer your heart cry. Listen to yourself this week. How often do you hear, "Me, myself, or I?"

Oh, that they would always have hearts like this, that they might fear me and obey all my commands! If they did, they and their descendants would prosper forever. DEUTERONOMY 5:29

 What Are You Afraid Of?

Avoiding dealing with issues can be a learned behavior, passed down in family trees. Take Abraham and Isaac, for example. Abraham was afraid, and it put others in danger.

When he was going to Egypt, he became concerned that his beautiful wife, Sarah, might put him at risk if the Egyptians thought that she was his wife. So Abraham lied and told them that Sarah was his sister. Because of his lie, the Egyptians treated him well, giving him all kinds of livestock and servants. But the Lord wasn't happy with the situation and inflicted diseases on Pharaoh and his household. They questioned why Abraham had lied and told them that Sarah was his sister when she was his wife.

Abraham couldn't trust God to take care of him and his wife, so he tried to handle his fear by his own methods. And a generation later his son Isaac handled fear the same way.

Isaac, afraid that he might be killed because of his wife's beauty, told the Philistines that Rebekah was his sister to try to save himself—just like his father, Abraham.

Your children learn how to make choices by watching yours. How much clearer can that process be than with the stories of Abraham and his son?

What are those around you learning from how you deal with fear?

TO READ
Isaiah 26:1-6

You will keep in perfect peace all who trust in you, whose thoughts are fixed on you! Isaiah 26:3

 ## Thought Control

Determination is a key ingredient in living out our dreams. But some days it seems everything goes wrong!

At those moments when bad news comes or my plans come to a screeching halt, my natural reaction is anger, fear, or depression. If life were a movie, dark foreboding music would be playing in the background to heighten the already strong sense of impending doom!

At those moments it is easy to believe Satan's lies: "You're going to fail. This will never happen! What were you thinking?"

Instead, I choose to take the thought captive and put the bad news in perspective. What's the worst-case scenario? Usually it is inconvenience more than failure. Then I also ask, "Is God still in control?" Looking to the many verses that declare God is sovereign Lord or supreme Deity, I can say the obvious answer is yes!

Then I ask, "What help is available to help me?" I don't usually have a clue, but God is wise. I am afraid of failure, but God is perfect and never fails. I may be without resources, but God created and owns everything.

As I recall the truth about God and review his strengths, I am forced to think thoughts beyond my own. That process helps me think differently. New, better, and even creative thoughts and options begin to appear.

And peace comes—and with it the ability to think more clearly.

TO READ
Proverbs 19:16-23

Listen to advice and accept instruction, and in the end you will be wise. PROVERBS 19:20, NIV

 Turn It Up!

It was happily ever after, or so Tammi thought. For eighteen years she and her husband had been the ideal couple, but one Sunday morning her world fell apart. Her husband confessed he no longer loved her and had been in numerous affairs over the past sixteen years. He was seeing another woman and planned to move out.

"I wanted to *die* and end the pain—but I knew God could pull me through. I ate, drank, and slept the Word. I believe God promised me that if I would be obedient to him, he would give me a marriage better than anything I had experienced."

So Tammi did everything God impressed upon her—even when it went in direct opposition to what friends and family were advising.

"I lost many friends for a time. Even my family disowned me, but I kept obeying God." Her husband was gone only a few days when he returned seeking her forgiveness. They lived apart for a short time while each received intensive counseling.

"Then God prepared me and told me to welcome him back with joy." He has now been clean from any addictions for over five years, and we have been happily married in an honest, growing relationship ever since. I feel like I am the happiest married woman on earth."

Is God's voice louder than any other voice in your hearing? Turn up the volume on his voice by getting into his Word, by listening to Christian tapes and music, and by attending Bible studies and church.

Turn up the volume!

| TO READ
Philippians 2:5-8 | He made himself nothing; he took the humble position of a slave and appeared in human form.
PHILIPPIANS 2:7 |

 ## *Turn Around*

Mary came to the retreat feeling like an outsider. All the women there seemed so beautiful, so together, and deeply spiritual. She felt like the little song I sang with my toddlers: "One of these things is not like the other; one of these things just doesn't belong. One of these things is not like the other; which one is wrong?" She felt wrong.

Of course all the women were happy she came and glad to have her as part of the group. They saw her as "in" the group, but Mary still felt "out."

The next morning she went with the group to the early morning worship. After worship, I was walking just ahead of Mary following some other women on what appeared to be a shortcut on the trail. It was a shortcut all right—but one with a tricky jump off a rock to a trail below. I navigated the jump and thought. *Hmm, this is a little treacherous. I wouldn't want anyone to get hurt.* So I simply reached back and helped the woman behind me, Mary. Then I stayed to help a few more who had followed us down.

Jesus did the ultimate reaching back. He became human to be able to relate to us and our struggles. "Your attitude should be the same as that of Christ Jesus: Who, being in very nature God, did not consider equality with God something to be grasped, but made himself nothing, taking the very nature of a servant, being made in human likeness" (Philippians 2:5-7, NIV).

On Sunday Mary came up to me and explained all that had transpired over the weekend, relating how she had gone from feeling like an outsider, with lots of spiritual questions, to someone who now had the "inside scoop" on how a person could have a personal relationship with Christ. She said she had enjoyed the talks I gave, but it was me turning around that helped her feel "in"cluded.

Turn around on the trail you are on. To whom can you lend a helping hand?

TO READ
Psalm 42:1-11

Why am I discouraged? Why so sad? I will put my hope in God! I will praise him again—my Savior and my God! PSALM 42:11

 ## *Determined*

When it comes to people in the public eye, we usually see the payoff, the pinnacle, but often we don't see the pit or the pain that so often proceeds God's payoff. There isn't really much distance between a pat on the back and a kick in the seat of the pants. Blessing often comes from brokenness.

I stood in the center of my kitchen one day after receiving a discouraging phone call. My husband and I held each other and sobbed, but these were not polite tears of frustration; they were sobs from the core of our being. I prayed, "God! We give up! We have done what we thought was right, tried to follow you, and right now it seems the payback for that is pain.

"Your Word does say, 'Here on earth you will have many trials and sorrows. But take heart, because I have overcome the world' [John 16:33]. We 'know the one in whom [we] trust' [2 Timothy 1:12]. God, you are able to make all grace abound to us, so that in all things at all times, we'll have all we need [2 Corinthians 9:8, paraphrased]. We are sick of the tears. Sick of the fears. Sick of the sadness. Sick of the madness. We are sick of the pain, and we cry out to you because our plans are in pieces at our feet. We are broken and spilled out. We are at the end of ourselves. We need you and only you. We are determined to turn the corner and leave this pain behind."

I picked up the nearest Bible and flipped open to Psalm 23:1-4. There I read: "I look to you, heaven-dwelling God, look up to you for help. Like servants, alert to their Master's commands, like a maiden attending her lady, we're watching and waiting, holding our breath, awaiting your word of mercy. Mercy, God, Mercy! We've been kicked around long enough" (*The Message*).

God's Word reflects his determined heart of hope to you. Be determined that the Word will win in your life.

TO READ
Psalm 122:1-9

All the people of Israel—the Lord's people—make their pilgrimage here. They come to give thanks to the name of the Lord as the law requires.

PSALM 122:4

 ## The Pity Party

On the wall in my kitchen is a sign that is six feet long. It says: Thou Shalt Not Whine. My kids think it's there for them, but it's really there for me. Serving women for over twenty years and being a woman myself, I know how easy it is to fall into a pity party.

When days get blue, one of the things I like to do is read about women who have gone before, those with great odds to overcome. I especially like to read about women who came west, selling nearly all their possessions, packing up their children, and braving the hard, long trails. Many of these women lost children to disease, the enemy, or wild animals. These brave women then held down the frontier, cooking, baking, washing, and sewing with the most primitive of tools in dugout homes made of sod.

At first these pioneers staked their claims a great distance from one another, but soon the settlers learned that when they built their homes on adjoining property lines, the four neighbors were close enough to gather for quilting, canning, and the birthing of babies. The pity party seemed to turn into a time of rejoicing with the support of just one other woman who could relate to her life.

Look at the early church's example: "All the believers were together and had everything in common. . . . Every day they continued to meet together in the temple courts. They broke bread in their homes and ate together with glad and sincere hearts" (Acts 2:44, 46, NIV).

Loneliness feeds the whining—friendship divides the sorrow.

TO READ
Psalm 119:41-48

I will walk in freedom, for I have devoted myself to your commandments. PSALM 119:45

Where Have You Been Walking?

When I was a young girl about eight years old, I walked to and from church because I just wanted to be where God "lived." I'd silently slip into the main sanctuary, surrounded by light streaming from the stained-glass windows. My feet would slide quietly over the deep burgundy carpet as I inched my way up to the front pew so I could be near the big white Bible that lay open on the Communion table. I didn't care that I had to walk blocks and blocks to get to church. It was peaceful there, and I felt as if heaven smiled on me each time I entered. I learned many truths there, including one found in a simple Sunday school song: "Be Careful Little Feet Where You Go."

As I grew up, I began to realize how easy it is for women to walk away from what is true, right, and healthy and how easy it is to walk toward what is wrong: wrong man's arms, wrong bar, or wrong party.

Some steps away from the truth are more subtle: spending more and more time with a persuasive friend who doesn't acknowledge Christ or his principles; reading magazines that make me feel inferior about my body; listening to songs that glorify casual sex; or even walking to the beach instead of church on Sunday morning.

Our prayer should be: "Teach me your way, O Lord, and I will walk in your truth; give me an undivided heart, that I may fear your name" (Psalm 86:11, NIV). And the result: "I will walk about in freedom, for I have sought out your precepts" (Psalm 119:45, NIV).

Retrace your footsteps over the past few days. Where have you been walking? Where would you like to walk?

TO READ
Proverbs 27:17-23

As iron sharpens iron, a friend sharpens a friend.

PROVERBS 27:17

 ## You Gotta Have Friends

"Would you like to bring a few of your healthy friends to the next meeting?" I asked.

"Healthy friends? What do you mean?"

"Do you have one or two friends who encourage you to make wise and godly choices? Positive people who believe in you, want the best for you?"

She stared back at me, drawing a total blank, and then she flatly responded, "Um, no. I don't think I do."

What a shame! It is really true that misery loves company and bad company corrupts good morals (1 Corinthians 15:33). People of severe dysfunction seem to be magnets for people with severe dysfunction.

Often when a woman desires to change her life, she may have to go outside her friendship circle to find help and support. Developing new, healthier friendships can feel a little frightening, especially if you are still battling old ghosts from your life and lies burned into your thinking. Lies like, "You aren't good enough, smart enough, or pretty enough."

How can you battle past the lies and gain some healthier friends?

- Hang out where healthy women hang out: Bible studies, support groups, career enhancement organizations, parenting classes, or places of education.
- Meet women in small groups or one-on-one in a neutral setting, like for coffee or with your children at a playground.
- Offer to help them achieve their goals. Healthy women are often busy women, so spend time in their world and observe how they interact with others, how they handle their responsibilities. Volunteer to serve on a committee they run, or offer to work a few hours in their office.
- Identify women who are a step or two ahead of you on the wellness trail, and be their encourager. You may find they will encourage you in return.

TO READ
Mark 12:28-34

You must love the Lord your God with all your heart, all your soul, all your mind, and all your strength. MARK 12:30

 Who's More Important?

"See you tonight at the meeting, Pam?"

That question, asked years ago, seemed simple enough, but I was full of excuses.

"I'm not sure. John, my boyfriend, is coming into town. It's my birthday, and he wants to take me to dinner."

"But the Bible study doesn't start until 8:30. You'd have time to come after dinner," said Tina, the young woman who was discipling me.

"Yeah, but I don't know if he'll want to come. He's just not into God like I am."

"Is he a believer, Pam?"

"I'm not really exactly sure."

"And you've been dating how long?"

"About two years."

"Pam, the Bible says we're not supposed to be unequally yoked. See?"

She pointed at 2 Corinthians 6:14: "Do not be yoked together with unbelievers. For what do righteousness and wickedness have in common? Or what fellowship can light have with darkness?" (NIV).

"Pam you've really been growing spiritually, and now this young man is encouraging you to break a commitment to Christ. Do you see a problem with this?"

I stared blankly back.

"Pam, who's more important to you? Jesus or John?"

I stuttered out, "J-J-Jesus, of course." Then, the Holy Spirit inside me whispered, *"Then why did she have to ask?"*

Who's more important to you?

TO READ
Psalm 127:1-5

Children are a gift from the Lord; they are a reward from him. PSALM 127:3

 Wisten to Me!

"Wisten to me, Mommy." My youngest son had placed his chubby, cherubic fingers on my checks and turned my preoccupied face toward his own.

Had I been "wistening"? Listening is a hard skill to hone. I prayed, *God, would you give me a listening heart?* Then I took it a step further. I prayed that God would send me reminders if my heart was drifting from the people priorities he had blessed me with.

God, show me a red flag in each son that will pop up if my heart drifts toward preoccupation with career or problems. God answered. Brock, I noticed, became independent and aloof. Zach became bossy and demanding, and Caleb became whiny or clingy, not wanting me to leave his side. Just as a red flag signals race cars to be aware of danger on the track, these flags are signals to me that if I don't correct my preoccupation and "wisten," my children will drift into danger.

To curb preoccupation, I place photo reminders of my children everywhere: on a locket around my neck, a page in my organizer, photo pages in my wallet, a photo cube on my desk, my bulletin board, a coffee mug, and now an alarm clock that not only holds their picture but records their voices saying, "Good morning, Mommy! We love you!"

So many things can distract us from our people priorities: work, conflict, negative or strenuous circumstances, and even the process of getting emotionally well. It is easy to get so focused on our well-being that we forget the well-being of those closest to us.

Buy a new picture frame; then make a memory with those you love to put in it!

TO READ
1 Chronicles 19:1-13

When Joab saw that he would have to fight on two fronts, he chose the best troops in his army. He placed them under his personal command and led them out to fight the Arameans in the fields.

1 CHRONICLES 19:10

 ## In the Fight

When my father passed away, I was a pastor's wife, an author under deadline for two new books, a director of women's ministry, mom of three athletes, director of Masterful Living, and a member of a dozen boards or committees. So many people were looking to me for leadership.

I knew grief was an unruly taskmaster. Like a weed, it could weave its way into every circumstance in my life, especially if there was any unfinished business left from my dysfunctional childhood.

Now that my father had passed away, I knew that any loose ends could whip back like a viper and sting me all over again. I didn't have time for that. In a war you have to have a triage unit to care for the wounded *now*. I prayed Psalm 18:34 (paraphrased), "Train my hands for battle."

Having always encouraged others to go find the help and information they needed, I knew the best path at this impasse in my life was the one to a good counselor. I needed one who had experience working with those in leadership and those in grief.

I went in with a list of what I needed from my counselor. Although I knew a lot of information before I went, I knew I should not go it alone in times of high stress. What I needed was a fresh point of view that was the result of years of experience working with people just like me.

You are in a war. Use the best people and resources to fight for you!

TO READ
Proverbs 19:17

He who is kind to the poor lends to the Lord, and he will reward him for what he has done.

PROVERBS 19:17, NIV

 ## *Try a Little Kindness*

"Please adopt me! Please, please be my mother." Carrine was one of the special education students in the class where I served as an aid. I was twenty, newly married, and heartbroken about Carrine.

I prayed for an answer. I talked with friends and professionals looking for an answer. I ran all kinds of scenarios through my mind. I knew there were all kinds of reasons I couldn't be Carrine's mom. She was only a few years younger than I and severely disturbed, so often she had to be restrained. I was smaller in stature, ill-equipped, and untrained. Financially, we were strapped college students heading to graduate school.

Carrine was the first—but not the last—person I wanted to help but couldn't in the way she wanted me to. But Carrine taught me some valuable lessons. Sometimes painful situations are not easily solved. I learned that I couldn't always "fix" problems but I could help make things better.

When I explained to Carrine that I couldn't be her mother but I would be her teacher and friend, she was upset at first. But when I asked how she was doing each day and really listened to her answers, she seemed happier and more focused that day. When she was upset, I stroked her hand or her hair, and she calmed. These small gestures were large acts of kindness for Carrine.

Kindness is like that. It may not solve the problem, but it does seem to make life better. I can't make a husband return, heal a disability, or turn back the clock on a terminal illness, but being kind and loving without reservation does seem to make moments sweeter for people in the midst of the crisis.

To whom can you show kindness?

TO READ
Jeremiah 32:17-20

O Sovereign Lord! You have made the heavens and earth by your great power. Nothing is too hard for you! JEREMIAH 32:17

 ## The Wedding Tape

A few weeks after Bill and I married, a dear friend who had been instrumental in bringing me back to a more personal relationship with Christ also married. There was a song in our wedding that she wanted in her own. She wondered if she could borrow the audiotape from our wedding so her soloist could learn the song. I was twenty and very trusting, so I didn't think twice about lending her the tape—the original. After she returned from the honeymoon, I called her up to ask about her trip. While I had her on the phone, I asked how I might get the tape back.

"What tape?" was her response.

Weeks went by. After numerous calls back and forth between the soloist, the church, and the friend, it became apparent that the only audiotape of my wedding was gone, maybe forever.

At that moment I had a choice. I could lambaste my friend, berate her soloist, cry uncontrollably, take my anger out on my new husband, or even blame him for "letting" me be so stupid as to loan out the original, or I could find another, more positive solution.

So I faced the facts: Did I need to have this tape to have a happy marriage? Absolutely not. Could my reactions and negative feelings, left unchecked, hurt my friendship with God? my husband? my friend? Definitely. Was there anything I could do to solve the problem? I had already tried all human options. I could not control this situation.

My only peace came when I rested in the sovereignty of God. We always have a choice when faced with a disappointment: rest in the sovereignty of God that somehow, someway, he will work for our best. The alternative of anguish, anger, and accusations will destroy our relationships and well-being.

When faced with a disappointment, ask yourself, *Is God still sovereign?*

The very hairs on your head are all numbered. So don't be afraid; you are more valuable to him than a whole flock of sparrows. LUKE 12:7

 You're Worth It

Mandy ran her own business. The work was rewarding, but the hours long.

Mandy began to put on extra weight because she never seemed to be able to make it to the gym and ate late at night to squeeze in a few more hours of work. Over the months she felt more tired, sluggish, and depressed as fewer and fewer of her clothes fit. The depression became so bad that she felt suicidal despite her apparent financial success.

"I hate myself. When I look in the mirror, I don't even recognize myself. I have more success than ever and am enjoying it less. I know the Bible says I am a temple of God (1 Corinthians 6:19), but I feel bad the temple's this big. I went to the doctor and found out my cholesterol is through the roof, and strokes and heart disease run in my family. I'm too young to die! But I can't squeeze one more thing in my day—I am already overwhelmed."

Her counselor said, "What if I showed you how working out could actually make you money?"

"I'd like to see that!"

"Let's say that working out gave you one more productive hour a day. How much do you think that hour would make you?"

"Oh, maybe $100."

"Now take that $100 and multiply it by 365 times for about ten years, because studies say those who work out live longer."

"That's $36,500 times ten or $365,000. I could buy a nice home with that!"

"And just think what you could do with those extra years!"

TO READ
Proverbs 7:1-5

Guard my teachings as your most precious possession. Tie them on your fingers as a reminder. Write them deep within your heart.

PROVERBS 7:2-3

 ## The Notebook

When Bill and I were dating, we lived two hours apart. On weekends I would drive to see him or he would come to see me. I'd stay with his friends from the women's leadership team, and he'd stay with my guy friends.

Each time we'd get together, Bill would pull out a notebook, and in it there would be a list of relationship questions or issues that he wanted to talk through. It wasn't something that he had learned; it was simply Bill's attempt to keep our relationship on the right track. To me it was a sign of an organized, focused, and caring man—all traits that I wanted in a life companion.

Now, nearly twenty-five years into marriage, I am even more grateful for that notebook. Bill now has a line he gives in most relationship seminars, "Relationships should be purposeful; if you live your life accidentally, just drifting, don't be surprised if your life and your relationships become an accident."

King Solomon, the wisest man to ever live, said, "Obey them [commandments] and live! Guard my teachings as your most precious possession. Tie them on your fingers as a reminder" (Proverbs 7:2-3). If it was important, it was written down!

List five relationship issues you can address. Make them questions you'd like to discuss or goals you'd like to achieve. Be sure you have a measure of control over them. For example, write: "I will set aside three hours each Thursday to focus on my husband and our relationship"; or, "Each Wednesday I will do something nice for my spouse."

Buy a notebook to write down what you learn and what you want to learn and achieve.

TO READ
Proverbs 23:12-19

For surely you have a future ahead of you; your hope will not be disappointed. PROVERBS 23:18

 ## *Painted with Hope*

Jen's marriage was falling apart, and the stress of that was causing her children's lives to unravel as well. She felt as if she were Humpty Dumpty; having fallen off the wall, she couldn't be put together again.

She and her husband were separated, and he wanted the kids for the day. She wasn't sure how to spend an entire day alone. Going home seemed like the responsible thing to do, but her house was echoing her own screams for help as she tried to clean and organize. Then she remembered a spring-cleaning day her women's ministry was holding to spruce up the church. That sounded like a nice distraction. She showed up, and only a few women remained who were working on some painting projects.

"Would you like to work with me?" said a friendly woman.

Glenna painted and shared her life, her stories, and her struggles. One struggle was her marriage that had been brought back from the brink of divorce. Glenna shared how she had prayed for years for her unbelieving spouse and then saw God transform him through a struggle with one of their children.

Jen couldn't believe what she was hearing. It was like seeing her life in fast-forward. She was hearing Glenna share what God could do. Jen had come in thinking she'd do a good deed for God, and instead, he had done a good deed for her.

She was given hope and a new friend who had faced some of the same things. She saw the woman she wanted to become: gracious, friendly, and nurturing.

The room had a coat of fresh paint, but her heart gained a coat of fresh hope.

April

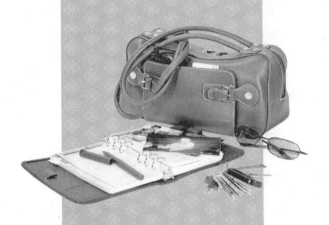

TO READ
1 John 5:1-5

Every child of God defeats this evil world by trusting Christ to give the victory. 1 JOHN 5:4

 ## *Word for Word*

Candace was being tormented by hostile, harassing phone calls from her estranged spouse. He was angry, raging at her over the phone just as he had done when he beat her before she and the kids fled for safety.

She tried to get the police to intervene, but they said that since no one was harmed, their hands were tied. She changed her number, but in no time her soon-to-be ex-husband had it again. She quit answering her phone and let the message machine pick up, but listening to the hateful messages was nearly as bad as hearing them live. She tried caller ID, but her husband used the phones of friends and family to call.

After each incident she felt wounded, frightened, and discouraged. As she listened to the messages, she would find herself sliding to the floor in tears. She felt trapped in her own apartment.

In her Bible study she was learning about the power of God's Word, so she decided to give God an opportunity to do battle for her. She asked her counselor and Bible study friends for verses they thought might help her when these harassing calls came. Then she borrowed a Strong's concordance and looked up key words like *victory, overcome, conquer,* etc. Then she typed all the verses out in big, bold font and posted them throughout her home, especially near the phone, with one laminated right in the middle of her kitchen floor!

The phone calls didn't stop, but she found that if she'd repeat the verses aloud, speaking God's Word over her husband's rhetoric, God won, and she remained peaceful and stable.

The churches here in the province of Asia greet you heartily in the Lord, along with Aquila and Priscilla and all the others who gather in their home for church meetings. 1 CORINTHIANS 16:19

Where's His Wife?

Bill and I had gone to a marriage conference at a large, respected conference center. We had heard biblically sound, important messages, all delivered by one man. One afternoon before we left the conference grounds, Bill and I went into the chapel to pray. As we prayed for our own relationship and the new baby that would soon be entering our home, both Bill and I felt a strong impression from God. One question kept ringing in our hearts: "Where was his wife?"

We thought back. We had received much marriage training through a Christian organization, delivered by a man; through seminary classes—professors—all men; and through marriage conference after marriage conference—all given by men. Great men, godly men, gifted men—but all men! We thought, "How can we help women understand what a godly, healthy marriage relationship looks like if we never hear from wives?"

We sensed that God was asking us to take our team approach to life and ministry on the road. We didn't know how or when, but that day we simply said, "God, we're here, ready and willing when you want to use us." We followed the example of many in the Old Testament who said, "Here I am" when God called: Abraham, Jacob, Moses, Samuel (Genesis 22:1; 46:2; Exodus 3:4; 1 Samuel 3:4). "Here I am!" is a good answer for both genders.

More than twelve years after we knelt and offered our lives to God to help build relationships as a team, we once again knelt in that chapel after teaching together at the same conference center.

TO READ
Luke 1:39-45

You are blessed, because you believed that the Lord would do what he said. LUKE 1:45

 Gasp!

I jumped out of bed in a fright. My throat was rapidly closing, and I couldn't breathe. I gasped for air. I must have hit Bill in my jump out of bed because he quickly jumped up.

"What's wrong? What's wrong?" I couldn't answer him. I couldn't even get one word out; I was scratching at my throat desperately hoping for air. Air! Air! *Lord, have mercy on me and send air!* my heart cried.

As Bill rushed to my side, I motioned for him to wrap his arms around me. All those years of working, speaking, and ministering together paid off because he seemed to read my mind: *Do the Heimlich.* His strong arms wrapped around me, and three times he tried to force air in and out of my lungs. Finally it worked and calmed my heart and spirit enough for me to point at my allergy medication.

I took some meds and stood shaking in Bill's arms. As my breathing slowed and became more regular, I sat down, my head filled with a weird mixture of thoughts:

I'm too young to die. I still want to raise my boys! I have a speaking engagement in the morning. God, thanks that I didn't die. That poor, sweet twenty-year-old director's first event would be traumatic if the speaker did not show because she died!

My house is a mess. Everyone would have seen the stacks of still-packed suitcases and books in the living room.

Then I got mad at Satan. Yeah, the only way to make me stop preaching, praying, and praising is to kill me! God's Word will go on! Books, tapes, videos, and influence last in people's hearts!

God's Word lasts!

TO READ
1 Corinthians 10:31–11:1

Whatever you eat or drink or whatever you do, you must do all for the glory of God.

1 CORINTHIANS 10:31

 ## *Make Me Look Good*

Some of the best advice I ever received I learned on my first job. I was eighteen, working at a new retail store because I wanted to buy a bicycle. After all, I was in college, and even though I had a car to drive, there were times that a coed just needed a bike (or so I thought). Needless to say, since I wasn't working to put food on my table, I was sure I could pick and choose my own hours.

I was in shock when the boss said, "I don't know what you have planned the next month—but cancel it. Expect to work twelve to fourteen or more hours a day, every day except one day off [I chose Sunday]. We have to get this store opened on time no matter what it takes." So much for having a life!

"And by the way, if you're wondering what your job description is—it is to make me look good." Make the boss look good. Sounds easy? No, but I set out to accomplish just that.

I had just rededicated my life to Christ, and one day in a quiet time, curious about work priorities, I began to look up verses having to do with work and authorities. I discovered that not only was my boss right, but God wanted me to go one step further: "Everyone must submit himself to the governing authorities, for there is no authority except that which God has established" (Romans 13:1, NIV).

Not only did God want me to make my boss look good, he wanted me to make God look good in the process! This paid off because when my car broke down, I was glad for the bike my first paycheck bought!

TO READ
Ephesians 4:14-16

We will hold to the truth in love, becoming more and more in every way like Christ, who is the head of his body, the church. EPHESIANS 4:15

 Am I My Brother's Keeper?

How do you show respect to parents, and how much should parents run your life? What is a person's responsibility toward a grown sibling? Should you lend him or her money? help them with constant marriage problems?

One woman shared how her parents thought she and her husband needed to buy her siblings new cars just because they had purchased a new car. Another had a sibling who thought her childless sister was obligated to pay for her three nieces to go to private school. Another sister was always at her house. Are you wondering how you can show love and respect and still maintain healthy boundaries?

Perhaps the most loving thing we can do is to give a loved one responsibility for his or her own life. I try to ask myself, *If love wants the best for another person, then what would love do?*

One mother, who realized her constant bailing out of her grown son was actually crippling his growth into maturity, wrapped up a note that read, "This is the best and most difficult gift I have ever given you. Enclosed you will find a check, the last one you will receive from me. This will cover your first and last month's rent and your bills for one month, but you also see that I have enclosed a set of apron strings. I am giving you the gift of being responsible for your own life, so I have cut the apron strings. Please enjoy this gift. All my love, Mom."

Real love makes the hard calls, does the brave thing, and encourages people to step up and step out. Love gives generously from a willing heart in a way that encourages responsible maturity. Sometimes the most treasured gift is the most difficult to give and impossible to wrap.

TO READ
1 Peter 4:7-11

Most important of all, continue to show deep love for each other, for love covers a multitude of sins.

1 PETER 4:8

 ## The Neighbor

When we first moved to San Marcos to take on our new pastorate, we were idealistic, wide-eyed twenty-eight-year-olds ready to build a church of a thousand overnight. We thought turning our small country church nestled in a growing suburb into a hubbub of megaministry would be a "piece of cake." After all, Bill and I had taken six teens at a Wednesday evening service and helped turn them into a thriving youth ministry of hundreds within a year—what could be so hard about growing a church?

When we moved, the housing prices escalated sixty thousand dollars over a six-week period. We were priced right out of the market. Nothing was in our price range—nothing but a small piece of land.

When we started hammering, curious neighbors began appearing. When a few found out we were in ministry, they didn't come back right away—except one: Ember. Ember was an intellectual giant to me. She used big words and had big questions. Nearly every day she'd come over and ask Bill some earth-shaking, cosmos-rocking, deep theological question.

I wasn't sure I could answer all her questions, but I was sure I wanted to get to know this mom of two who lived right across the street. As I prayed one morning in a quiet time, God reminded me of one of his seemingly simple commands: "Love thy neighbor."

But how could I love my new neighbor if I felt intimidated by her? The reply came back: *Listen*. So that's what I did. By the time our home was built, so was Ember's refound faith, and built right in was a forever friendship. Ember then went on to become a key leader in our fledgling new ministry.

I thought God had sent us to build a church, but I learned that if you build relationships, God uses those to build his church.

TO READ
Psalm 17:1-8

Show me your unfailing love in wonderful ways.
You save with your strength those who seek refuge
from their enemies. PSALM 17:7

 Tell Me What I Need to Hear

Sheryl Ann was struggling to overcome fears that were holding her back.
She had come in for counseling, and we had created a life-coaching support
group to take her calls when she felt her fears were holding her back from
being the kind of mother she knew she needed to be. As a single mother,
there was no one to bail her out, so when fear won, her children lost.

One day Sheryl Ann needed to take her children to a large school event,
but her insecurities were getting the best of her. She felt panic, her heart
racing; she felt dizzy, as if her heart would explode in her chest. All kinds
of thoughts ran through her mind, one of which was advice from the life-
coaching group: "When you feel fear, pick up the phone and call one of
your support team."

Usually fear would have prevented her from doing it. Thoughts of
unworthiness crossed her mind. I can call Carol—no, she'd be too busy.
Or Sandy said call her—no, she'd think I was being stupid. Then the counselor's words crossed her mind: "You'll think you shouldn't call—fight that
feeling. Don't think. Just pick up the phone, call, and say, 'Sandy or Carol,
tell me what I need to hear. Tell me the truth.'"

Fingers shaking so badly she could barely dial, Sheryl Ann picked up the
phone and punched the numbers scrawled on her life-coaching folder. She
choked out the words, "Hi, Sandy, this is Sheryl Ann. I am so sorry to call
and interrupt your day, but I need you to tell me what I need to hear.
Sandy, can you tell me the truth?"

"Sheryl Ann, so glad you called! Fear number one is out of the way—you
called!"

TO READ
Hebrews 6:9-12

We want each of you to show this same diligence to
the very end, in order to make your hope sure.

HEBREWS 6:11, NIV

 ## Eighteen Hundred Dollars

I had been the registrar for a sports camp and had been given eighteen hundred dollars in registration funds. It was Wednesday evening, and at 5 A.M. Thursday I was flying out of town and hadn't packed a thing. Before I left camp, I had to put away the uniforms. I carefully carried the folder of money on top of the clothes and set it on the center shelf, where I was stacking uniforms.

I was preoccupied about the rest of the evening: one son's appointment, taking the other home, fixing dinner, and packing books, clothes, and conference supplies. I gathered the boys and headed home. I brought everything in from the car and began my travel preparations, thinking I would get the money to the volunteer coordinator after I arrived home from my trip. I always leave my most important papers on my kitchen counter. However, when I got home four days later, the money wasn't there. It wasn't anywhere in my house. The coaches were on vacation, so I couldn't totally retrace my steps, nor could I let them know of the misplaced money.

I rethought my last day; I could see no place where I could have put the money, and I had looked everywhere. But it was nowhere to be found.

"God, I am going to choose to believe you know where the money is, and I believe you have protected it. I will reimburse the football program (eighteen hundred dollars!) if I don't find it, but I will live as if the money is already in the bank. I'll keep looking but living, too. I have too much that needs done for you this week to use up all my time in worry."

When the coach returned, I went in to break the news. I began my remorseful confession, and the coach interrupted, "I found the money, Pam, on the shelf. It's already been deposited!"

TO READ
Ezekiel 36:22-27

I will give you a new heart with new and right desires, and I will put a new spirit in you. I will take out your stony heart of sin and give you a new, obedient heart. Ezekiel 36:26

 ## A Change of Heart

What does a change of convictions look like? What is the process God takes us through to give us a change of heart? One of my friends described the process this way:

> After twenty-two years of walking away from God, I went back to church and rededicated my life. God started the process of molding me into the woman he created me to be. I must admit that I wasn't very pliable in the beginning, and because I hadn't been in his hands for so long, I was pretty stiff. It took a while for me to allow God to soften me, and I continually questioned him. *Are you sure this is what you want me to look like? Why? What purpose will I serve?*
>
> One such example is when God asked me to give up alcohol. He had brought it to my attention frequently. I had already cut down, but I knew he was asking more. I stiffened up again and stubbornly questioned him. Then during a prayer time in a Bible study, God graciously showed me a picture I could understand. It was a picture of an old western style saloon. There was a long bar with a huge mirror hanging on the wall behind it with a long shelf above the mirror. On top of the shelf were liquor bottles labeled "Spirits."
>
> God asked me, "Do you want to be filled with those spirits or with my Holy Spirit?" What a clear picture God gave me, what a contrast in choices. He made the choice obvious to me; I wanted to be a vessel molded by him and filled with his Spirit.

God sent Saul a blinding light; God sent Peter a vision of a sheet from heaven; God wrestled with Jacob; and a donkey talked to Balaam. When God wants to get your attention to change your life, he has the resources. It is just so much easier when his Word speaks to your heart like it did when he spoke to my friend's heart.

Is God trying to send you a message? Tell him you want a new heart and a softer soul, and you'll hear him speak through his Word.

TO READ
Psalm 16:5-11

Lord, you alone are my inheritance, my cup of blessing. You guard all that is mine. PSALM 16:5

 ## A Cup Full of Love

My friend Natalie relayed a story that helped me grasp a glimpse of God's love on a day I needed to hear it!

Last Christmas we were planning to celebrate a week early with Randy and Sarah (our son and daughter-in-law) because they were going to the Midwest for Christmas. I learned that Sarah's mom was going to be there, and I wanted to bring her a gift. I have a cupboard where I keep gifts, and I pulled a few out and placed them on the bed. When my son, Nic, walked by, I asked his opinion on what he thought Sandy would like. His reply was that he didn't think any of them were nice enough for a Christmas gift, and I had to agree.

It was too late to purchase anything, so I went to my china cabinet—I had just recently purchased a lovely teacup made in England at an estate sale. I hesitated briefly, then pulled the teacup out of the cabinet and wrapped it for Sandy. When she opened her gift, I could see the delight on her face.

She said, "How did you know? Did Sarah tell you? I just made the decision a couple of weeks ago to start a teacup collection; this one is beautiful!"

It was so fun to have made someone so happy. God knew it was the perfect gift for her. I was so glad I had given her the teacup instead of the original "make do" gift.

A few weeks later I received a call from a dear friend and mentor who had moved away but was coming to visit. "I have a little gift," my friend said, "I want you to have one of my mother's teacups."

Tears immediately came to my eyes. God is so personal. The teacup from a dear friend's mother is so much more meaningful and treasured than the cup I had purchased at an estate sale.

Are you holding on to something God has intended for someone else (a possession, an opportunity, a dream, a role, a calling, or a title)? Release it, and see what cup full of love he has in store for you.

TO READ
2 Thessalonians 1:3-12

All this is evidence that God's judgment is right, and as a result you will be counted worthy of the kingdom of God, for which you are suffering. God is just: He will pay back trouble to those who trouble you and give relief to you who are troubled, and to us as well. This will happen when the Lord Jesus is revealed from heaven in blazing fire with his powerful angels. 2 THESSALONIANS 1:5-7, NIV

Pulling Up Short

Pulling up short, quitting, throwing in the towel, giving up, or walking away—we all want to do it much more than we are willing to admit. So what do you do when you've run out of steam but the train station of rest is at the top of the next mountain?

What did the apostle Paul do? He reminded himself and others of the following:

- What we suffer now is nothing compared to the glory he will give us later. (Romans 8:18)
- We don't look at the troubles we can see right now; rather, we look forward to what we have not yet seen. For the troubles we see will soon be over, but the joys to come will last forever. (2 Corinthians 4:18)
- I once thought all these things were so very important, but now I consider them worthless because of what Christ has done. Yes, everything else is worthless when compared with the priceless gain of knowing Christ Jesus my Lord. I have discarded everything else, counting it all as garbage, so that I may have Christ. (Philippians 3:7-8)
- Dear brothers and sisters, I am still not all I should be, but I am focusing all my energies on this one thing: Forgetting the past and looking forward to what lies ahead, I strain to reach the end of the race and receive the prize for which God, through Christ Jesus, is calling us up to heaven. (Philippians 3:13)

Paul didn't look at the task, at the work, or at the suffering. He looked beyond, farther down the trail to the finish line. Are you tired? Do you feel like throwing in the towel? Change your gaze.

| TO READ | In your strength I can crush an army; with my God I |
| Psalm 18:25-36 | can scale any wall. PSALM 18:29 |

 ## *A Fake*

Amanda is a smart cookie! She graduated eighth in her class, yet for years she felt like a fake. She graduated from college with honors, and landed her first job in a male-dominated field, but she was full of fear:

"It is not like you can just go up to a coworker or boss and say, 'You hired me to be an expert, but every time I make any decision, I second-guess myself. My paperwork all says I have the brains for this job, but I feel like such a fake. I am so afraid every time I have to make a decision or give an answer.'

"One night, driving home, I heard a speaker on Christian radio talk about women and self-esteem and how many women believe lies about themselves and are full of self-doubt. Then she said, 'They feel like a fake.' I couldn't believe it—that was exactly how I felt! How did she know? As I listened, I learned many women feel this way. I wasn't alone, but I was buying into Satan's sham. And with God's help, I could fight this battle!"

To battle negative thoughts, replace them with positive ones about God and his view of you. I like to paraphrase verses and string them together, like:

I have no fear of sudden disaster or of the ruin that overtakes the wicked, for the Lord will be my confidence and will keep my foot from being snared.[1] In him and through faith in him I may approach God with freedom and confidence.[2] Being confident of this, that he who began a good work in me will carry it on to completion until the day of Christ Jesus.[3] I will approach the throne of grace with confidence, so that I may receive mercy and find grace to help me in my time of need.[4] This is the confidence I have in approaching God: that if I ask anything according to his will, he hears me. And if I know that he hears me—whatever I ask—I know that I have what I asked of him.[5] I am confident of better things . . . things that accompany salvation.[6]

TO READ
Luke 10:25-37

"Love the Lord your God with all your heart and with all your soul and with all your strength and with all your mind"; and, "Love your neighbor as yourself." LUKE 10:27, NIV

 ## Lack in Love

A collegue was talking about discipling and training leaders. "When I see that a person has a deficit in his or her relationships with people, I know they have a deficit in their relationship with God. When we are rightly relating to God, we gain the ability to rightly relate to others. The key is to discover what is missing in their relationship with God."

What's missing in your relationships with people?

Short with people? Maybe you are angry at God about his provision or timing.

Noncommunicative? How much are you praying and talking with God?

Distant? Maybe you have a hurt you haven't allowed God to heal.

Keep running away from commitments? How are you doing keeping your commitments to God?

Hiding in drugs, shopping, or booze? What are you hiding from God? Pain? Disappointment? Trauma?

Always nagging? How's your trust level with God? Feeling like you need to help him out?

Resentful? Your underground anger will go deeper unless you let God meet the need you feel the person near you is supposed to meet.

Look at your relationships—is there an unhealthy pattern? Now transpose that to your relationship with God. Invest in your primary relationship (with God), and you may see improvement in all your secondary ones (with people).

TO READ
Psalm 31:1-5

Since you are my rock and my fortress, for the sake of your name lead and guide me. PSALM 31:3, NIV

 A New Path

Insanity is doing the same thing over and over and expecting a different result. Perseverance is one thing—stupidity is another. Sometimes we totally ignore the directional signs God places along our path.

One friend of ours was told by several seminary professors that he was great at research, and that he had the talent and skills to be a graduate assistant, but he wanted to be a senior pastor. All of his friends saw his lack of charisma and his struggle with recruiting and leading people. We all suggested he continue in the professor tract, but he ignored us.

His first pastorate was an interim, and they let him go early. His second church plant never got off the ground, so he took a position at a Christian school teaching a few Bible classes. His students loved him. He was offered a full-time position. Then other schools heard of his reputation and wanted him to train their teachers.

But he still wanted to be a senior pastor until one day, a friend asked, "Why would you want to go to a church when God has given you so much success teaching?"

"I want to teach the Word."

"You are," the friend said.

"I want to impact lives."

"You are."

"I am!"

A calling or passion can take many forms. What are your life goals? Boil down your hopes and dreams to the core values; then list all the ways you can live out your core values. You might decide a new path with the same old values is a better option.

TO READ
Psalm 26:2-3

Put me on trial, Lord, and cross-examine me. Test my motives and affections. PSALM 26:2

 ## Does a Pattern Emerge?

"What's up? All my relationships are exploding on me!" Sharon had been married twice; her children, now in college, made excuses for never calling, never coming home. She was passed over for a promotion at work, and now her fiancé was getting cold feet—he wanted to postpone the wedding.

"He told me I am high maintenance! What does that mean? Am I, Pam? Am I high maintenance?"

Telling a high-maintenance woman she is high maintenance is an explosive situation and may or may not lead to change. However, change is more likely if a high-maintenance woman with emotional issues realizes it herself.

"Why don't you look at all your relationships? Go back and write down what you think happened to strain the relationship. Better yet, go ask them why the relationship is strained. You need to be like a court reporter or journalist. Take notes on what they say; don't react—no matter what they say. Set up some interviews, and see if you can gather enough information to see a pattern."

"What do I ask? I don't think I can do this! It's too hard!"

"Harder than losing all the people you love, over and over again?"

"Well, when you put it like that—okay—can you help me? What do I say to them?"

"Just ask each of those people to go to coffee with you. I'll give you a few questions to ask, but it's more important that they hear your heart. They need to hear that you are sorry your relationship is strained and that you want to see if you can change or do something to rebuild the relationship. Your most important job will be to listen and not react."

TO READ
Judges 4:4-16

Then Deborah said to Barak, "Get ready! Today the Lord will give you victory over Sisera, for the Lord is marching ahead of you." So Barak led his ten thousand warriors down the slopes of Mount Tabor into battle. JUDGES 4:14

 A Skirt on a Platform of Suits

Hitting the glass ceiling? Feeling outnumbered by the guys? Feel like the good old boys' club is giving everyone else the edge? As women, sometimes we can feel out of the loop or passed over, and Judge Deborah could have felt that way too. She is the only woman judge included in the Bible.

But God had obviously called her, for people would travel long distances just to have her judge their cases. Her wisdom and fairness were known throughout the kingdom. Even Barak wouldn't go into battle without her:

She sent for Barak son of Abinoam from Kedesh in Naphtali and said to him, "The Lord, the God of Israel, commands you: 'Go, take with you ten thousand men of Naphtali and Zebulun and lead the way to Mount Tabor. I will lure Sisera, the commander of Jabin's army, with his chariots and his troops to the Kishon River and give him into your hands.'"

Barak said to her, "If you go with me, I will go; but if you don't go with me, I won't go."

"Very well," Deborah said, "I will go with you. But because of the way you are going about this, the honor will not be yours, for the Lord will hand Sisera over to a woman." So Deborah went with Barak to Kedesh. (Judges 4:6-9, NIV)

And that is exactly what happened: Jael lured the king in for a bite to eat and a nap, then "nailed" him with a tent peg through the temple. God gave the opportunity and the credit to a woman. As you seek what God has for you to do, stay focused on his wisdom and encouragement.

Know that God hasn't forgotten you because of your gender—keep being yourself, and like Deborah and Jael, your moment will come.

TO READ
Mark 10:35-45

Whoever wants to be a leader among you must be your servant. MARK 10:43

 A View from the Muck

Many of today's Christian leaders were once very humble servants. Josh McDowell left a law practice to come on staff with Campus Crusade for Christ and was assigned to facilities where he found himself scrubbing toilets. Jill Briscoe cleaned homes as a maid. I held a job shoveling manure in horse stalls. Very glamorous!

But it is these servant roles that best prepare us to serve in other roles that may appear more "glamorous," more powerful, or more prestigious—but are in all reality just another way to serve. What are the questions that a "servant" of God asks when interacting with others?

- What can I do for you? Not, What can you do for me?
- How can I help you feel really good about the way God made you? Not, How can I get you to feel really good about who God made me?
- How can I share what I have to help you get what you need? Not, What can I get from you to get what I need?

What did I learn while shoveling manure with my brother each week? Life is messy, and someone has to clean it up. Some of life's best, most meaningful conversations happen as you work alongside others who are also cleaning up the mess. The right tools help. There are many tasks that don't look fun but can be made fun. Messes happen over and over again. Many hands make light work. Singing, joking, and humor help. Sometimes the most beautiful sunsets and rainbows can be seen when you are standing in the worst circumstances. Cleaning stalls keeps pride from setting in.

Now that I am in the business of helping people clean up emotional messes and teaming with others to clean up the mess we see the world in, I rely on those lessons learned long ago when I stood in the muck.

TO READ
Romans 12:6-11

Love each other with genuine affection, and take delight in honoring each other. ROMANS 12:10

 ## When You Think of Me

Staying connected to the people you love can be a challenge in a busy world. But it doesn't have to be if you plan ahead for connection. Keep every address, including e-mail, and every phone number—cell, office, etc., as a way to get hold of people you want to stay connected to. Buy a PDA or a planner and keep all that information in one place. This way, if you have a cell phone and think of someone, you can call that person from anywhere. Another way to stay connected is to carry postcards and when you are caught waiting for a daughter to get out of ballet or a son to get done with soccer practice, jot a quick note, an encouraging verse, or a funny joke. You get bonus points if you carry stamps in your purse because then you can address, stamp, and mail your note on the way home. I also place reminders in my planner so that I don't forget to e-mail, call, or stop and see people. By placing reminders in my schedule, I remember to stop by a nursing home or hospital.

Often when I think of people and am praying for them, I call them and leave a voice-mail prayer on their answering machine. Why just pray when you can pray *and* encourage a friend, spouse, sibling, parent, or child at the same time! Keep surprises on hand (greeting cards, coffee cards, fast-food coupons, etc.), and when you feel a person in your world needs a quick gift of encouragement, toss one in the mail. By consciously preparing to be kind and show affection, you will actually see progress and growth in showing the depth of emotion you feel toward those special people in your world, no matter how crazy and busy life gets!

| TO READ
Psalm 119:59-64 | I pondered the direction of my life, and I turned to follow your statutes. Psalm 119:59 |

 *Adrift*

"We just drifted apart." This is the most common excuse a person gives when she wants out of a marriage. It is the foundation for no-fault divorce and the legal term "irreconcilable differences." Most differences can be reconciled, and usually it is a "*both*-fault" divorce. There is no drifting apart; rather, it is a series of decisions, choices, and attitudes that distance two people. Just as it is choices that made you "drift," choices can also move your hearts back toward each other.

If you are feeling stressed in a relationship, retrace your steps, just as you would if you lost your car keys. Love, like lost keys, can be found.

Review your history: When do you last remember being happy, emotionally connected, and in love? What was going on in both of your lives then? What changed: a job? an attitude? a circumstance? a set of responsibilities? Try to specifically discern what changes occurred.

Once, Bill and I found we were growing impatient with each other. Everything we did seemed to irritate the other. Yes, we were carrying a heavy load of responsibility, but that was characteristic of our entire married life. What was different?

As I retraced my steps, I observed that we had always carried a full plate of responsibility, but until the past year, we had carried much of it together. Our current ministry and work responsibilities had us functioning independently too often. So we made choices and decisions to cause change. We moved our offices next to each other, scheduled in ministry we could do together, and delegated ministry responsibilities that would keep us apart. Just as choices moved us apart, choices brought us together.

TO READ
James 1:2-5

Whenever trouble comes your way, let it be an opportunity for joy. For when your faith is tested, your endurance has a chance to grow. JAMES 1:2-3

 Turmoil or Triumph—You Choose!

"Adversity doesn't build character, it reveals it."

"What doesn't kill you makes you stronger."

Do you agree with these statements? I think both statements are true if you don't waste your pain. Pain, obstacles, and adversity can be the anvil on which your character is forged. However, if you fail to learn from the pain, choosing bitterness and anger instead, then the next adversity will reveal the shallowness of your pain.

Try the Job method: "[Job] replied, '. . . Shall we accept good from God, and not trouble?' In all this, Job did not sin in what he said" (Job 2:10, NIV).

Job lost his children, his livestock, his home, and his health. His own wife wanted him to curse God and die. And Job's response was to accept both good and trouble from God's hand.

He refused to whine, refused to complain, refused to give in and give up. He refused to sin and chose to worship instead.

How do you handle the trouble and the good that comes into your life? Ask God to help you accept everything that he gives you.

TO READ
Exodus 20:2-18

Do not worship any other gods besides me.

EXODUS 20:3

 ## *All about You!*

Satan wants your eyes off God. To get you distracted, he doesn't move your eyes to himself; rather, he subtly moves them to *you*. He twists the truth so that you are now the object of worship. To illustrate the point, let's see what would happen if we rewrote the first six of the Ten Commandments so that instead of God being the focus, you were:

1. You are the lord of your own life. Don't let anyone else tell you what to do!
2. Create your own religion. Use whatever god you want if you think it will get you ahead.
3. Have as many idols as you want. Follow sports teams and movie stars, spend time and money on cars, drugs, music, sex—whatever you want. It's your life, your money, and your call.
4. Swear whenever you want. In fact, say anything you want, whenever you want. Don't let social mores, your parents, church, or anything else keep you from expressing yourself any way you want to.
5. Don't get hung up on going to church—it's just a building. Besides, they are just a bunch of hypocrites anyway. Be "spiritual" any way you like!
6. Don't listen to your parents. Those old people will just hold you down. Family is like a noose around your neck. If you feel like being with your family, fine, but don't feel obligated. No guilt trips!

Have any of those thoughts crossed your mind? It's amazing how when we actually say those things, we can see how self-centered and evil they sound. God wants us to honor him by obeying his Word. It's not all about you but rather all about him—the Lord your God.

TO READ
John 8:31-47

[The devil] was a murderer from the beginning, not holding to the truth, for there is no truth in him. When he lies, he speaks his native language, for he is a liar and the father of lies. JOHN 8:44, NIV

 ## Twisting

Satan is a deceiver. Let's continue rewriting the last of the Ten Commandments and notice how he wants to feed your lust and your desires, while leaving out the consequences. Satan might say:

"Murder might be a gift. Death isn't really so bad. Death is a great escape, suicide a statement." The Bible says Satan comes to kill, steal, and destroy. Satan rarely tells someone in a rage, bent on self-mutilation, self-destruction, or suicide, "Wait, consider the consequences." No, he wants you to go with the emotion of the moment.

"Have sex with whomever you want. If it feels good, do it! Marriage is overrated—look, hardly anyone is happily married. Fulfill all your desires, right now, any way you want." The Bible says that marriage is the best place for sex because it is a committed relationship. Trust is the key to sexual fulfillment, and trust is built by commitment. Satan wants you to use others and to be used. He wants you to get hooked on sex, not hooked on love because love reflects God.

"Take what you want. If someone is stupid enough to leave it right there in open sight, they are just asking for you to take it. You need it more than they do." I don't think Satan brings up jail sentences while tempting.

"White lies are all right. Say whatever you need to cover for yourself. If you want it, go after it: someone's house, car, boyfriend, husband, clothes, or status. Take them down. Your needs are most important." Satan won't mention to you that a certain statement or action could destroy a friendship or work relationship. He wants to put you on the hook, not take you off the hook. He wants to leave you twisting in the wind.

> **TO READ**
> 2 Thessalonians 3:10-13

Even while we were with you, we gave you this rule: "Whoever does not work should not eat."

2 THESSALONIANS 3:10

 ## *All the Answers and No Action*

When my father was laid off for medical reasons, he lost his identity. His work had been everything to him. All our ice chests, tool chests, mugs, cups, and many of my dad's clothes had the company logo on them. He *was* the company!

I was an idealistic newlywed, and I thought if he got a new job, started his own business, or volunteered for a worthwhile organization, it would boost his self-esteem. And I thought if he'd just get connected to God through a local church, it might help when I, being so far away, couldn't help.

I did hours of research. I got lists of churches from the chamber of commerce. I received newspapers from his city and circled want ads and mailed them. I called all the helping organizations, like the Salvation Army and Goodwill, looking for ways he might volunteer. I sent page after page of help—but he sat day after day in his recliner declining.

Then it hit me: I was doing his work. He needed to want the information I was IV dripping into his life. He would get well only if he got up off the recliner and let his own fingers do the walking in the Yellow Pages.

Are you doing someone else's work? Are you letting someone else do your work?

Be silent, and know that I am God! PSALM 46:10

 Courage to Stay

Alma and Steve had dreamed of being missionaries in Japan since their youth. They arrived in 1969, and all three of their children were born and raised in Japan.

However, in 1991, Alma found herself sitting next to Steve's hospital bed in tears the night before his cancer surgery.

"There are three things that we should keep in mind: (1) God is here. (2) God is in control. (3) And we can trust him. If we can remember these three things, we will get through this," Steve said.

Four years later Alma's son graduated from high school, her beloved Steve had gone to be with the Lord, and the unknown lay before her:

> New Year's Eve came, and I found myself alone in a large living room by the fire. I prayed, *Lord, I just can't go on as I am. You have got to do something for me.*
>
> I began to read about the work of the Holy Spirit in a book by Charles Stanley. My heart was stirred. I remember sitting in the chair for some time just thanking the Lord that *he*, Almighty God, was living in me through the Holy Spirit, and that I did not have to struggle to keep the family together, be both mother *and* father to my son, and make decisions about my future. As I surrendered to the Lord, he would lead me and take care of the family and me. Galatians 2:20 just kept going over and over in my mind. "I have been crucified with Christ." God, in all his greatness and power, was living in me and would direct my life as I submitted to his will for me.
>
> I thought, *God is there and I can trust him, and he is living in me.* I sat for a long time in that cozy living room with the fire in the fireplace going to embers, but the fire in my heart burning brighter and brighter.

So bright were Alma's hope and renewed calling that she returned to Japan and later married a wonderful, godly man, Larry, and together they continue to minister there.

TO READ
Matthew 9:18-29

He touched their eyes and said, "Because of your faith, it will happen." MATTHEW 9:29

 Already Answered!

On my flight home from a conference for pastors' wives, I decided to try to live as if all my prayer requests were already answered. I knew if all my requests for more time, more financial security, more opportunity, more obedient and successful children, and more time with my husband were answered, I would be a whole lot easier to live with. I need to be easier to live with now! *Jesus, I will seek to live as if you have answered my requests.*

I had just done that when an announcement came over the speaker: "This flight is cancelled!" It seems that the delay we experienced in Phoenix, waiting for a crew, put us over the landing curfew of my city. Instantly, I wanted to cry. I was already going to have only a few minutes to kiss my husband and sons before they left on a father-son trip at 4 A.M. Now I would have no time to see them in person, and it would be more than a week until I would see and talk much to them.

Live as if I have answered, whispered the Holy Spirit. So I deplaned with a smile. I got in line to get a hotel voucher. It was 12:30 A.M. People around me were not happy! But I decided to befriend those in line by me and help them choose joy.

When I got up to the counter, I announced to the six overworked and underpaid clerks, "Thanks for helping us. I know you wanted to go home, be with your families, and get some sleep. I know this is hard on you, too. So thanks! I'm praying for you!" They smiled.

A sweet young woman of maybe twenty was helping an angry, unkind businessman; I winked and mouthed, "Hang in there." He walked away. I complimented her. "You did very well. He wasn't easy to deal with."

If I truly believed God had already answered my prayers, I could focus on the opportunity at hand to encourage someone else!

TO READ
John 4:34-38

Do you think the work of harvesting will not begin until the summer ends four months from now? Look around you! Vast fields are ripening all around us and are ready now for the harvest. JOHN 4:35

I'll Just Write One!

When my son Brock was five, he asked Christ into his life. Because I thought it was the most important decision he would ever make, I went directly to the Christian bookstore to find a book, a certificate, a wall hanging—something to commemorate the event and to follow up on the decision—but there was nothing!

So I went to another store and another. This was in the days before the Internet, but a large Sunday school convention was near us, so I went there—and in all the racks and racks of books there was nothing to celebrate and follow up a child's decision to come to Christ. I was shocked! I didn't want to wait any longer to commemorate and follow up the decision with some good kid-friendly training, so I went home and wrote a book for him.

The Big Decision is a scrapbook and workbook that commemorates a child's decision and then gives the key elements of information that a child needs to grow with God in a personal relationship.

As you seek to make a difference, you'll hit some roadblocks—and you might be the solution that God uses to remove a roadblock not only in your life but in the lives of others!

Just as in John 4:35, where Jesus says the fields are ready for harvest, we are called, even as new believers, to come to work in the harvest.

I wanted my son to know that God already had planned a way to use him in his work. This is something that new Christians need to know right away, God loves you and has a purpose for your life.

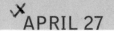

TO READ
Colossians 2:6-10

Let your lives overflow with thanksgiving for all he has done. COLOSSIANS 2:7

 ## *Show Appreciation*

When I was in Bible Study Fellowship, I was always amazed at the wonderful end-of-the-year gifts the class would pull together for the teaching leader. One was a block quilt done by a member of each small group, depicting the moments in Genesis.

The quilt was priceless.

One of my favorite parts of speaking is the kind creativity that has gone into the thank-you gifts. I never expect them, but they are such an encouragement at the end of a long week when I am short on sleep and long on responsibility. One of my favorite ones recently was a hand-carved, inscribed wooden pen. The woman who made it was also in charge of the outreach. When did she have time to carve?

Another gift was an inductive Bible, ready for me to study! The best gifts are always ministry tools or days to rest and recover to do more ministry.

God wants us to reward those who have sacrificed to help us grow:

- The elders who direct the affairs of the church well are worthy of double honor, especially those whose work is preaching and teaching. (1 Timothy 5:17, NIV)
- Give everyone what you owe him: If you owe . . . revenue, then revenue; if respect, then respect; if honor, then honor. (Romans 13:7, NIV)

Whom do you need to thank? A host of people has helped you. Did you ever thank that sixth-grade drama teacher or the coach who taught you to work hard? Have you thanked the person who led you to Jesus? The counselor who helped you overcome? A few well-chosen words of gratitude go a long way.

TO READ
Hebrews 11:1-40

Now faith is being sure of what we hope for and certain of what we do not see. HEBREWS 11:1, NIV

 ## *Living by Faith*

At a conference for pastors' wives, I heard Jill Briscoe recount a painful circumstance in her family life when she prayed frantically, asking and demanding of God. She caught herself and said, "I am praying like a woman who has no faith." Then she began to praise God for what she knew to be true about him instead of praying her feelings.

She said, "I asked myself, How would I live if all my prayer requests were answered?" Prior to this she had felt anxious, frustrated, discouraged—but after she decided to live as if all her prayer requests were answered, she found new peace and hope.

That is really the essence of faith. *Faith* is defined as: "persuasion, moral conviction (of religious truth, or the truthfulness of God or a religious teacher), especially reliance upon Christ for salvation."

Taking the definition apart, faith is living fully persuaded of God's abilities and character. Faith is a conviction, a full commitment to the truth and living out what you know intellectually. Faith is relying consistently on God because you believe.

How are you living? Are you shouting at God? Are you angry at his plan? at his timetable? What prayer requests are dominating your days and keeping you up at night?

Write out how you would live if God answered them all. Would you be less preoccupied? Would you be able to "be in the moment" rather than always planning and fretting? Would you have a longer fuse? Would you treat people differently? Write it out—then live it out!

Live as if God has answered—that's what a walk of faith is all about!

If you need wisdom—if you want to know what God wants you to do—ask him, and he will gladly tell you. He will not resent your asking. JAMES 1:5

 ## *Ask Me!*

Women are full of great ideas, but so few of us really ask God to make the ideas happen. God commands us to come to him for advice, direction, and wisdom.

Ask. He knows you want it. "For your Father knows what you need before you ask him" (Matthew 6:8, NIV).

Ask in agreement with another. "I tell you that if two of you on earth agree about anything you ask for, it will be done for you by my Father in heaven" (Matthew 18:19, NIV).

Ask, especially if it will bring glory to God. "I will do whatever you ask in my name, so that the Son may bring glory to the Father" (John 14:13, NIV).

Ask, and remain in God's Word for the answer. "If you remain in me and my words remain in you, ask whatever you wish, and it will be given you" (John 15:7, NIV).

Ask with right motives. "You want something but don't get it. You kill and covet, but you cannot have what you want. You quarrel and fight. You do not have, because you do not ask God. When you ask, you do not receive, because you ask with wrong motives, that you may spend what you get on your pleasures" (James 4:2-3, NIV).

Ask if it's in God's will; he will answer. "This is the confidence we have in approaching God: that if we ask anything according to his will, he hears us. And if we know that he hears us—whatever we ask—we know that we have what we asked of him" (1 John 5:14-15, NIV).

All he can say is no; then you're in the same spot as you are now. But God may say yes! Our vulnerability in asking will only strengthen and grow our relationship with him. Just ask!

Your unfailing love is higher than the heavens. Your faithfulness reaches to the clouds. PSALM 108:4

 Fully Rely on God!

I have a bright green toy frog sitting on my bed. My friend Kendyl gave it to me when I was going through a really tough place emotionally. Around this frog's neck is an acrostic from a talk given by Daisy Hepburn:

- **F**ully
- **R**ely
- **O**n
- **G**od

Those toy frogs have been the perfect encouragement for many of my friends and me to remember to fully rely on God in hard times: when a spouse leaves, a child is in crisis, a friend disappoints us, a teen rebels, a home burns down, or other trials. There are many reasons why we women need to fully rely on God. And there are many ways to do that. I once gave my friends bracelets shaped like a set of mountains with a note that I would pray for them in the ups and downs of life. Having a friend pray over you can be very powerful. It helps to study the attributes of God or get the Bible on CD and play it day and night. Write a letter to Jesus, completely surrendering to him and asking him to take over the situation. Sing a favorite hymn or praise chorus until you actually believe it. And spend time praying these verses: "Bend down and listen to me; rescue me quickly. Be for me a great rock of safety, a fortress where my enemies cannot reach me. You are my rock and my fortress. For the honor of your name, lead me out of this peril" (Psalm 31:2-3).

May

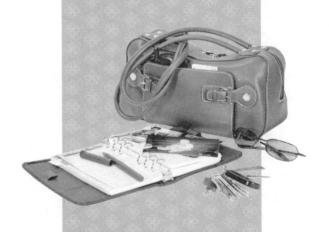

MAY 1

TO READ
Psalm 54:1-7

I will sacrifice a voluntary offering to you; I will praise your name, O Lord, for it is good.

PSALM 54:6

 ## At What Sacrifice?

Priorities are worth sacrifice—even personal sacrifice of great measures if the priority is high enough. Samson's mother is a supreme example. A man from Zorah, named Manoah, had a wife who was infertile and had no children. "The angel of the Lord appeared to Manoah's wife and said, 'Even though you have been unable to have children, you will soon become pregnant and give birth to a son. You must not drink wine or any other alcoholic drink or eat any forbidden food. You will become pregnant and give birth to a son, and his hair must never be cut. For he will be dedicated to God as a Nazirite from birth. He will rescue Israel from the Philistines'" (Judges 13:3-5).

God had a big plan for this baby—but Mom would have to do her part. She had to go without wine (a very common drink, especially at celebrations and weddings), and she had to eat according to the Mosaic law (very specific cleaning and cooking, which was very time consuming and detailed).

Then she had to watch over her son's upbringing according to a Nazirite vow: no wine; no grapes or anything made from grapes; no cutting of hair or shaving; and never going near anything dead (not even to bury your own relative!). If a person accidentally made a mistake, there was a detailed ceremony to "purify" oneself.

Samson's mother made a great personal sacrifice to raise a man for God. But her sacrifice and willingness to work produced a great deliverer for Israel.

Are your priorities worth some work and hassle to ensure? Are they worth your personal sacrifice? Do you have a "get the job done" attitude?

TO READ
Proverbs 15:1-10

A gentle answer turns away wrath, but harsh words stir up anger. PROVERBS 15:1

Bad Attitude

This gal was so bad that it is still a slur to be called a Jezebel!

After Ahab married Jezebel, he began to worship Baal. He even set up an altar for Baal in Samaria. You can imagine how angry God was with Ahab's choice of a bride and with his choice to worship other gods (1 Kings 16:31-33).

Talk about a bad influence! Ahab was no saint, but Jezebel pushed him to be worse: "Now Ahab told Jezebel everything Elijah had done and how he had killed all the prophets with the sword. So Jezebel sent a messenger to Elijah to say, 'May the gods deal with me, be it ever so severely, if by this time tomorrow I do not make your life like that of one of them.' Elijah was afraid and ran for his life" (1 Kings 19:1-3, NIV).

She was full of threats and pure evil. I can only imagine "the look" she could give. Elijah was a powerful man of God who had just single-handedly killed one hundred evil prophets, and she had him running scared!

Although you may not be "evil" like Jezebel, what do people do when you walk into a room? Have you let pressure and stress get the best of you in certain situations with your friends or coworkers?

Observe how people react to you. If you are brave, ask a few employees or subordinates what people say about you when your back is turned. Is that what you want said?

TO READ
Proverbs 22:1-4

Choose a good reputation over great riches, for being held in high esteem is better than having silver or gold. PROVERBS 22:1

 Bankrupt

Sheryl was on the brink of financial collapse.

I was in debt twenty thousand dollars from credit-card spending beyond my means. I would buy on impulse, thinking, *Oh, I'll pay this off later.*

Then I was fired from a job wrongfully, hit by a drunk driver, and two years later, after barely feeling better from the first accident, was hit again and had to have surgery. I was also responsible for a one-hundred-thousand-dollar home loan. I had no means to pay, but I didn't want to declare bankruptcy—I wanted to pay off my debts. I knew God had promised to bless me, but I also knew I had to change my lifestyle and live within my means.

I prayed and called my creditors, and because of my willingness to pay, they all decided to cut the debt in half! Then the miracles really started happening! I got a check for taxes I had overpaid the year before. Then I got a partial settlement from the accident so I could pay the doctor's bills. I still had one thousand dollars in debt, and although I had seen him pay off thousands in debt, I still worried over paying this last thousand dollars. I finally surrendered control and prayed, *I trust you, Lord!* Within three days the debt was paid!

 God cares about your finances. More verses are written about money than almost any other topic in the Bible. Seek God's answers about your finances, and he will lead you!

You can find financial freedom.

TO READ
Isaiah 42:10-16

I will lead blind Israel down a new path, guiding them along an unfamiliar way. I will make the darkness bright before them and smooth out the road ahead of them. Yes, I will indeed do these things; I will not forsake them. ISAIAH 42:16

 ## *Miracles on the Diamond*

My friend Debbie is quiet, reserved—shy, even. But one day when she was praying for her disabled son, Tim, and looking at his empty summer calendar, God impressed upon her the need to start a baseball league for disabled kids. Although Debbie knew nothing about baseball, she remembers, "The call was clear. The passage was Philippians 4:13. I knew I couldn't—but God could."

She called the city recreation department. They weren't interested. She prayed, and when someone mentioned a school principal who had a disabled child, she gave a call. The principal called a meeting of all the "exceptional parents" of kids with disabilities at his school; lots of parents said they'd help, but no one would coach.

"Lord, we need a coach!" She sent out announcements to the churches asking for special buddies to help, and only one reply came: a coach!

Now they needed a field with a dirt infield so the wheelchairs would roll. Debbie prayed as she drove, and outside Loveland, Colorado, was a church with a baseball field—and it was delighted to host the league!

The kids needed uniforms, so she called the Little League in the area. The league sent free uniforms and equipment. But the uniforms were all the same size—small! So she prayed and God provided a sweet grandmother who took the uniforms and created new shirts out of the old ones in all sizes!

The best payment for all her time was seeing a child swing the bat for the first time and the parents who said, "We look forward to this day each week. It is the one time we feel normal as a family."

If God's in it, it will succeed!

TO READ
1 Thessalonians 4:1-5

God wants you to be holy, so you should keep clear of all sexual sin. 1 THESSALONIANS 4:3

 ## Before I Say I Do

Love is a passionate and many-splendored thing. God gives sexuality to married couples as cement, a bond that helps hold hearts together.

However, couples who accept the counterfeit and give in to a sexual relationship before marriage divorce at twice the rate as those who wait until marriage for sexual intimacy. Most couples, especially those who live together, never even make it to the altar to say, "I do." In fact, the earlier a woman experiences sex, the less satisfied she is sexually when she marries. The more sexual partners she has experienced, the less fulfilled she is in her adult sexual life. The women who gave their sex life the highest possible rating of fulfilling and passionate were married women who waited until marriage and expressed a deep faith in God.

So practically speaking, how can you succeed at waiting so you can gain a lifetime of sexual fulfillment?

- Decide your boundaries ahead of time.
- Set up consequences. One couple decided to phone their youth pastors when they were tempted, or if they crossed a certain line in their physical relationship. Another was a bit more creative. They would take a week break from seeing each other if they crossed the boundary. Bill's line while we were engaged was, "I love you too much; you have to go home—now!"
- Date in public places. You are more likely to maintain your boundaries in a crowded restaurant than in an apartment watching a movie.
- Stay active. Exercise, work on projects, or help others.
- Share a purpose. Couples in service, ministry, or volunteer work have a reason bigger than themselves to stay pure. Be a role model.

TO READ
Psalm 1:1-6

Oh, the joys of those who do not follow the advice of the wicked, or stand around with sinners, or join in with scoffers. But they delight in doing everything the Lord wants; day and night they think about his law. They are like trees planted along the riverbank, bearing fruit each season without fail. Their leaves never wither, and in all they do, they prosper.

PSALM 1:1-3

Bless You!

We hear that phrase when people sneeze. I might sign a card, "Blessings! Love, Pam." Perhaps someone has prayed that God might bless you. But what is a life that God can bless? The psalmist explains it in Psalm 1:1-3.

Let's break it down: (1) Don't listen to people who are living sinful lifestyles. (2) Don't hang around with people going nowhere because they won't commit to Jesus. (3) Do delight in God's rules, in God's Word.

Why? Because your life will look like a tree planted by a stream: (1) Your life will have good fruit and plenty of it. (2) Your life will not wither, even when the heat comes in the form of oppression, frustration, obstacles, etc. (3) You will prosper because you have what you need to grow (water is a symbol for spiritual truth).

A tree with plenty of water is one that produces fruit, looks good, gives shade, and has a strong root system so adversity doesn't shake it.

So be sure to plant yourself near the water, the nourishment of God's love and his Word.

TO READ
Matthew 13:44-52

The Kingdom of Heaven is like a treasure that a man discovered hidden in a field. In his excitement, he hid it again and sold everything he owned to get enough money to buy the field—and to get the treasure, too! MATTHEW 13:44

 ## But How?

Spending time in God's Word has been shown to be the key to overcoming challenges and experiencing success. However, some need new tools to keep the journey to God's heart as interesting as a treasure hunt.

A friend of mine shared a simple system she learned from the Navigators while she was a student in college. It's as easy as saying your vowels:

- A—Ask questions. Read the verse and see if you can come up with ten questions to ask of the text.
- E—Emphasize. Find definitions for key words; look up the meanings of key phrases. (You will need a dictionary, a Bible dictionary, or maybe a Bible encyclopedia.)
- I—In your own words paraphrase the verse or part of the passage.
- O—Other references. Use cross-references to lead you to other verses, and/or use commentaries.
- U—You! Make it personal. The sooner you can apply the verse, the better!

Studying the Bible doesn't have to be complicated—it just needs to be done! Enjoy the treasure hunt!

TO READ
Isaiah 43:18-21

I am about to do a brand-new thing. See, I have already begun! Do you not see it? I will make a pathway through the wilderness for my people to come home. I will create rivers for them in the desert! ISAIAH 43:19

 ## Change Agent

How do we know when God is bringing change? When are we to make a midstream correction? How do we decide to turn off onto a new road in business, family life, or ministry? What's the difference between running away and God leading away? If you feel you are at a fork in the road, ask these questions:

Am I Running Away?

- Am I avoiding the path because I will have to face down a personal demon or weakness if I stay the course?
- Am I just lazy, and this path looks like too much work?
- Am I in conflict, and if I stay on the path, will I have to resolve it—and I feel unwilling or unprepared to do so?

If the answer is yes, stay the course and see how God will provide.

Is It Time for a Real Change?

- Is God using personal discomfort to bring new opportunities across my path?
- Am I getting repeated encouragement or affirmation regarding a different course?
- Am I sensing leading from God's Word, and/or am I seeing answered prayers leading me in a different direction?

If the answer is yes, investigate the new options more, and pray that God will confirm or put up fences or roadblocks repeatedly if you are not to proceed.

You may be doing a good thing, but God might want you to do a new thing!

TO READ
Psalm 25:1-6

Lead me by your truth and teach me, for you are the God who saves me. All day long I put my hope in you. PSALM 25:5

 Forward Focus

I was in extreme emotional pain. A friend had betrayed my trust, and the biggest hit I took was in my ability to hang on to hope. I was waiting to go onstage for a national interview when something reminded me of the pain, and I had to go to the restroom and pray as I blinked back the tears: *God, I can't cry. It would be so unprofessional! This pain is so immense, and it is so near the surface. Please show me what to do with this pain. But for right now, help me to focus on the people you have called me here to reach and serve.*

That was it! As I "focused forward" on the task immediately ahead, I gained peace. Later I wrote out a prayer of forgiveness and filled five pages with my hurt and pain. Then I laid it at Jesus' feet. *Lord, here it is—all the pain of the past few months. I have been waiting for an apology that I don't think I will ever get. I have been waiting for justice, and this side of heaven it may never come. I release the past and embrace the future you have for me.*

Then peace overwhelmed me. I went home and made posters. On them was a beautiful and serene scene with the word *hope* and these verses: "I don't mean to say that I have already achieved these things or that I have already reached perfection! But I keep working toward that day when I will finally be all that Christ Jesus saved me for and wants me to be. I am still not all I should be, but I am focusing all my energies on this one thing: Forgetting the past and looking forward to what lies ahead, I strain to reach the end of the race and receive the prize for which God, through Christ Jesus, is calling us up to heaven" (Philippians 3:12-14). I included a reminder from a dear friend: "You can't drive forward looking through your rearview mirror."

TO READ
Isaiah 43:1-4

When you go through deep waters and great trouble, I will be with you. When you go through rivers of difficulty, you will not drown! When you walk through the fire of oppression, you will not be burned up; the flames will not consume you.

ISAIAH 43:2

 ## Ablaze

The wildfires whipped through the neighborhoods. In the worst fire in San Diego's history, families with only a few minutes to pack grabbed treasures—or just each other—and escaped with their lives. One elderly couple was busy packing their car when they realized that the fire was rapidly moving toward them and they might not make it out. The two senior citizens crawled into their pool, which was far too cold to swim in but warm enough to save their lives.

One pastor's family was away on vacation and returned to no home and no church building, and discovered that every family in their church except one had lost their homes to the fires. When our organization took some supplies to them, the pastor's wife was amazingly cheery. "I am thankful because all my family made it through and we are together. Times like this make you realize what is really of value."

Of course, it's a good idea to make a list of what valuables you'd pack in an emergency, but while you're doing that, check your list against what God sees as valuable. Romans 5:8 explains, "God showed his great love for us by sending Christ to die for us while we were still sinners." People are of value to God. Make a list of the people you want to make sure are safe. Once you have it, you also have a list of the people who deserve the bulk of your time this year, and perhaps some who need to hear about God's love, too.

The Lord is my strength, my shield from every danger. I trust in him with all my heart. He helps me, and my heart is filled with joy. I burst out in songs of thanksgiving. PSALM 28:7

 ## Choosing Joy

In one particularly stressful season of life, when we were going through a very public difficulty but most of the details were either too complicated or too personal to share, people would ask me, "How are you doing?"

I would answer, "I am choosing joy!" Most of us have only a few friends we trust enough and feel safe sharing intense emotion. So that response seems to protect both the person asking and the person answering. The best part of answering, "I am choosing joy!" is that it helps you do just that.

A quick scan of the Hebrew and Greek words translated "joy" shows that when you choose joy, you are choosing exceeding gladness, pleasure, rejoicing, cheerfulness, and calm delight. Those are definitely the things I want from life! So how do you choose joy? Choose Jesus instead of the emotion at hand. Make a conscious choice to worship instead of worry. Here are some great statements about what Jesus will do for you when you choose the joy he gives:

- You have turned my mourning into joyful dancing. You have taken away my clothes of mourning and clothed me with joy. (Psalm 30:11)
- When doubts filled my mind, your comfort gave me renewed hope and cheer. (Psalm 94:19)
- I pray that God, who gives you hope, will keep you happy and full of peace as you believe in him. May you overflow with hope through the power of the Holy Spirit. (Romans 15:13)

The next time you're experiencing a time of stress, choose joy!

I meditate on your age-old laws; O Lord, they comfort me. PSALM 119:52

 Cozy Comforter

Do you have a memory like this? You're outside playing in the snow. Your clothes get all wet and frozen. You run inside, and your mother peels off the frozen clothes, wraps you in a cozy comforter, and places you next to a fireplace with a cup of hot chocolate. That's comfort!

Sometimes people need that kind of comfort for the soul. In the Bible, Isaac was grieving after his beloved mother died. His father arranged for a servant to go retrieve Rebekah to be Isaac's wife.

After the wedding, the Bible describes their new relationship: "Isaac brought her into the tent of his mother Sarah, and he married Rebekah. So she became his wife, and he loved her; and Isaac was comforted after his mother's death" (Genesis 24:67, NIV).

Comfort in this passage means "to give strength or staying power." Who in your world needs strength or staying power? Do you need comfort? God can be that cozy comforter.

God's love, sent through the promises of his Word, is a blanket of hope. Like a quilt, there is a piece of the Word to wrap your heart in today.

TO READ
Mark 2:1-12

"I will prove that I, the Son of Man, have the authority on earth to forgive sins." Then Jesus turned to the paralyzed man and said, "Stand up, take your mat, and go on home, because you are healed!" The man jumped up, took the mat, and pushed his way through the stunned onlookers. Then they all praised God. "We've never seen anything like this before!" they exclaimed. MARK 2:10

 ## *Crumbs of Time*

The more you have to give, the more people will want from you. You may feel bad about the little time you can give friends old and new. Jesus knows how you feel. But look at what happened in a few brief moments with Jesus:

> When Jesus had entered Capernaum, a centurion came to him, asking for help. "Lord," he said, "my servant lies at home paralyzed and in terrible suffering."
>
> Jesus said to him, "I will go and heal him."
>
> The centurion replied, "Lord, I do not deserve to have you come under my roof. But just say the word, and my servant will be healed. . . ."
>
> When Jesus heard this, he was astonished and said . . . , "I tell you the truth, I have not found anyone in Israel with such great faith. . . ."
>
> Then Jesus said to the centurion, "Go! It will be done just as you believed it would." And his servant was healed at that very hour. (Matthew 8:5-13, NIV)

> A Canaanite woman from that vicinity came to him, crying out, "Lord, Son of David, have mercy on me! My daughter is suffering terribly from demon-possession." . . .
>
> He answered, "I was sent only to the lost sheep of Israel. . . . It is not right to take the children's bread and toss it to their dogs."
>
> "Yes, Lord," she said, "but even the dogs eat the crumbs that fall from their masters' table."
>
> Then Jesus answered, "Woman, you have great faith! Your request is granted." And her daughter was healed from that very hour. (Matthew 15:22-28, NIV)

When you are pressed, pray that God will empower your crumbs of time.

TO READ
Proverbs 27:15-27

A nagging wife is as annoying as the constant dripping on a rainy day. PROVERBS 27:15

 Nag, Nag, Nag

Delilah was a nag: "Delilah said to Samson, "Tell me the secret of your great strength and how you can be tied up and subdued."

He gave an answer, but not the right one, so she asked again: "You have made a fool of me; you lied to me. Come now, tell me how you can be tied."

Samson dittoed another false answer, so Delilah nagged, nagged, and nagged: "Until now, you have been making a fool of me and lying to me. Tell me how you can be tied."

Again Samson gave a fake answer, so Delilah upped the whining ante: "'How can you say, "I love you," when you won't confide in me? This is the third time you have made a fool of me and haven't told me the secret of your great strength.' With such nagging she prodded him day after day until he was tired to death" (Judges 16:6, 10, 13, 15-16, NIV).

He was sick and tired of her nagging, whining, and constant pressure—so he caved. The Philistines took him, cut his hair, and gouged out his eyes.

Delilah got what she wanted, an answer that put her in good graces with the Philistine leaders. She must have been front and center in the arena when Samson took the two pillars and brought the house down. Thousands were killed, and the Bible never mentions Delilah again. Maybe she got what she wanted, but it looks like she also got what she deserved.

TO READ
1 John 2:15-17

Stop loving this evil world and all that it offers you, for when you love the world, you show that you do not have the love of the Father in you. 1 JOHN 2:15

❋ Distracted

Anyone who has read the Bible is familiar with the apostle Paul, author of a majority of the New Testament. He gathered a committed group around him and set off on several missionary journeys, spreading the gospel and laying a foundation for the church as we know it today. However, not all of those companions were as committed as Paul. Take Demas, for example: "Demas has deserted me because he loves the things of this life and has gone to Thessalonica" (2 Timothy 4:10).

He loved the world and deserted Paul, and perhaps he even deserted the faith. How would you like it if all that was written about you was your desertion?

Jesus warns against this distraction in the parable of the sower. In Matthew 13:22 Jesus explains: "The thorny ground represents those who hear and accept the Good News, but all too quickly the message is crowded out by the cares of this life and the lure of wealth, so no crop is produced."

Jesus' admonition is clear: When God's Word is choked out, worldly things like making money, entertaining sinful behaviors, and distracting relationships grow in the void.

John describes the distraction as a craving: "For everything in the world—the cravings of sinful man, the lust of his eyes and the boasting of what he has and does—comes not from the Father but from the world" (1 John 2:16, NIV).

A craving is something you are desperate for, a longing that screams for attention and pushes you to fulfill it. We see cravings in addicts. The only way to really combat a craving that is a distraction is to crave God's Word more.

Be desperate for God. There's a choice: be a Demas who ends up distracted or a woman who is desperate for Jesus and ends up hearing, "Well done!"

TO READ
Psalm 143:8-12

Teach me to do your will, for you are my God; may your good Spirit lead me on level ground.

PSALM 143:10, NIV

Do It by Ones

In the game Cricket you can move ahead, then win the game in small increments, or "ones."

While traveling and preaching in a foreign country that was challenging and dangerous, Jill Briscoe felt overwhelmed by the task at hand. Her husband, Stuart, said, "Do it by ones."

Elisabeth Elliot, whose husband Jim was killed by a tribe she later went back to minister to, was asked, "How do I know God's will?" Elisabeth responded, "Do the next thing."

My husband, Bill, believes that it is in the small, daily, even mundane decisions of life that we gain ground for God.

Often we want victory to be won once and for all! We want a dramatic rescue or an exciting event to change our lives. However, we gain ground and move from chaos to change in small steps. Galatians 5:25 says, "If we live in the Spirit, let us also walk in the Spirit" (NKJV).

The word *step* means "to march or keep step, like in the military. Think about marching—it isn't dancing; it is just one foot in front of the other, over and over and over again.

Victory comes if we "do the next thing," if we "do it by ones," and if we live one day at a time. Level ground is the goal. When we can get out of the drama and chaos and onto level ground, we can go full speed ahead. If we have lofty goals, they will be attained if we can daily do the next thing. It is like we are biking up the mountain and soon we'll be on the flatland, where we can make great gains and distance ourselves from past failures. One day at a time—"Do it by ones!"

TO READ
Psalm 9:9-16

The Lord is a shelter for the oppressed, a refuge in times of trouble. PSALM 9:9

 Does God Care?

Sexual harassment, rape, molestation, being a battered girlfriend or battered wife, men cheating. All these are fears, real fears. Does God care if these things happen to women?

Check out the list of consequences for men who hurt women:

- Cheats on his wife: death (Leviticus 20:10)
- Sex with mother or daughter-in-law: death (Leviticus 20:11-12)
- Bigamy and incest: death (Leviticus 20:14)
- Incest with his sister: cast out (Leviticus 20:17)
- Rape: death (Deuteronomy 22:25)

God does care. Sometimes it seems life just can't go on when someone inflicts sexual pain on you. It hurts even more when it seems there is no justice. But God does see. He does care. He will bring justice about—in his way and in his timing: "This is what the Lord says to the dynasty of David: Give justice to the people you judge! Help those who have been robbed; rescue them from their oppressors. Do what is right, or my anger will burn like an unquenchable fire because of all your sins" (Jeremiah 21:12).

God's anger burns against those who rob and oppress. He does care, and he will care for you. There will be justice on your behalf—if not here, in the courts of heaven.

TO READ
Mark 14:3-9

She has done what she could. MARK 14:8

She Did What She Could

Over coffee my friend Marilyn Williams shared her excitement about a message she had just given at a women's tea that day. She shared her insights about the woman who anointed Jesus with oil before he was crucified.

When Jesus was in Bethany at the home of Simon Peter, a woman came with a very expensive bottle of perfume, and she broke it open and poured it on Jesus' head. Now some of those who were in attendance thought this was a waste of resources that could have been given to the poor, but Jesus responded by asking why they were bothering her. He said she had done a beautiful thing. Look at Mark 14:8-9: "She has done what she could and has anointed my body for burial ahead of time. I assure you, wherever the Good News is preached throughout the world, this woman's deed will be talked about in her memory."

"See, Pam, she was ordinary. She couldn't do everything—she just did what she could!"

So many times we think we have to do everything to please God, but sometimes it is our simple act of worship that pleases him most.

The verse reminds me of some advice I heard a seasoned pastor, Chuck Smith, say: "I do my best and commit the rest." Be faithful, doing what you can—not frantic in serving Jesus.

Today, just do "what you can."

TO READ
Matthew 14:22-32

When [Peter] looked around at the high waves, he was terrified and began to sink. "Save me, Lord!" he shouted. MATTHEW 14:30

 ## When the Boat Is Rocking

I once heard John Maxwell, founder of Injoy Ministries, say that those who are busy rowing the boat seldom have the time or energy to rock it.

If God places you at the helm of an event or organization, keep the people rowing and their eyes set on the goal, and the sailing will be smoother.

What happens to people when their eyes are off the goal? Peter and the disciples saw Jesus walking on the water in the middle of the night, and they were afraid, thinking he was a ghost. But Jesus encouraged and calmed them, telling them not to be afraid. And then Peter decided he would walk out on the water to meet Jesus. As long as he kept his eyes focused on Jesus, he was walking on the water, but when he looked out at the wind, he immediately began to sink and cried for help (Matthew 14:25-30).

Things will start sinking if your eyes or your crew's eyes are on the circumstances rather than on Christ. If you feel your idea, dream, company, or future sinking, turn your eyes and the eyes of your team back to Christ.

Pray together, study the Word, or bring in a godly specialist or teammate who can point the team back to God and his purpose. This is especially true if the crew starts turning on each other or on you!

Before you have a mutiny, lead your team to look to the horizon!

TO READ
James 1:6-8

When you ask him, be sure that you really expect him to answer, for a doubtful mind is as unsettled as a wave of the sea that is driven and tossed by the wind. JAMES 1:6

 ## *Doubt Does Us In*

When we know what is right, then doubt it, we slide down a slippery slope. The serpent in Genesis 3 was "more crafty" than any other animal God had created. He used a question to get Eve to doubt God's commandment about what to eat in the Garden.

Satan is more likely to use doubt than straight out contradict God to get you off track. He doesn't have many tricks, just different versions of the same. He told Eve, "Are you sure God said that?" He plants those same seeds of doubt in our minds: Are you sure you can do this? Are you sure people will follow you? Are you sure this was God's idea?

And then this crafty animal goes a step further. Now that woman has a bit of doubt—he lies. Eve tells him that they are not to eat from the tree in the middle of the Garden, for God has told them that they will die. The serpent's response: "'You will not surely die,' the serpent said to the woman. 'For God knows that when you eat of it your eyes will be opened, and you will be like God, knowing good and evil'" (Genesis 3:4-5, NIV).

With a seed of doubt: "Did God really say . . . ?" and a lie: "You will not surely die," Eve looked at the fruit differently. It was pleasing and desirable, so she ate it. Her doubt took her a step further, and she gave some to her husband, too.

Their perfect world was turned to pain—for her and for all of us. Doubt can be the beginning of a downward spiral in our faith with God. Don't let doubt even get started in your heart.

TO READ
Matthew 7:6;
1 Corinthians 13:1-13

"Don't give what is holy to unholy people." Don't give pearls to swine! They will trample the pearls, then turn and attack you. MATTHEW 7:6

 ## Place Some Space

The Bible gives us some great principles to follow when it comes to our relationships with others. Think about the following statements:

- Love is patient and kind. Love is not jealous or boastful or proud or rude. Love does not demand its own way. Love is not irritable, and it keeps no record of when it has been wronged. It is never glad about injustice but rejoices whenever the truth wins out. Love never gives up, never loses faith, is always hopeful, and endures through every circumstance. (1 Corinthians 13:4-7)

- If another believer sins against you, go privately and point out the fault. If the other person listens and confesses it, you have won that person back. But if you are unsuccessful, take one or two others with you and go back again, so that everything you say may be confirmed by two or three witnesses. If that person still refuses to listen, take your case to the church. If the church decides you are right, but the other person won't accept it, treat that person as a pagan or a corrupt tax collector. (Matthew 18:15-17)

You may be wondering, *Where does not giving pearls to swine come in?* If you have tried to follow the relationship principles above and a person who sinned against you won't acknowledge the wrong or apologize or repent, then, to paraphrase God's instructions to you in Matthew, *place some space* between you. If you keep sharing your heart, that person will know exactly how to hurt you the next time. The time may come when you need to treat that person like a stranger on the street: Be polite and respectful and obey what the Bible says about praying for your enemies, but give the relationship some breathing space and wait for God to intervene.

TO READ
Luke 22:1-6

Satan entered into Judas Iscariot, who was one of the twelve disciples, and he went over to the leading priests and captains of the Temple guard to discuss the best way to betray Jesus to them. LUKE 22:3-4

Portrait of Betrayal

Betrayal. It happened to Christ: Judas was paid thirty pieces of silver for betraying Jesus to the chief priests. And it will happen to us as Christ's followers. Satan loves to get in between people. It's hard to recognize Satan's entrance, but you can see his fingerprints in the lives of people. "When you follow the desires of your sinful nature, your lives will produce these evil results: sexual immorality, impure thoughts, eagerness for lustful pleasure, idolatry, participation in demonic activities, hostility, quarreling, jealousy, outbursts of anger, selfish ambition, divisions, the feeling that everyone is wrong except those in your own little group, envy, drunkenness, wild parties, and other kinds of sin" (Galatians 5:19-21). Another early warning sign is reflected in the way Satan acted toward God: "You [Satan] said to yourself, 'I will ascend to heaven and set my throne above God's stars. I will preside on the mountain of the gods far away in the north. I will climb to the highest heavens and be like the Most High'" (Isaiah 14:13-14). Pride was Satan's downfall, and it is almost always involved in betrayal.

A betrayer asks, "What's in this for me?" Matthew 26 shows Judas tipping his hand and showing the intent of his heart when he asks the chief priests, "How much will you pay me to betray Jesus to you?" and they give him thirty pieces of silver (v. 15). This is the opposite of what the Bible teaches: "Be humble, thinking of others as better than yourself" (Philippians 2:3). If we follow Jesus' example of love, we will likely experience betrayal because loving others makes us vulnerable. But loving and following Christ will protect your character so that you won't become a Judas too.

TO READ
Colossians 3:12-17

Let the words of Christ, in all their richness, live in your hearts and make you wise. COLOSSIANS 3:16

Dumbing Down

In education they call teaching to the test "dumbing down the curriculum" because a teacher isn't teaching students everything they need to know, just what they will be tested on. We also see "dumbing down" in the easy A's given because educators may not want to hurt a student's self-esteem by giving a lower grade than others in the class, even if the student has done inferior work.

However, once children reach adulthood, they quickly find that employers and others don't dumb down or grade on the curve. The corporate work environment demands that employees do their job with excellence, or they are fired. Talk about hurting self-esteem! I would rather work hard learning early all I need to know, regardless of the grading system, because the real test is in the real world.

We may be tempted to dumb down spiritually, too. We may tell ourselves, *I am not as bad as Sally,* or, *I know more Bible verses than most.* But God isn't interested in our comparisons; he has an individual learning plan for each of us because he wants us to be the best we can be for him.

He wants us to follow the plan he has set out for us. Maybe we aren't living lives of blatant immorality, but are we hiding sins like pride, self-righteousness, anger, or resentment in our hearts? How is your Bible study and knowledge of God? Are you comfortable resting on what you learned five years ago, or are you striving to learn more every day? Are you challenging yourself to memorize, pray, and live a disciplined life that might include answering God's individual call to fast, do an inductive study, or pray at a certain time each day?

Don't dumb down—strive to be the best you can be through Christ.

TO READ
Philippians 4:6-9

Don't worry about anything; instead, pray about everything. Tell God what you need, and thank him for all he has done. If you do this, you will experience God's peace, which is far more wonderful than the human mind can understand. His peace will guard your hearts and minds as you live in Christ Jesus. PHILIPPIANS 4:6-7

Entitlement

"Why do bad things always happen to me?"

The young mother looked into my eyes, pleading for an answer. She had rattled off a list of "woes." We never have enough money. My husband didn't buy me an anniversary gift. We have only one car, and I am stuck at home with three screaming toddlers.

"Life sounds hard," I commented. She nodded, thinking she'd gained a sympathetic audience. "And it sounds like you are in a strenuous stage of life." Again she nodded. "And it all sounds normal."

"Normal! This is normal?" She was not happy with the answer.

"Yes, these are normal growing pains. Most every woman goes through lean days as well as days of plenty. Do you think money issues might be why your husband didn't get you a gift? Did he get you a card; did he somehow wish you a happy anniversary?"

"Well, yes—he did say 'Happy Anniversary' on a screen saver he put on my computer."

"Having little ones and no car is a challenge, but I think you are looking at the glass as half empty instead of half full. Nowhere in the Bible does God promise an easy life, but he does say he will bless you when you give thanks.

Instead of looking at what you don't have—look at what you do have. There are no special entitlements. Everyone must grow up, and often there are growing pains. But a thankful heart makes growing up a bit easier.

> **TO READ**
> 2 John 1:1-13

I have much more to say to you, but I don't want to say it in a letter. For I hope to visit you soon and to talk with you face to face. Then our joy will be complete. 2 JOHN 1:12

✳ *Face-to-Face*

The more intense the emotion, the more sensitive the topic, or the more unknown the outcome, the more a conversation needs to happen face-to-face.

When a challenge needed to be laid out, Amaziah sent messengers to Jehoash, "Come, meet me face to face" (2 Kings 14:8, NIV). The harder the road ahead or the bigger the mountain, the more the challenge needs to be explained face-to-face, followed by plenty of time for questions and lots of time to encourage, comfort, and instill vision and confidence.

When a vital transaction or negotiation needed to happen, Zedekiah king of Judah was handed over to the king of Babylon to speak with him face-to-face (Jeremiah 32:4). The more tenuous the transaction, the more room there may be for misunderstanding; thus, the more those negotiations should be handled in person. And if there is any question of character, those talks need to be in person so you can discern the person's motives.

When correction or punishment is given, God says he wants to see his people face-to- face to judge them (Ezekiel 20:35). Jesus tells us that if someone sins against us, we should go to him or her in person (Matthew 18:15). Words that are hard to hear should be given in person.

Life is hard, and those moments need to be shared in person. But the best moments should also be shared in person: announcing an engagement, news of a pregnancy or birth, congratulations over a raise, a new job, or an award. Good news is rare; make the moment count!

TO READ
Exodus 34:29-35

Whenever [Moses] went into the Tent of Meeting to speak with the Lord . . . the people would see his face aglow. EXODUS 34:34-35

 ## *Facing God*

The Lord spoke to Moses face-to-face, just like a friend (Exodus 33:11). Moses had a real, deep friendship with God. What were the results of his friendship with God?

Moses overcame insecurities. When God first called him, Moses felt insecure. "O Lord, I have never been eloquent, neither in the past nor since you have spoken to your servant. I am slow of speech and tongue" (Exodus 4:10, NIV).

But the Lord encouraged him by saying that he would help him speak and teach him what to say. God walked Moses through numerous scenarios that might happen with Pharaoh and told him how to respond.

Moses reorganized his strengths to accomplish God's plan. God helped Moses see he was the man for the job, since Moses knew the language, beliefs, and customs from growing up in the palace. God gave him the insight to see how to use all these skills, talents, and experiences for God's people.

Moses gained faith to lead, then delegate. He gained supernatural strength from his meetings with God, like when he was given the Ten Commandments for the people. Only a strong leader can lay out rules—people are resistant to rules. Then Moses was able to take good advice from his elders, appointing representatives to share leadership. Only a secure leader can share position and power.

Meeting with God regularly prepared Moses for the next step. What's your next step? Don't know? Get away with God. Know the next step but feel afraid? Get away with God. To face it, face him.

TO READ
Romans 6:15-23

You are weak in your natural selves.

ROMANS 6:19, NIV

 Failure

We hate the word *failure,* don't we? The thought of having to say it aloud sends shivers up the spine, ties our stomach in knots, and gives us a head-ache! However, if you never say you are wrong, then you can never figure out what would be right! There is no sin in saying you have failed.

If you are not matching up to the Bible and God's plan in one area of your life, it is not news to God. He already sees it! "All have sinned; all fall short" (Romans 3:23). Left to yourself, using all your own strength and power, you will fall short. Paraphrased, it might be, "You were wrong. You failed. You are not perfect." It is no sin to acknowledge you fell short—that is just agreeing with God. God likes it when you live in agreement with him.

However, there is a sin if you say, "I am a failure." He came down and died in our place so we'd never have to see ourselves as a failure. Instead of playing that same old tape of lies that Satan has strung together, reject the lie and state the truth.

"The truth is I have failed here. The truth is that God sees me as a win-ner, so what do I need to change to get my reality to match up with God's picture of me?"

Is there a sin to avoid, a habit to unlearn, a new skill to learn, or a piece of information I need? If I did this all over again, what would I do differently this time?

He alone is my rock and my salvation, my fortress where I will never be shaken. PSALM 62:2

 ## Pressure Turned Priceless

Cindy, my college roommate, seemed to have it all—beauty, brains, and boys! But more than anything, she had a blossoming relationship with Christ. She modeled growth in godliness each day we shared that dorm room. But it was years later that she modeled the meaning of deep faith under the most difficult circumstances. Cindy describes it best:

> As a young girl, I remember being timid, shy, and fearful. Growing up into a teenager, I learned to hook into the hope of being a people-pleaser in constant worry of the impression I made and how people perceived me. I believed the lie that God wasn't enough for me, and that I had to have more to be complete.
>
> Then when our first baby was full term stillborn and our second child died of a genetic neurological disease, it rocked my world and sent the false foundation that I stood on into oblivion. Through that time, in spite of my weak faith, God proved himself faithful to me over and over again. The lights came on for me one day when I realized that the fear was no longer dominant. I had come to know that if God could get me through this, he could get me through anything. He is my hope and the Rock I stand on, and he is now my firm foundation.

Deep changes in our lives are like diamonds—they are very often formed under intense pressure. Just as coal is transformed into a diamond, so your fears can be formed into a firm foundation. When your fears feel like they are shaking your world, run to the doorway of hope—Christ, your firm foundation.

TO READ
Romans 8:21-28

The Holy Spirit helps us in our distress. For we don't even know what we should pray for, nor how we should pray. But the Holy Spirit prays for us with groanings that cannot be expressed in words.

ROMANS 8:26

 Translator

We pray many prayers. We toss them up like basketballs heading toward the basket, and, of course, we expect God to answer all of them! We see only each individual ball as we toss it up in hope and faith:

- Lord, help me to find a better job.
- Lord, please bring me a godly man to marry.
- Lord, please give us a child.
- Lord, help my sons and daughters grow to be godly adults.
- Lord, give my daughter a godly husband.
- Father, help my children to achieve their dreams.
- Jesus, use them to touch others, to make the world a better place.

From our perspective, it would seem like a good thing to answer our prayers just the way we pray them. But only God knows what those prayers might look like from *his* point of view. God sees the big picture, the eternal priorities and plan he has already carved for a child or spouse or even for ourselves. Some of our prayers may actually conflict with one another. If God were to say yes to our request for acceptance at a particular college or to a job opportunity, perhaps the spouse he has planned for us would not cross our path. Too often when we pray, we are really just telling God—in a nice way—what to do! Today try, "Father, you know best!" The Spirit will translate all those prayers you've prayed so fervently, and God, who "causes everything to work together for the good of those who love [him] and are called according to his purpose for them" (Romans 8:28) will make sense of all the desires you have directed up to him.

TO READ
Luke 12:22-34

Look at the ravens. They don't need to plant or harvest or put food in barns because God feeds them. And you are far more valuable to him than any birds! LUKE 12:24

 ## For the Birds

A young woman who had graduated from college wanted to do something in business, but the jobs were scarce. So she took a job substitute teaching "until the job she wanted came along." After a couple years of substitute teaching, she was discouraged, wondering why God didn't give her the job *she* wanted.

One day in her garden she noticed how her peach tree was loaded with peaches that weren't quite ready for harvest, so she propped up the over-loaded branches, pampered the tree, and waited.

After a couple weeks went by, she went out to pick peaches, and to her surprise, many of them were on the ground half eaten. She was angry, thinking her neighbors were sneaking in, eating them, and just throwing them on the ground. But then she noticed the peaches on the tree had bite marks in them, too.

The birds had been eating her peaches! Those birds didn't do anything to help her grow them! They didn't pay the water bills! They didn't put fertilizer on the tree, but they came and ate! Then it came to her, God cares for the birds and provides for them, just like it says in Matthew 6:34: "Do not worry about tomorrow, for tomorrow will worry about itself. Each day has enough trouble of its own" (NIV).

She realized that if God provided for birds, he would provide for her—and he did. The substitute teaching job quickly turned into a full-time teaching position, which she loves now, years later.

TO READ
2 Corinthians 1:8-11

He will rescue us because you are helping by praying for us. As a result, many will give thanks to God because so many people's prayers for our safety have been answered. 2 CORINTHIANS 1:11

 Friend in Need

A friend in need is a friend indeed. When you need a friend, one of the best things a friend can do is pray or intercede for you before the throne. A friend who prays with you and for you is a gift in times of transition and crisis.

In the Bible Job lost his income, family, and health. He had plenty of friends who pointed out all the reasons he might be in this tough place. But Job didn't need critics; he needed friends—praying friends. He expresses this desire: "My intercessor is my friend as my eyes pour out tears to God; on behalf of a man he pleads with God as a man pleads for his friend" (Job 16:20-21, NIV).

Who cries with you? Who prays with you? Who pleads your requests when you are growing weary of doing it yourself?

How is this kind of relationship formed? This kind of friendship is intense, deep, and trusting. Time spent in like-minded activities develops trust.

My intercessory friends are those with whom I have studied the Bible, served in ministry, worked alongside, and more than anything, prayed together weekly for several years. They have the ability to read my emotions. They are not shy about praying, and if they see me struggling emotionally, they stop and pray—right then.

When women succeed in life, work, and ministry, it's because they have one or more praying friends.

June

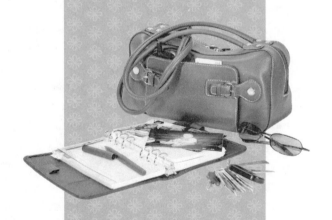

TO READ
2 Kings 4:19-37

Elisha summoned Gehazi. "Call the child's mother!" he said. And when she came in, Elisha said, "Here, take your son!" She fell at his feet, overwhelmed with gratitude. Then she picked up her son and carried him downstairs. 2 KINGS 4:36-37

Get the Best

The Bible tells a story of a rich woman who built the prophet Elisha a room in her home. One day her only son grabbed his head in pain and collapsed. The woman held her son on her lap as he died. For a parent, this is a crisis of great proportion. There was nothing this woman could do to help her son. The problem was far beyond her own limited power or ability. What did she do? She promptly went to someone who could help her:

> When she came to the man of God at the mountain, she fell to the ground before him and caught hold of his feet. Gehazi began to push her away, but the man of God said, "Leave her alone. Something is troubling her deeply. . . ."
> Elisha returned with her. . . .
> He went in alone and shut the door behind him and prayed to the Lord. Then he lay down on the child's body, placing his mouth on the child's mouth, his eyes on the child's eyes, and his hands on the child's hands. And the child's body began to grow warm again! Elisha got up and walked back and forth in the room a few times. Then he stretched himself out again on the child. This time the boy sneezed seven times and opened his eyes! (2 Kings 4:27, 30, 33-35)

This woman in need went after the best help she could think of. She needed someone who had the *ability* and the *desire* to help her. We can learn an important lesson from this woman's example. When we face a crisis, we can go to the One with the greatest ability to help and the greatest desire. Our heavenly Father's heart wants his children to cry out for his help when their path takes them through difficulties. We can find no better help and no more loving heart than his. When you're in a tight spot, look for help with a heart.

TO READ
Ezekiel 34:11-16

I will be like a shepherd looking for his scattered flock. I will find my sheep and rescue them from all the places to which they were scattered on that dark and cloudy day. EZEKIEL 34:12

 ## In the Flock

When I grew up on a Suffolk sheep farm, I witnessed the brutal attack of wolves and wild dogs on the sheep. They would chase the flock, trying to separate out one lamb from the rest. Then they would rip and tear at the lamb's flesh, eating it alive.

Satan attacks in much the same way, usually trying to separate us from the body of Christ with lies:

- They don't want you at small group.
- You aren't qualified to be a leader. What are you doing at the training?
- You don't need to be at church today—you're too tired.
- If those people really knew you, they'd reject you.

These lies build when no one is around to tell you the truth. Any time you are feeling lonely, alone in your responsibility, or isolated due to lack of confidence or self-esteem issues, run *to* people, not away from them. Run to a trusted leader or friend and ask him or her to tell you the truth and pray.

One friend experienced this kind of attack at a large gathering of Christian leaders. She felt so discouraged and her self-image so shaken, she ran back to her room to cry.

"I didn't expect that kind of attack in this setting."

I empathized with her surprise. "Yes, I know, we expect to be safe from Satan at a large gathering of Christian leaders—but what better place for Satan to attack. If he can get leaders shaken and discouraged by taking their eyes off of God and putting them on self, then he's won by distracting us from the purpose of changing and reaching the world."

Get back to the flock; it's safer there.

Trust me in your times of trouble, and I will rescue you, and you will give me glory. PSALM 50:15

 ## *God plus One*

Andy was struggling to scan my purchases—but determined to get it done. As he talked, I could tell he had been through a trauma, probably a head injury and much more.

I commented, "Wow, that must be hard to do with one arm."

"Yes, but you do what you have to, and I guess that's what I get for riding motorcycles."

"God must really have a plan for you since you are alive."

A few words were slurred in his answer, but the message was clear.

"You have no idea. I died four times at the hospital, and they had to revive me. I was in a coma for weeks. The doctors told my mom the first night, 'Sorry, there's not much hope for him.' Yes, God has a plan for me."

I smiled; then Andy's real hope shone.

"I have a math problem for you. What is one cross plus three nails? Four-given!"

He might have been disabled in body but not in spirit!

I was reminded of a favorite quote: "God plus one is a majority."

Then Andy said as we left the checkout, "The doctors didn't know who they were dealing with. It wasn't just me, but my mom and her prayers—my mom plus God—you don't mess with that!"

TO READ
Proverbs 11:16-20

A kindhearted woman gains respect.

PROVERBS 11:16, NIV

 ## Good Attention from a Good Man

We've all witnessed it—or maybe we've resorted to it. You know, those desperate methods of getting a man's attention. But what does a good man look for in a good woman? We can learn much from Ruth, the daughter-in-law who followed Naomi back to Israel. What was it about Ruth that caught Boaz's attention? "Boaz asked his foreman, 'Who is that girl over there?' And the foreman replied, 'She is the young woman from Moab who came back with Naomi. She asked me this morning if she could gather grain behind the harvesters. She has been hard at work ever since, except for a few minutes' rest over there in the shelter'" (Ruth 2:5-7).

In Ruth, Boaz saw a respectful, polite, hardworking woman willing to sacrifice for her family. So Boaz told his crew to watch over her safety and help her glean. He offered her rest, food, and water; then he asked for a lunch date!

When he got her alone, he told her all he knew about her leaving her homeland and coming with her mother-in-law to care for her. She had made quite an impression on Boaz, and he blessed her. "May the Lord, the God of Israel, under whose wings you have come to take refuge, reward you fully" (Ruth 2:12).

Boaz saw Ruth's heart for God and others before he ever enjoyed seeing her heart for him.

Do your actions reveal your heart?

TO READ
Ephesians 5:10-20

Be careful how you live, not as fools but as those who are wise. EPHESIANS 5:15

 Good-Girl Syndrome

After the strain of a marital separation and the stress of divorce hearings, many women who have been good, moral, and strong mothers, can fall into behavior that I call the "good-girl syndrome."

These women tend to be the parent who has been consistent for the children even if their father has left, cheated, or abused alcohol or drugs. These women rallied for the strain of separation and divorce, but once the divorce is final, they can easily feel entitled to some "fun."

I have observed a pattern of nights out with "the girls" that often end up at bars or dance clubs, talking—or more—with men. These relationships with men can develop into dates or rebound relationships, and the character and quality of these men are not the same caliber as men met through business, church, or community volunteer work. These women may even recognize this pattern but say things to their friends or counselor like, "But I've earned it!" or "When is it my turn to have some fun?"

If a woman recovering from a divorce is not careful, she can fall into the "good-girl syndrome" by establishing unhealthy habits that expose her to more unhealthy relationships that will only cause more hurt. The wise woman reestablishing her life will look for ways to enjoy life and relationships in more healthy ways: college classes, divorce-recovery classes, Christian singles' Bible studies, sports, or hobby classes.

Remember it is "good" to be "good"! Psalm 37:3 promises: "Trust in the Lord and do good. Then you will live safely in the land and prosper."

Make a list of "safe," fun activities—and enjoy.

TO READ
Psalm 51:1-7

Purify me from my sins, and I will be clean; wash me, and I will be whiter than snow. PSALM 51:7

 ## *Good-Bye to the Ghosts*

It was terrifying, and it was healing. Janine knew God wanted her to face the ghosts of her past choices, but she was so afraid her husband and children would reject her.

She had tried to live a Christian life before them. Her husband had recommitted his life to Christ right after she did when they were dating in college. They wanted to create a new legacy, far different from the broken homes in which they were raised.

Their three children all attended Sunday school, Awana, and youth group and had heard numerous talks on sexual integrity. As a family they had also participated in Walk for Life and other pro-life fund-raisers to support crisis pregnancy centers. They were well trained to wait until marriage for sex, but they had never heard Mom's whole story. They didn't even know there was a story.

Through her involvement with crisis pregnancy centers, she had heard of a support group that helps women who have chosen abortion to heal from the trauma of their choice.

She had been so young, just a freshman. She was told it was just tissue, not a baby. And the more she had learned the truth from God's Word and the medical literature, the more she felt she had been deceived. Yet the blood was still on her conscience. She knew somewhere deep inside there had been a small voice begging her to choose life, but she ignored the voice. The shame and guilt was unbearable; she had to find help and healing.

Through the abortion recovery group, she felt true forgiveness from God—and an unquenchable desire to share her story to help other women. She was afraid to tell the whole story, but she was more afraid not to.

"I can't live in the shadows anymore. I want God to reign in my life, not the ghosts."

I am sure that God, who began the good work within you, will continue his work until it is finally finished on that day when Christ Jesus comes back again. PHILIPPIANS 1:6

Groundhog Day

In the movie *Groundhog Day,* the main character finds himself living the same day over and over again. At first he thinks he is going crazy; then he decides to improve himself, make better choices, and thus see if he can change the monotonous cycle and break out into reality again.

The saying goes, "Insanity is doing the same thing over and over while expecting different results." Are you "stuck"? Has your career reached a plateau? Relationships not working? Are you making the same mistakes spiritually and morally?

Then make a change. Once we accept Christ, we are redeemed. We are now a work in progress, so we aren't aiming at perfection—rather, movement. Any forward movement, even the tiniest baby step, is progress. God can help with that forward movement: "I will put my Spirit in you and move you to follow my decrees and be careful to keep my laws" (Ezekiel 36:27, NIV). God gives his Spirit; listen to it. The Spirit will help you follow God's "decrees."

"Small steps taken consistently over time equal big results," my friend Danna Demetre says.

Sometimes steps to change look too big. You need to break them down into smaller steps. If you break them down small enough, even climbing a mountain seems possible. Each step is just slightly higher than the step before, a gentle incline—like a ramp.

Build a ramp to your dreams.

TO READ
Psalm 92:1-8

It is good to give thanks to the Lord, to sing praises to the Most High. It is good to proclaim your unfailing love in the morning, your faithfulness in the evening. PSALM 92:1-2

 Hanging Out with God

I am the parent of teens. Their cell phones ring constantly with requests from friends to "hang out." Their friends say, "Let's go to the movies, a Christian concert, or a friend's house to swim, etc."

They simply enjoy being with their friends, as long as the activities are moral and productive.

The outcome of time spent together is that my sons have deep and authentic friendships. One day I thought about how Zach lights up when a friend calls and invites him someplace, and I wondered if I respond to God with the same delight.

We, too, can find a great, deep, and authentic friendship with God, but we have to make him a priority. Look for time, create time, carve out time with God, and put it in pen in your date book.

Press forward, no matter the obstacle, and find ways to gain time with God. List the distractions, hindrances, and obstacles; then brainstorm solutions to acknowledge God, and God's presence will appear in your life naturally.

Just like the spring brings rain, time with God will bring positive results. You will enjoy the benefits of this kind of relationship.

TO READ
Psalm 71:19-24

You have allowed me to suffer much hardship, but you will restore me to life again and lift me up from the depths of the earth. PSALM 71:20

 ## Hope for the Brokenhearted

Kristina didn't think she could breathe, let alone live. Her fiancé had just broken the bad news: He wanted out. All her hopes and dreams were gone, dashed to pieces with one sentence. How could she possibly go on?

I had a broken heart and a mind full of questions. *Why me? Why now? Was something wrong with me?* I was so hurt and confused, and I didn't even want to get out of bed. I heard about a Bible study called *Divine Surrender*. I wasn't sure if surrender was what I needed, but so many of my friends had been helped by the Bible study, I decided to give it a try. *Why not?* There I learned that my life was not my own and that my plans weren't always best for me, but God's plans were. I learned to surrender my will, plans, and life to God. . . . He would work with all I gave him.

I learned to trust God, not myself. I learned that no matter how many times I go through hurt, God is always there. He will restore my life again, and I will find comfort in him.

I learned to love God first and foremost: "Because your love is better than life, my lips will glorify you. I will praise you as long as I live, and in your name I will lift up my hands. My soul will be satisfied as with the richest of foods; with singing lips my mouth will praise you. On my bed I remember you; I think of you through the watches of the night. Because you are my help, I sing in the shadow of your wings. My soul clings to you; your right hand upholds me" (Psalm 63:3-8, NIV).

Without God to heal her broken heart, Kristina couldn't have gone on, but with the hope of his Word and her surrender to him, she found the will and love to go on.

Do you need a bit of hope today?

TO READ
Psalm 107:39-43

Those who are wise will take all this to heart; they will see in our history the faithful love of the Lord.

PSALM 107:43

 How Could Anything Possibly Go Wrong?

Eve was created by a perfect God and placed in a perfect environment, and Adam sure seemed like a perfect husband. After all, when he first laid eyes on Eve, he broke into spontaneous praise of his new wife. And he had a great job: tend a perfect Garden. They didn't call it Paradise for nothing! So how could anything possibly go wrong?

A small thing: Eve wasn't perfect! She wanted more out of the Garden. Waking up every day next to a handsome man wasn't good enough. (I am assuming Adam was handsome, because God was the creator and the Fall had not happened.) And living in a perfect setting wasn't good enough (it hadn't even rained yet!). No, Eve wanted more; she wanted to have God's ability, God's power to know good from evil.

Now this is a lofty goal—wanting to know what God knows—and a finite being can never know what an infinite one does. Eve wasn't designed to be God; she was designed to be Adam's helpmeet. But she didn't take her job very seriously—she got Adam into trouble right off the bat!

What can we learn from Eve? Here are a few principles I have gleaned from her:

- Self-improvement is a good goal *if* I do it God's way, in his time, and according to his principles.
- Listening carefully and obeying can save me a lot of trouble. Eve added to God's rule not to eat the fruit; she told the serpent she couldn't touch it! It's easy to get an attitude about rules that don't make sense to us—Eve's addition may have made her vulnerable to the serpent's persuasive words.
- Be careful to whom you listen. Why was she talking to a snake when she had God to talk to? She hadn't even been in the Garden long enough to get bored with Adam's company.

TO READ
Hebrews 10:32-36

Do not throw away this confident trust in the Lord, no matter what happens. Remember the great reward it brings you! HEBREWS 10:35

 ## Think about Something Else

When things are tough, we are tempted to think only about how tough things are. What else can we think about?

- *Remember the gospel is not chained to your pain.* "I am suffering even to the point of being chained like a criminal. But God's word is not chained." (2 Timothy 2:9, NIV)
- *Remember there are some possessions that can never be taken away.* "Remember those earlier days after you had received the light, when you stood your ground in a great contest in the face of suffering. Sometimes you were publicly exposed to insult and persecution; at other times you stood side by side with those who were so treated. You sympathized with those in prison and joyfully accepted the confiscation of your property, because you knew that you yourselves had better and lasting possessions." (Hebrews 10:32-34, NIV)
- *Remember there is a reward for hanging in there.* "Do not be afraid of what you are about to suffer. I tell you, the devil will put some of you in prison to test you, and you will suffer. . . . Be faithful, even to the point of death, and I will give you the crown of life." (Revelation 2:10, NIV)

When we're going through dark days and everything looks gray, it may help to focus on the fact that we are surrounded by "a huge crowd of witnesses," who have gone before us (Hebrews 12:1). They, too, suffered, but now they are cheering us on as they watch us walk in faith. As we keep our eyes on Jesus, who suffered to the point of death, we will begin to think less about our own troubles and more about the great gift Jesus gave us in suffering for us.

God has not given us a spirit of fear and timidity, but of power, love, and self-discipline. 2 TIMOTHY 1:7

 *I Flew*

I flew on September 11, 2002.

People had all kinds of opinions. "You are crazy. It's the one-year anniversary of the terrorist attacks! Well, they probably won't hit the same place twice."

It was an orange-alert day, just one step down from the red alert, the highest alert level the President's Council on Homeland Security developed. Why did I go?

On September 11 the year before, I was slated to speak to a local seniors group, but when the planes crashed, they cancelled the event and stayed in their homes to pray. For the seniors, the day was a sober reminder of the attack on Pearl Harbor.

I was supposed to go to New York a few days after September 11, 2001, to speak on being a woman of influence—being a difference maker. I was determined to make it to my speaking engagement if at all possible because if ever there was a time to rally women to make a difference, this seemed like it! Instead, planes were grounded, and I arranged a local speaker and counselor friend to substitute for me.

I was frustrated that the terrorists made even these small changes in my life. I would not give them the satisfaction of creating fear in me too. Besides, in light of all the real pain, suffering, and sacrifice surrounding the true heroes of 9/11, flying a year later seemed as trivial as a hangnail. God says his perfect love expels all fear (1 John 4:18).

If I kept my heart connected to his perfect love, I could fly without fear, especially to an event to speak to hundreds of women about being difference makers.

I can face down fear as I stand face-to-face with God.

TO READ
Galatians 6:7-10

Don't get tired of doing what is good. Don't get discouraged and give up, for we will reap a harvest of blessing at the appropriate time. GALATIANS 6:9

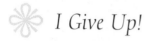 *I Give Up!*

I have felt it, and I have heard it:

"Why bother? It's just going to fail anyway."

"Why call? They won't come."

"Why try? It's like beating my head against a brick wall."

"This wasn't worth the work."

"All this effort—for this outcome?"

"I give up."

Giving up is easy. Giving in takes no effort. There is pain in the struggle, especially in the struggle to live a holy and healthy life. There is work, hard work, involved in taking back darkness.

Our youth pastor calls himself a "hell rescuer" based upon Colossians 1:13: "He has rescued us from the one who rules in the kingdom of darkness, and he has brought us into the Kingdom of his dear Son."

Have you ever looked at a police officer after a shoot-out? a firefighter after he has carried someone out of a burning building? a search-and-rescue leader after she has rapelled down a cliff to save a stranded and injured person? a lifeguard after he has saved someone from drowning in the ocean? They look tired! Rescuing is hard work!

Being God's instrument in his work of rescuing others takes tireless prayer and an intense drive to "be there"—inviting, reminding, giving healthy options, and training. It is work.

Exhausting? Yes!

Rewarding? Yes!

Necessary? Definitely!

TO READ
Hebrews 11:1-3

What is faith? It is the confident assurance that what we hope for is going to happen. It is the evidence of things we cannot yet see. HEBREWS 11:1

 ## *I Stand on the Truth*

Stacy walked into the bedroom in her brand-new home. She loved this house! She loved tucking her three sons into bed each night. But on this night she walked into her room to find her husband in bed with her best friend.

Things went from bad to worse in her marriage. She wanted the marriage to be saved, but he was feeling guilty about an affair and was running fast. Stacy began to read *The Power of a Praying Wife,* and she started praying the verses for her husband every day.

"Those verses made me stay. I knew I could leave because the Bible allowed it, but I wanted the marriage to work. I wanted my children to have their dad—and a family. I felt convinced I needed to stand on the truth and calmly answer my husband no matter what he said or did. One day he said, 'I want a divorce,' and I calmly answered, 'I don't believe that's true.' Then he said, 'I want to move out,' and I said, 'I don't think that you really do want to move. I think the truth is you want to stay and you want to be a good family man.'"

Week after week she prayed and stood on the truth until her husband came to her one day.

"You are right. I don't want a divorce. I don't want to leave. I was afraid that you wanted to leave, that I wasn't good enough, and that I couldn't be who you wanted me to be. I wanted to leave you before you left me. But now I see you are not going to leave me, and I don't want to leave you— and that's the truth."

TO READ
2 Corinthians 13:5-9

Our responsibility is never to oppose the truth, but to stand for the truth at all times.

2 CORINTHIANS 13:8

 I Tell You the Truth

About eighty times in the Gospels Jesus says, "I tell you the truth." Over and over again he says it. Why? Is it because telling the truth, the whole truth and nothing but the truth, is so hard for us to do? The movie *Liar, Liar* was a big box-office hit because it showed just how hard it is for some people to tell the truth.

Numerous marriages have crumbled because the foundation of love was eroded when a lie came to light. For example, Marc said to my husband, Bill, in a counseling session, "I don't care how beautiful she is anymore. I can't live like this. She has told so many lies to me and everyone else. She has gotten us so far in debt with her lies that I don't even know what's real anymore. Everything she says to me I immediately think is a lie because that seems to be all she's done for the past seven years—lie!"

Try it for one whole day. Tell the *complete* truth—no white lies allowed. Say with the psalmist, "I have chosen the way of truth; I have set my heart on your laws" (Psalm 119:30, NIV).

Then try something radical: See how often you set people up to shade the truth when you put them in a no-win situation with questions like, "Do I look fat in this?" or "Honey, did you notice what that woman was wearing?" (He knows he's in trouble if he even noticed another woman! How is he supposed to answer that?)

Try to ask only the questions you want honest answers to, and try to give honest answers when asked.

TO READ
Psalm 119:127-135

Guide my steps by your word, so I will not be overcome by any evil. Psalm 119:133

 Growth on the Go!

How do you keep so many people in a family all going in God's direction when everyone is going in different directions? The book of Deuteronomy gives us an answer to that question: "Commit yourselves wholeheartedly to these commands I am giving you today. Repeat them again and again to your children. Talk about them when you are at home and when you are away on a journey, when you are lying down and when you are getting up again. Tie them to your hands as a reminder, and wear them on your forehead. Write them on the doorposts of your house and on your gates" (Deuteronomy 6:6-9).

When you are "at home": Look for posters, framed Scripture verses, Scripture memory-verse holders, and screen savers to remind everyone what values are most important to you. As parents, the principles we want our kids to "get" are framed on their walls and hang on handcrafted wall hangings. Our family mission statement with verses included is by the front door.

When you are "away on a journey": Let's face it—when we are on the road today, we're driving, so a version of the Bible on CD, praise music that is Scripture set to music, sermon tapes, and dramatic presentations that include Scripture are all handy things to keep in the car. We also keep Bible games, and Bible-based card games, and even last week's Sunday school papers in the glove compartment so that there is always something to talk about or listen to that will focus our hearts on Christ.

When you lie down and when you get up: Surround your child's bed with the tools he or she will need to stay connected to Christ: a cassette or CD player, an age-appropriate Bible, journals, devotionals, etc. The key is to select several key verses from Scripture that your family "owns" and personalizes to keep on track spiritually.

TO READ
Philippians 2:5-18

In everything you do, stay away from complaining and arguing. PHILIPPIANS 2:14

 ## If You Hate It, Change It!

"I hate my job."

"I hate this tiny apartment!"

"I hate this rat race!"

What are you complaining and grumbling about? While in a worship service, a two-year-old, tired of sitting and waiting, threw herself down and gave a full-blown tantrum right in front of the pulpit! Of course her parents picked her up and carried her out of the service, but I thought to myself, *How often do grown-ups look like that?*

We whine, complain, moan, and make a scene, but we make no change! How often am I throwing a spiritual tantrum?

What are the things you hate about your life? Think about what the opposite would be. For example: "I hate my menial and routine job; a job I might love would be challenging and full of variety." "I hate the constant deadlines and having no time to reflect or relax; a career that would allow me time to smell the roses—that I would *love!*"

First Corinthians 10:13 explains, "God is faithful; he will not let you be tempted beyond what you can bear. But when you are tempted, he will also provide a way out so that you can stand up under it" (NIV). Some Bible translations say that God provides a way of escape, or an exit.

Instead of complaining, write out four or five of your top "dislikes"— then write a positive solution. Look for the escape route. God has probably already provided one. The next step is to brainstorm how to move from list one, what I hate, to list two, what I would love.

Don't whine; move forward.

TO READ
1 Samuel 25:23-31

When the Lord has done these great things for you, please remember me! 1 SAMUEL 25:31

 ## It's Not My Fault!

Abigail was married to a jerk—a selfish, ungrateful jerk whose actions were about ready to cause a battle. Abigail could have stood by and said, "It's not my responsibility!" She could have let it come to blows and still claimed, "It wasn't my fault." And technically, she was right.

But victories come when we humbly assume responsibility and do what needs to be done for the good of the many instead of doing just what makes life easier for us.

Abigail leaves Nabal (who is home drinking) and intercedes with David on behalf of her worthless husband. Even though Nabal doesn't deserve it, Abigail realizes that all those who are working for Nabal, everyone in her family, and all David's men may have to pay the consequences for Nabal's evil. So she intervenes to save innocent lives: "When Abigail saw David, she quickly got off her donkey and bowed down before David with her face to the ground. She fell at his feet and said: 'My lord, let the blame be on me alone. Please let your servant speak to you. . . . And let this gift, which your servant has brought to my master, be given to the men who follow you'" (1 Samuel 25:23-27, NIV).

Abigail saved lives by coming in humility and taking responsibility. Successful women daily say, "I don't care who gets the credit or whose fault this is; someone needs to do something right now, and that someone is me."

TO READ
Proverbs 22:17-29

Do you see any truly competent workers? They will serve kings rather than ordinary people.

PROVERBS 22:29

 Jesus, CEO

As a boss and leader, I keep my eye out for talent and a strong work ethic. If I can delegate something to someone, walk away, and know with 100 percent certainty that he or she will get the task done well, I will invest in and encourage that person so he or she keeps rising on the ladder.

However, nothing is more frustrating for a leader or employer than to find out work you thought was accomplished wasn't. And nothing is more devastating than to delegate and then find out at the last minute that you must do the task because someone dropped the ball.

Just how hard is a person supposed to work? The wisdom of Colossians 3:22, while written to slaves—those who were indentured to serve—also contains a main point that can serve us well today: "You slaves must obey your earthly masters in everything you do. Try to please them all the time, not just when they are watching you. Obey them willingly because of your reverent fear of the Lord."

Work as if God is watching (he is) even when the boss isn't. Even if your boss is not your best friend, Jesus is, so work to please Jesus. Let pleasing Jesus be the standard.

If your boss is good and godly, pleasing Jesus should please him or her. If your boss is unreasonable, then by pleasing Jesus, your conscience will be clear.

TO READ
Ephesians 2:13-18

Now you belong to Christ Jesus. Though you once were far away from God, now you have been brought near to him because of the blood of Christ.

Ephesians 2:13

 ## Cling-Ons

When I was growing up, we watched *Star Trek*. On one planet the crew was attacked by creatures that stuck on their bodies and sucked the life out of them. To go with the Star Trek metaphor of the alien race called Klingons, we named the "suction creatures" Cling-Ons.

If you are living in an environment that is hostile to your emotional and spiritual health, those you live with can be like Cling-Ons. But you don't necessarily have to leave the relationship(s)—sometimes you just learn how to peel the Cling-Ons off.

Diagnosis: Confess that, like leeches, the impact of their hostility is clinging to you. You can't go forward if you don't even realize you are going backward! Are you feeling more distant from God? from your local church? from Christian friends? from family members who love God? Are you finding it easier to just go along with the hostile person's belief system so as not to make waves? Wake up! You may have Cling-Ons all over you!

Rx: The prescription for defeating these Cling-Ons is:

- *Quietly turn up the volume.* Get back in God's Word. Read; listen to Christian music or the Bible on tape. (For privacy, you may need your own headset.)
- *Look for strong friends who are already in your world.* Is there a woman at work or your health club, or another mom at your child's sports or dance lessons who has a strong faith in God? Start sitting by her. Tell her your plan of trying to get back to God. Ask her to pray with you.
- *Take small steps forward.* When your unbelieving spouse is out of the house, watch a Christian video or listen to sermons on the radio. Housecleaning can wait for when he is around—or do it while you listen!

Take a step back to God, and he'll take a step toward you. As you do this, you'll begin to see those Cling-Ons fall off.

TO READ
1 Corinthians 4:2-5

When the Lord comes, he will bring our deepest secrets to light and will reveal our private motives. And then God will give to everyone whatever praise is due. 1 CORINTHIANS 4:5

 Lights Flashing

One Saturday morning I read a newspaper story about a man I'll call John Smith. He was driving erratically, so the highway patrol pulled him over. They gave him a battery of sobriety tests: walk a straight line, touch your nose, etc. When they were about ready to administer a breath test, an accident happened on the other side of the freeway. So they said to John Smith, "Stay right here!" But Smith got in the car and drove home, parking the car in the garage.

He told his wife to tell anyone that he was home sick all day. A few hours later there was a knock at the door. Mrs. Smith answered to find two highway patrol officers.

"Does John Smith live here?" She nodded the affirmative, and they asked to see John Smith. John came out of the bedroom, faking a cough.

"What can I do for you fine officers?"

"Were you pulled over for a highway citation today?"

"Oh no, I've been sick all day," John said, coughing.

"Well, someone using your identity and your address was pulled over today. May we see your car and clear this up?"

"Sure, officers." John confidently walked out to the garage. He was thinking, *It's been hours. That engine is nice and cool, and I am totally going to get away with this!*

John threw open the garage door, and there in the garage was the *patrol car* with the lights still flashing!

What are you thinking you'll get away with? Where are you cutting corners? What lights are flashing in your garage?

TO READ
Luke 13:10-13

When Jesus saw her, he called her over and said, "Woman, you are healed of your sickness!"

LUKE 13:12

 ## *You Can!*

Sometimes our best, most innovative ideas come because others see our potential when we do not. I met Lisa at the bottom of her life. Her marriage was ready to break up; her spouse eventually left her for another woman. Lisa had a two-year-old and had experienced years of brokenness, abuse, and abandonment. Her biological mother left her; then her stepmother couldn't take living with Lisa's drug-addicted dad, so she left. Then Lisa's biological mother wanted Lisa's sister—but not Lisa. Her father was a drug dealer who went to prison, then died of an overdose. She was on her own at sixteen. She thought she had married Prince Charming, only to realize he was a frog.

I helped Lisa pick up the pieces of her life by being her counselor and then a discipler and mentor. Somewhere in all of it, we became friends. I challenged Lisa to start a ministry to help women overcome, just as she had.

One day when I was driving in the car praying for another counselee, God reminded me of Lisa. He told me, *Lisa is an example of how to overcome. Tell her, "Shine your light!"* I grabbed the phone and excitedly told Lisa all God had put on my heart.

"Lisa, why don't you start a ministry for all those women who fill counseling offices. So many stall, but you overcame. Why don't you call the ministry 'You Can!' because through Christ we *can* do anything through him who strengthens us!"

Lisa was hopeful but still doubted her readiness for the challenge.

"You *can,* Lisa! I'll be beside you all the way, and more important, God will be beside you!"

What have your friends, family, and mentors been telling you?

TO READ
1 Peter 4:10-13

Most important of all, continue to show deep love for each other, for love covers a multitude of sins.

1 PETER 4:8

 Looking for Love in All the Wrong Places

I asked a group of women I was speaking to if they would share stories of overcoming. This one stood out to me:

> I realized I was out of control when I woke up next to a man and I had no idea where I met him or what his name was. Sex was not worth that risk anymore!
>
> The road back is hard but worth it. I have messed up a few times, but not since I met Mary after that morning when I woke up next to "Mr. What's His Name?"
>
> I called a counselor who recommended a twelve-step program. That's where I met Mary. She was my sponsor, my mentor, and my accountability partner.
>
> Accountability works with Mary because she says it like it is, and I decided that we'd always be completely honest, and I would never take offense. I chose to never become angry at anything Mary said.
>
> I am getting better, learning I am worthy of love, and looking at some hurts I have buried for years: incest, date rape, and my own poor choices. I feel I can say anything to Mary, and then we can look at whatever it is, pray through it, talk through it, and then I can get through it.
>
> I was finally able to open up to Mary, to be totally honest, because one night, right after I started going to a Twelve Step Overcomers group, Mary said to me, "I love you, regardless of what you struggle with."

Who loves you regardless of how honest you are or what you struggle with? Find that kind of support. We all need that kind of love.

TO READ
Matthew 18:2-6

Therefore, anyone who becomes as humble as this little child is the greatest in the Kingdom of Heaven. And anyone who welcomes a little child like this on my behalf is welcoming me. MATTHEW 18:4-5

 ## *Make It Simple*

When our oldest son was a little over two, I was teaching at a leadership conference. My husband, Bill, had finished his session and was sitting in the back. The child-care worker slipped in and tapped Bill's shoulder, and he went out to take care of Brock.

It seemed that Brock had a boatload of questions, and only Dad would do for the answers! Brock was asking big theological questions for a little guy. He'd been watching the *JESUS* film over and over and over. And he wouldn't let us turn it off until after the prayer at the end that leads people into a relationship with Christ (and the verse at the end and the credits).

Brock had all kinds of questions about Jesus that night, and as Dad and son sat under the stars on a cabin step, Bill thought, *This must be the moment. Brock must want to ask Christ into his life.* So he asked, "Brock, do you want to ask Jesus to come into your heart?"

Brock pondered for a moment then piped out, "No! When Jesus gets out of the Bible, then I'll ask him into my life!"

And that became our mission as parents and leaders—get Jesus out of the Bible, off the pages, and make him real to people.

Can you state your mission in terms that a child would understand? Jesus could: "I, the Son of Man, have come to seek and save those like him who are lost" (Luke 19:10).

If a child can comprehend the purpose, anyone can and will follow.

TO READ
Psalm 90:14-17

Satisfy us in the morning with your unfailing love, so we may sing for joy to the end of our lives.

PSALM 90:14

 ## Make the Most of Morning

The annoying alarm, the quick stop at Starbuck's for coffee, a bit of breakfast—if you are lucky! Is this your morning ritual? Want to trade it in for a new routine?

Here is some inspiration: "The next morning Abraham was up early and hurried out to the place where he had stood in the Lord's presence" (Genesis 19:27). "Listen to my voice in the morning, Lord. Each morning I bring my requests to you and wait expectantly" (Psalm 5:3). "But as for me, I will sing about your power. I will shout with joy each morning because of your unfailing love" (Psalm 59:16).

Wouldn't you rather start your day this way? If you currently aren't spending time with God in the morning, try to give him five minutes before anything else gets in the way:

- Pray through your day before you get out of bed, and ask for his help.
- Rise to the sound of Christian radio rather than the buzz of an alarm.
- Read a psalm a day or a proverb a day. Write down a phrase to post on your mirror or desk, and meditate on it all day.
- Read a devotional such as *Daily Light for the Daily Path.*
- Record your prayers in a journal.

What are the results? A heart that rejoices and sings throughout the day.

TO READ
John 12:23-28

The truth is, a kernel of wheat must be planted in the soil. Unless it dies it will be alone—a single seed. But its death will produce many new kernels—a plentiful harvest of new lives.

JOHN 12:24

Metamorphosis

When a caterpillar is on its journey to becoming a butterfly, it goes through an amazing change, a metamorphosis. But what is perplexing is that the change requires the caterpillar to go dormant. The caterpillar spins itself into a cocoon and stays there—seemingly dead to the world.

Sometimes we have cocooning times. We usually don't like them. They may seem boring, and you may even feel that God isn't moving fast enough. You might be tempted to question God, "He gave me this vision, right?" or "If you gave me this plan, why don't you do something to move it forward, God?" You may even be tempted to rip the cocoon apart yourself and take matters into your own hands, running ahead of God's timing.

But the cocoon is all part of the plan. If you tear open a cocoon too soon, science tells us that the wings of the butterfly will be underdeveloped, that it is the act of struggling to get out of the cocoon that strengthens them. It is in the stillness that we hear God. It is in the waiting that character is formed. Psalm 37:34 instructs us what to do while we wait: "Travel steadily along his path." Then the results are given: "He will honor you, giving you the land."

If we wait, nuzzled close to God, when he releases us, we will have a beautiful flight, producing an abundant harvest.

TO READ
Matthew 17:1-9

Jesus came over and touched them. "Get up," he said, "don't be afraid." MATTHEW 17:7

Mobilize

Rudy Giuliani was named *Time* magazine's Man of the Year in 2001. There was some controversy about why, but to me it seemed clear. As I watched the mayor of New York, America's largest city, run for his life right at the site of the World Trade Center while he gave directions to save the city, it just seemed right to give him an award for clarity and compassion under pressure. He mobilized millions on a day when the impact of his own personal losses could have immobilized him.

What do you do when you lose a job? a dream? hope? Many freeze, unable to move, think, or function. Others spiral downward into self-pity or self-destruction.

I recommend that you make your pain work for you. Frustration and anger have some emotional energy behind them; turn that negative energy into a positive in your life. Get going.

Over fifty times in the Bible people are told to "get up"! So do something, anything—make the bed, clean the house, gather friends to pray, go help someone else, or make a list. Then start doing the task that seems easiest, and work your way to the harder tasks.

You don't want to lose twice. If you spiral down, you are compounding loss upon loss; however, if you do something, you turn pain inside out. And your pain becomes a platform, the first step out of despair.

O Lord, rescue me from evil people. Preserve me from those who are violent. PSALM 140:1

 Don't Mess with Mama Bear

My husband affectionately says that men are not wise when they mess with mama bear because a mother, in the wild or in humankind, protects her own.

God told Deborah that Sisera was a bad man, and Barak was to go take him out. However, Barak was too afraid to go alone, so Deborah predicted God would give Sisera into a woman's hands.

Deborah and Barak sang a song of praise that tells the story:

"Arise, O Barak! Take captive your captives, O son of Abinoam." . . .

The princes of Issachar were with Deborah; yes, Issachar was with Barak, rushing after him into the valley. In the districts of Reuben there was much searching of heart. . . .

Most blessed of women be Jael, the wife of Heber the Kenite, most blessed of tent-dwelling women. He asked for water, and she gave him milk; in a bowl fit for nobles she brought him curdled milk. Her hand reached for the tent peg, her right hand for the workman's hammer. She struck Sisera, she crushed his head, she shattered and pierced his temple. At her feet he sank, he fell; there he lay. At her feet he sank, he fell; where he sank, there he fell—dead. (Judges 5:12, 15, 24-27, NIV)

A mother may seem an unlikely candidate in war; however, God prompted Jael, the "mama bear" to protect her family, her friends, and her people from evil.

This is a drastic picture because Jael was called to do what hopefully we will never be called to do. However, the principle of a mother protecting her own is a sound one.

What child or children has God asked you to protect?

TO READ
1 Samuel 2:1-10

Then Hannah prayed: "My heart rejoices in the Lord! Oh, how the Lord has blessed me! Now I have an answer for my enemies, as I delight in your deliverance." 1 SAMUEL 2:1

 ## *Need a Breakthrough?*

Hannah was a woman who needed a breakthrough. First Samuel 1:15 has Hannah explaining, "I am a woman who is deeply troubled" (NIV). Other Bible translations say she was oppressed in spirit.

Did she stay troubled and oppressed? What did she do to get out of her trouble and oppression? She looked up, and she poured out.

Look up: She went to the Temple, where she knew she could talk to God openly and honestly.

Pour out: Hannah tells Eli, "I was pouring out my soul to the Lord" (NIV). She was so free with her feelings that when the priest, Eli, saw her, he thought she was drunk. She had no inhibitions as she expressed her pain and sorrow.

Where do you go when you need to hold court with God? When I am experiencing incredible sorrow, pain, or overwhelming responsibility, I look for a place to talk, cry, pace, and maybe even rant and rave a bit to God.

This honesty gained a breakthrough for Hannah. She made a commitment to God and then kept that commitment. From her barrenness of womb and emptiness of soul, she came to a level place where she had the strength to give her beloved only son to God for full-time ministry.

She went from weakness to strength, and it started with an honest heart-to-heart with God.

TO READ
Zephaniah 3:14-17

The Lord your God has arrived to live among you. He is a mighty savior. He will rejoice over you with great gladness. With his love, he will calm all your fears. He will exult over you by singing a happy song. ZEPHANIAH 3:17

 ## The MRI

In those unknown moments of waiting, God can do some of his best work. Nicky shares her story:

> I had a scare that I might have cancer. The doctors called for an MRI. This is a sort of X-ray done while you are virtually enclosed in a tube the size of your body. I am claustrophobic! I knew the only way I could make it through the MRI was to keep my eyes closed, never opening them until the forty-five to sixty-minute procedure was over, and *pray.*
>
> I had recently finished the Beth Moore study *A Women's Heart—God's Dwelling Place,* in which we studied the finite details of the Tabernacle. As I was moved into the MRI tube, I closed my eyes and began to pray. I had to stay perfectly still. I wasn't even supposed to swallow, as it was mostly my throat they were taking film of. The MRI equipment makes extremely loud banging sounds as it takes the images. I prayed and pictured myself in my heavenly Father's lap with my head against his chest, and the pounding became his comforting heartbeat.
>
> My thoughts began to turn from the MRI to a "tour" of the Tabernacle. It felt as if God and I were walking its perimeter, recognizing each pole, ring, and curtain as described in our study. Then I entered the Tabernacle and revisited all the minute details that had come to life and meaning in our study, and I truly felt the presence of the Lord.
>
> When I was finally removed from the "tube," my husband, knowing my concerns, asked me how it had gone. I told him, "That was the most incredible experience of my life. I have never felt so close to God before!" He just looked at me and could not grasp what I had experienced in that tube I had so feared.

July

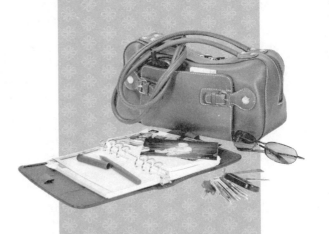

TO READ
Ephesians 6:10-18

In every battle you will need faith as your shield to stop the fiery arrows aimed at you by Satan.

EPHESIANS 6:16

 ## *Only You!*

Because of my positions in the helping profession, I have offered all kinds of assistance to facilitate life change and help women achieve their goals. But in the end, it is a *one-woman* show. Only *you* can:

- Make a phone call.
- Make an appointment.
- Make it to the Bible study.
- Make the counseling session.
- Do the homework.
- Pray.
- Care that the change happens.

Decide to make it different:

- Decide you want a change in your life.
- Choose to ask for help.
- Ask for help. Research options of where help can be found: churches, friendships, counseling (small group, professional, or pastoral), women's resource organizations, achievement networks, community/social service organizations, or governmental agencies. Most of this information can be found in a phone book or on the Internet.
- See a person face-to-face, and ask for help. There are many kinds of help, including mentoring, counseling, discipleship, Bible studies, networking groups, accountability partners, and prayer groups.

Now it's up to you!

TO READ
1 Corinthians 14:26-33

God is not a God of disorder but of peace.

1 CORINTHIANS 14:33

 Order in the Court!

St. Augustine defined peace as "the tranquility of order." How much peace do you have? Is your desk in order so that you can find what you need when you need it? How about those drawers and closets?

My frustration is the refrigerator, where I always hope that we will actually eat most leftovers. Then there's the car, everyone's mobile life-support system these days!

You don't have to be the one who creates the order—you are just responsible for seeing that you have it in your life. Perhaps hiring a housekeeper or a teen helper can help you gain a little order. And it is amazing just what your kids can do to keep order if you train and trust them. Give them the training, tools, and time to do it—their way!

If you never can find what you thought you filed or can't find the file, you are less efficient. If you can't find a tool and have to buy another, you are less profitable. If you have to spend time hunting for your keys, your purse, or your sweater, you are less calm. If you have to go without because you hunted and hunted but still couldn't find what you were looking for, you are less prepared.

Ezekiel 38:7 records the prophet's word of the Lord to his people: "Get ready; be prepared! . . . and take command of them." Many military commanders down through the ages have said it: Get ready. That's what order does—it readies us for service.

One of the ways I can tell when I don't have enough margin is when I feel my surroundings are out of order. Everyone has a different definition of order, but when I turn Augustine's quote inside out, I know tranquility is order that brings peace.

TO READ
Acts 20:32-35

You should remember the words of the Lord Jesus: "It is more blessed to give than to receive."

ACTS 20:35

 ## *Out of the Deepest Need*

What a challenge. The Sunday school teacher laid down the gauntlet: "Give out of the area of your greatest need. In the world's economy, when you are running short, you horde what little you have left; however, in God's economy, you give out of your deficit."

Carolyn heard, but she wasn't sure how she could give. What she wanted more than anything was a baby. That was her greatest pain. She and her husband had been trying for five years. She avoided baby showers, cringed at the sight of a newborn, and avoided the church nursery. But God was calling her to give out of her place of pain.

Carolyn called the neonatal center. She had heard they needed people to just come in and hold drug-addicted crack babies. No special skills, just loving arms. Day after day Carolyn faced her own pain to alleviate the pain of the tiniest of God's creation. She found a place of peace, peace that she never thought she could experience. She would be all right if she never carried her own baby.

At her annual checkup five months later, the doctor told her she was pregnant, and she didn't believe him! "But I can't have children, you said so."

"Then I guess it must be a miracle."

Everyone's miracle is different. Without a child of her own, Ruth thought it was a miracle that she felt contentment loving the junior high girls she worked with. Teresa thought it was a miracle when God provided a child for her to adopt. Terry thought it was a miracle to find an international child who needed a home.

Each gave out of her deepest need and found that God met her own need in the process.

TO READ
Psalm 119:171-176

Stand ready to help me, for I have chosen to follow your commandments. PSALM 119:173

 Good Company

A woman is known by the company she keeps, and, girl, we're in good company:

- George Washington: "It is impossible to rightly govern the world without God and the Bible."
- John Quincy Adams: "So great is my veneration of the Bible, that the earlier my children begin to read it, the more confident will be my hope that they will prove useful citizens of their country and respectable members of society."
- Charles Dickens: "The New Testament is the very best book that ever was or ever will be known in the world."
- Andrew Jackson: "That book, sir, is the rock on which our republic rests."
- Abraham Lincoln: "I believe the Bible is the best gift God has ever given to man. All the good from the Savior of the world is communicated to us through this book."
- Woodrow Wilson: "I ask every man and woman in this audience that from this day on they will realize that part of the destiny of America lies in their daily perusal of this great Book."
- Douglas MacArthur: "Believe me, sir, never a night goes by, be I ever so tired, but I read the Word of God before I go to bed."
- Herbert Hoover: "The whole of the inspiration of our civilization springs from the teachings of Christ and the lessons of the Prophets. To read the Bible for these fundamentals is a necessity of American life."
- Dwight D. Eisenhower: "To read the Bible is to take a trip to a fair land where the spirit is strengthened and faith renewed."

Your belief in the Bible puts you in the super-leader league. That's a crowd I want to hang around!

TO READ
Luke 6:36-42

If you give, you will receive. Your gift will return to you in full measure, pressed down, shaken together to make room for more, and running over. Whatever measure you use in giving—large or small—it will be used to measure what is given back to you.

LUKE 6:38

 Pay It Forward

Mandy confided to me over coffee that she was worried, very worried. She held an eviction notice in her hand.

Mandy's decisions had led her from bad to worse. Unhappy in her marriage and suffering from the loss of a baby, and a son in juvenile hall, Mandy escaped to start again. However, leaving her marriage meant leaving her security. And it wasn't only Mandy who was suffering—her children were suffering most. Dad was angry and not paying child support. Mom was in pain, Dad was in pain, and the kids were in peril!

I felt God wanted me to give her enough money to pay a month's rent and buy a month's food so she could get a job and provide for herself and her three children. Mandy might have deserved to be on the street, but her innocent children didn't. I made Mandy a business deal: Get into counseling, and I would lend her money to pay her rent and buy groceries for four weeks to get on her feet. She would have to be serious about getting well and getting right with God.

"What is the repayment plan? What is the interest rate?"

"Zero, principle only. Someone once loaned us funds while we were in a tough place between ministry positions, and he offered the same rate with a condition: that we would do it for someone else in need sometime. So pay it forward by paying us back the principle; then offer, when you are financially strong, to help another in need for zero interest.

"By paying it back, we can use that same money to help someone else at zero interest, and we will also know you will be doing the same! Twice as many people will be helped. Can you commit to this?"

TO READ
Lamentations 3:22-27

It is good for the young to submit to the yoke of his discipline. LAMENTATIONS 3:27

 Pay the Price

When Bill and I received a call into ministry, we were both very young—nineteen. We had not finished (barely started) our education. We both gave up majors that would have provided great starting salaries and career ladders to climb. We traded security for seeking God's call.

We married at twenty and owned very little. On our wedding day, Bill's apartment (which became ours after the ceremony) had a twin daybed that served as a sofa, an old stereo (both from Bill's room growing up), a set of bookshelves that were cinder blocks and unfinished boards, a dresser Bill made in the high school wood shop, and a bed—the only thing we bought. We had to wait until after our wedding to afford a dining-room table and lamps.

My car went to my sister (that was the deal since we shared it). Bill owned a green Vega with a blue back door that soon broke down so we rode our bikes everywhere. We wanted to finish Bill's degree and get him to seminary and me to Bible college. If we had to eat tuna casserole and macaroni and cheese every day and walk to and from school to get that degree done—then so be it! The call was more vital than comfort.

No one owes you a car, rent, money for food, or shoes for your kids. If the body of Christ gives generously, great, but *no one owes you your dream.* It feels sweeter when you work for it.

TO READ
1 Kings 17:1-7

Elijah did as the Lord had told him and camped beside Kerith Brook. 1 KINGS 17:5

 Stop!

A commercial shows a little pink battery-operated bunny beating a drum with the slogan "The Energizer Bunny keeps going, and going. . . ."

Many of us think we are that bunny, driven to keep going, going, and going. While hard work is admirable, and diligence is necessary, so is stopping. Even race-car drivers in the lead have to take a pit stop and have their crew change tires and refuel.

My favorite example from the Bible is Elijah, the prophet who had to constantly battle evil kings who were in leadership in Israel: "The Lord said to Elijah, 'Go to the east and hide by Kerith Brook at a place east of where it enters the Jordan River. Drink from the brook and eat what the ravens bring you, for I have commanded them to bring you food.' So Elijah did as the Lord had told him and camped beside Kerith Brook. The ravens brought him bread and meat each morning and evening, and he drank from the brook" (1 Kings 17:2-6).

God told him to stop, so he stopped. He completely unplugged. The ravens' feeding him is a precursor to our room service. He pulled away from all people and stopped all activity. The only things he could do in this isolated spot were eat, drink, rest, and worship. (He might have done a few stretches, but there's no record of any aerobic activity!)

Take out your yearly calendar, and mark off rest periods with stop signs. Look for times of fast pace, demanding deadlines, or significant life changes (like a child being married or leaving for college), and place a stop sign— a break—after those activities or transitions.

Like the wise race-car driver who strategically plans pit stops, you, too, might find yourself in the winner's circle.

TO READ
1 Peter 3:8-12

All of you should be of one mind, full of sympathy toward each other, loving one another with tender hearts and humble minds. 1 PETER 3:8

 Plan, Don't Panic!

Over the years I have noticed that one of the biggest obstacles that prevents a woman from achieving her God-given potential is panicking when family or friends hit a tough transition or make unwise choices. The panic distracts her calling because she desperately tries to put out the latest emotional fire.

How should you, the woman who is called, whose passion has been ignited by God, act toward a loved one who may not be making wise choices? Get angry? Yell? Preach? Give the silent treatment? Take over all his or her decisions?

None of the above! Love, and create a plan that expresses that love toward yourself and the person in pain.

Did Jesus panic when his disciples didn't get the fact that feeding five thousand people wasn't a problem for the One who had created the world? Did Jesus pace the ship deck in a storm? Did Jesus whip out his sword in the garden so he could escape?

Jesus knew the gospel going out to the world was dependent on the twelve disciples "getting it," but he didn't panic, not even when one betrayed him. He didn't panic because he knew the Holy Spirit was coming. "I will send you the Counselor—the Spirit of truth. He will come to you from the Father and will tell you all about me" (John 15:26).

Instead of panicking, plan. When a woman comes into our offices for help, we have her create two plans: a short-range emergency plan to get her through the next twenty-four hours or the next counseling session and a long-term plan to help her or those close to her gain the resources needed to move forward.

TO READ
Matthew 17:14-20

"You didn't have enough faith," Jesus told them. "I assure you, even if you had faith as small as a mustard seed you could say to this mountain, 'Move from here to there,' and it would move. Nothing would be impossible." MATTHEW 17:20

 ## Let's Pray about It

I like being part of a miracle! I love being part of a prayer movement that sees results. I get a thrill over answered prayer. Seeing mountains moved through prayers of faith builds my faith. When I see God answer in other people's lives, it impacts my ability to believe him in my own.

So how can we pray for and with others even when we are busy with our own responsibilities?

Pray it now. When the request is given, don't say, "I'll pray." Pray right then!

Pray it the same time each day. Set aside a specific time of day, and set the alarm on your palm pilot or your clock radio to remind you to pray.

Pray in the natural rhythm of life. Commit to pray each morning on your way back from driving the children to school, when you first sit in your desk chair, or during a work break. Find a blank space, and fill it with prayer. You might need a little reminder like a note on the dashboard, bathroom mirror, or your computer at work.

Pray it through technology. Use e-mail, fax, or voice mail to pray. The prayer coordinator of our ministry, Masterful Living, places a sentence at the bottom of all her e-mails sent each day. It is the Masterful Living prayer request for the day and a verse. She reminds everyone she communicates with to pray.

Pray it with company. Get your husband, your children, a coworker, or a friend on board. If you don't remember, they might!

TO READ
Luke 22:39-46

"Why are you sleeping?" [Jesus] asked. "Get up and pray. Otherwise temptation will overpower you."

LUKE 22:46

 Pray to Win

What does God think important enough to pray for? What are the areas God sees as vital for success in life? We get a glimpse from the scriptural prayer requests below.

Pray:

- For your enemies and those who persecute or mistreat you (Matthew 5:44; Luke 6:28).
- For strength to not fall into temptation (Matthew 26:41).
- For reconnected relationships (Romans 1:10-11).
- You are rescued from unbelievers (Romans 15:31).
- You won't make mistakes (2 Corinthians 13:7).
- Your heart will be enlightened to understand the wonderful future he has promised (Ephesians 1:18).
- You will be strengthened by the Holy Spirit (Ephesians 3:16).
- You will be rooted and established in love (Ephesians 3:17).
- You will open your mouth and be given words to fearlessly and clearly share the gospel (Ephesians 6:19; Colossians 4:4).
- God will count you worthy of your calling and fulfill every good purpose of yours prompted by your faith (2 Thessalonians 1:11).
- You will be generous because of your faith and have a full understanding of all the good things you can do for Jesus (Philemon 1:6).
- You will have a clear conscience (Hebrews 13:18).
- If you have trouble or sickness (James 5:13-14).
- To confess sin (James 5:16).
- For good health (3 John 1:2).

TO READ
Luke 22:31-39

Simon, Simon, Satan has asked to have all of you, to sift you like wheat. But I have pleaded in prayer for you, Simon, that your faith should not fail. So when you have repented and turned to me again, strengthen and build up your brothers.

LUKE 22:31-32

 ## *Preparing for the Attack*

Starting a new business or going into ministry is new, fun, and exciting, but it can also be really difficult. There is the stress that comes with the volume of work that accompanies a new venture, but there is also emotional and spiritual stress. The closer you get to completion or lasting eternal impact, the more spiritual attacks you should expect.

Physical setbacks. Satan loves to rob our effectiveness with unexpected illness or simply irritating physical problems like a back problem or waking up with your eye swollen shut. (Just check out the book of Job!)

Technical setbacks. Rarely do I go through a book deadline without a major computer problem. A friend of mine got a computer virus that crashed her system. The virus listed the sender as "Darkman." In John 14:30 Satan is called the prince of this world.

Preoccupation. My own preoccupation with an event or deadline makes me more likely to run out of gas, drop my PDA, or forget to turn off the iron. Satan was an angel who got off track, so his favorite tool is getting us off track with him.

Heaviness of heart. By far, this is the hardest to pinpoint and the most common, I believe. An overwhelming heaviness for the event's success or feelings of oppression or burden make you feel like you are carrying the weight of the whole world. You may also wonder if it is really going to work or sense you are battling something evil or pushing a massive boulder uphill. These are the most common attacks among my peers in leadership. (Look at Elijah and Jonah—they wanted to die just because they were spiritually exhausted.)

The first step out of the attack is to identify the irritation or setback as an attack.

TO READ
1 Timothy 5:17-21

Elders who do their work well should be paid well, especially those who work hard at both preaching and teaching. 1 TIMOTHY 5:17

 ## *Priorities That Pay*

Success brings a new question: What do I do with all this money? Taking care of the leaders God has put in place in your life is a good place to start. Second Kings 4:8-9 explains: "One day Elisha went to Shunem. And a well-to-do woman was there, who urged him to stay for a meal. So whenever he came by, he stopped there to eat. She said to her husband, "I know that this man who often comes our way is a holy man of God. Let's make a small room on the roof and put in it a bed and a table, a chair and a lamp for him. Then he can stay there whenever he comes to us" (NIV).

When leaders are cared for, they notice and want to give something in return for your generosity. Often that something is what money cannot buy:

> One day when Elisha came, he went up to his room and lay down there. He said to his servant Gehazi, "Call the Shunammite." So he called her, and she stood before him. Elisha said to him, "Tell her, 'You have gone to all this trouble for us. Now what can be done for you?'" . . .
>
> Gehazi said, "Well, she has no son and her husband is old."
>
> Then Elisha said, "Call her." So he called her, and she stood in the doorway. "About this time next year," Elisha said, "you will hold a son in your arms."
>
> "No, my lord," she objected. "Don't mislead your servant, O man of God!"
>
> But the woman became pregnant, and the next year about that same time she gave birth to a son, just as Elisha had told her. (vv. 11-17, NIV)

Who is ministering to you? How are you ministering in return?

TO READ
Psalm 37:23-29

The Lord loves justice, and he will never abandon the godly. Psalm 37:28

 Provision

When you are busy doing God's work, it seems he gets you what you need when you need it.

I was packing for Japan and ran out of room in my suitcases and boxes. I was not going to be able to take the bouquet of fake flowers I used as a prop.

God, you are just going to have to get me some flowers, I prayed. I then promptly forgot all about it until midnight the night before the event when I was previewing the talks in my head as I rested in bed. God would just have to provide, or I would do without. I walked into the church, and there on the podium was a bouquet of fresh flowers.

Another time recently my literary agent was going to meet us for lunch. A few minutes before we left the house, we got a call from his secretary in Colorado asking us to bring a tape recorder.

"Honey, do we even have a tape recorder anymore? Do any of the boys' CD players also play tapes?"

"Why?" Bill asked, and I explained.

Bill then picked up a blue box. "What's this?"

"I have no idea."

"I was cleaning your car, Pam, and it was in the car."

"Oh. It's probably something someone donated to the ministry. I think there was a box of stuff like that in the back, but I haven't had time to go through it yet."

"Pam, it's a brand-new tape recorder!"

"Cool! God provides!"

TO READ
Romans 11:25-36

God's gifts and his call can never be withdrawn.

ROMANS 11:29

 ## *Red Marks the Spot*

Rahab believed the Hebrew spies. She learned about the true God from them. She believed enough to let them down to escape through her window on the wall. Now it was time to act on her belief. The instructions were clear

She and her family had to be in the house, and the red cord must hang from the window. No matter what was happening around them, she must believe and then act on this information (Joshua 2:17-18). The troops of Israel marched around her city.

For seven days she wouldn't let her family leave. Some may have complained, some may have doubted her, but she stood firm. They had to stay and wait there. The red cord was their safety line to freedom.

God has called you to freedom. He has laid a dream on your heart. You have a calling—are you going to act on it? Some people may criticize you, others may doubt, and some may complain.

Will you still stand firm in your call and act on it? Doing so will lead to freedom.

TO READ
Proverbs 9:1-9

Teach the wise, and they will be wiser. Teach the righteous, and they will learn more. PROVERBS 9:9

 Regroup

Our oldest son, Brock, was the leading quarterback in our area and had been honored with numerous awards. At six feet, he had been recruited by many Division One teams but always landed further down on the lists because of his height.

He looked toward the Ivy League after several coaches flew out to talk with him. It looked as if Dartmouth was going to sign him, but then the call came, "Brock, we ran out of spaces on your academic index."

The door was closed. It was time to regroup!

Look forward to the goal, not the particular path. His long-term goal was to have football (coaching, playing, or managing) as a platform for the gospel.

Look for alternatives. We sent Brock on a trip to consider six colleges as alternatives. An informed decision is a safeguard against regret.

Look at yourself. Brock had to take a hard look at his skills, talents, and obstacles. At six feet, he would really have to prove himself to play Division One football. He could take safer routes (Division Two or Three), but that felt like "settling for second best" to Brock. In the end he chose the junior college route. He tied a school record his first season and was voted the season's MVP. Then came season two, and the performance wasn't coming as easily. He wondered if the dream was going to happen for him to earn a scholarship to a "big football school." On the darkest day, midseason, Brock said, "I will have no regrets on the path I've chosen; going for the dream by a different path is better than no dream at all."

Regroup if you need to, but hold on to your dream.

TO READ
Luke 19:11-26

"Well done, my good servant!" his master replied. "Because you have been trustworthy in a very small matter, take charge of ten cities." LUKE 19:17, NIV

 ## The Small Things

God has used some pretty obscure methods to move our ministry forward. He used a little heart-shaped box I bought to put romantic conversation starters in to move a publisher's heart to sign us.

I spoke at a women-in-leadership event to a handful of women. One was a missionary home on furlough, and she invited me to Japan two years later. I have ministered to groups of one (really, *one* in the audience!) and have spoken to thousands or millions through television. Many times I can see the piece of the puzzle that moved us forward, but just as many times I can't.

God is the master chess player who moves the pieces around for the good of the Kingdom. Our job is to remain faithful in the little things. If we are honest we all have asked, "Why her? Why not me?"

God's answer is simply "because." In *Woman of Influence,* I include a poem a friend gave me after my husband and I left a job in a megachurch to take a senior pastorate of a sixty-person church. It's called "A Little Place," and it encourages my heart when I am wondering at my lot in life:

Where shall I work today, dear Lord?
And my love flowed warm and free.
He answered and said,
"See that little place?
Tend that place for Me."

I answered and I said,
"Oh no, not there,
No one would ever see
No matter how well my work was done,
Not that little place for me!"

His voice when He spoke,
Was soft and kind,
He answered me tenderly,
"Little one, search that heart of thine,
Are you working for them or Me?"

"Nazareth was a little place,
And so was Galilee."[1]

TO READ
Mark 6:30-44

Jesus said, "Let's get away from the crowds for a while and rest." There were so many people coming and going that Jesus and his apostles didn't even have time to eat. MARK 6:31

 ## Run Away

A group of mothers chatted: "I was so upset and stressed the other night, I felt like running away from home!"

"I hear you! Once, I was so mad at my husband I wanted to run away. It was late at night, so I couldn't figure out where to run. I didn't want to spend the money for a hotel or drive to one myself at that hour. The beach isn't safe, so I just went and sat in the car! Then I was afraid even sitting in the car alone. I thought, *This is stupid! Why do I want to run away? Everyone I love is in that house!* So I went back in and went to sleep. Things looked better in the morning."

"I know. One time I was so stressed, so frustrated with my family I wanted to go on strike and leave them on their own. Then I thought, *They will think I am crazy if I up and leave at 2 A.M.* So I stayed, and over breakfast I said, 'I want everyone to know that I am going to spend today and tonight at a health spa. I need a day off, and you'll be on your own for meals.'

"Their response, including my husband's was, 'That's great, Mom! You deserve it!' I couldn't even be mad at them anymore, but I did go to the spa anyway. It was great!"

Maybe you need a break, instead of an emotional breakdown.

Plan some time that will restore and replenish you.

TO READ
Job 37:1-18

Listen . . . stop and consider the wonderful miracles of God! Job 37:14

 Bad Attitude

He had a day most leaders dream of. One hundred and twenty thousand people repented and turned to God because of a simple, poorly delivered, half-hearted sermon of just one line: "Forty more days and Nineveh will be overturned" (Jonah 3:4, NIV).

The right response would be elation! But Jonah hated the Ninevites. When they repented, he pouted:

> "Didn't I say before I left home that you would do this, Lord? That is why I ran away to Tarshish! I knew that you were a gracious and compassionate God, slow to get angry and filled with unfailing love. I knew how easily you could cancel your plans for destroying these people. Just kill me now, Lord! I'd rather be dead than alive because nothing I predicted is going to happen."
>
> The Lord replied, "Is it right for you to be angry about this?"

Are you angry because God isn't doing things your way or in your timing or with the people you want him to be using or blessing? Find a friend to tell your woes to in thirty minutes or less, then leave the pity party and get on with life.

TO READ
Psalm 75:1-10

We thank you, O God! We give thanks because you are near. People everywhere tell of your mighty miracles. PSALM 75:1

 ## Say Thanks

How can you thank God? He is so good, holy, and awesome. He needs nothing, not even our thanks, but he longs to hear us give thanks.

Notice how Hannah gave thanks:

"Hannah prayed: 'My heart rejoices in the Lord! Oh, how the Lord has blessed me! Now I have an answer for my enemies, as I delight in your deliverance'" (1 Samuel 2:1).

She expresses her delight. "No one is holy like the Lord! There is no one besides you; there is no Rock like our God" (v. 2).

She acknowledges God's character. "Stop acting so proud and haughty! Don't speak with such arrogance! The Lord is a God who knows your deeds; and he will judge you for what you have done" (v. 3).

She gives a warning. "The Lord brings both death and life; he brings some down to the grave but raises others up. The Lord makes one poor and another rich; he brings one down and lifts another up" (vv. 6-7).

She exalts God for his power. "For all the earth is the Lord's, and he has set the world in order. He will protect his godly ones, but the wicked will perish in darkness. No one will succeed by strength alone. Those who fight against the Lord will be broken. He thunders against them from heaven; the Lord judges throughout the earth. He gives mighty strength to his king; he increases the might of his anointed one" (vv. 8-10).

Make your own list of why you delight in God and what you have seen him do for you. Observation and remembrance are great forms of thanks.

TO READ
Genesis 39:1-6

The Lord was with Joseph and blessed him greatly as he served in the home of his Egyptian master.

GENESIS 39:2

 ## Share the Wealth!

As God rewards your life, all those who surround you receive rewards.

Your spiritual health will be blessed by God, but that blessing will spill over the borders of your life into the lives of all those who interact with you. And then those blessed interactions turn into more opportunities for success.

Take Joseph, for example. The Lord blessed Joseph as he lived with his Egyptian master, who could see that the Lord was with him, giving him success in all he did.

Joseph's boss saw God was with him, so he basically turned the running of the entire business over to Joseph. All Potiphar was concerned with was what he ate (Genesis 39:2-6).

Potiphar seemed to be on a constant vacation or taking early retirement!

This is a huge level of trust for a boss to give any employee, let alone an employee who was not even an Egyptian. Is this how your boss or your ministry or volunteer supervisor feels about you?

Invest in your relationship with God. Your raise may not come, and your job advancement may not happen until you first see God as your boss and seek to please him.

TO READ
James 2:14-20

Do you still think it's enough just to believe that there is one God? Well, even the demons believe this, and they tremble in terror! Fool! When will you ever learn that faith that does not result in good deeds is useless? JAMES 2:19-20

 She's Up Again!

One of the loves of my life is encouraging and equipping women to reach their potential. Over the years God has brought many women across my path. Some were a broken heap of hurt when I met them; others were further on the path to wellness.

A few years back several women with speaking and writing gifts approached me for mentoring. I knew I could never give them what they needed if I tried to find time to meet one-on-one. No, I would need to gather them together and teach them together. And more important, they would need to learn and lean on one another.

And they did—I mean, we did. I taught them, but I also learned much. One day on a retreat, Tami, the newest member of the group, and I were talking. I told her how I loved being with the group because in place of their fears they chose faith. They refused to let anything keep them down. We talked about how vital it is to know how to battle the enemy of our souls.

Tami said that one of her favorite quotes was from Joyce Meyer's teaching on victory over the enemy.

"When they see my feet hit the floor in the morning, I want the demons to be shaking in their boots and say, 'Oh no! She's up again!'"

How do you make demons shudder? James 2:19 says, "Do you still think it's enough just to believe that there is one God? Well, even the demons believe this, and they tremble in terror!" The context of this verse is a discussion of action.

"Show me your faith without deeds, and I will show you my faith by what I do" (James 2:18, NIV). Our faith *in action* is evidence we believe God. *Believe* is a verb. Act as if you take God at his Word; that's what makes demons shudder!

TO READ
Mark 6:7-13

[Jesus] called his twelve disciples together and sent them out two by two, with authority to cast out evil spirits. MARK 6:7

 Side by Side

The wall was down in Jerusalem. Nehemiah led the charge to build it up again, thus providing much needed protection from enemies on all sides. However, rebuilding the wall was no easy task. To accomplish the task, he divided up the wall and gave families charge of sections of the wall. He found that the builders felt safer and worked better when one other ingredient was in place. See if you can spot it in the text below:

> Next to him, Ezer son of Jeshua, ruler of Mizpah, repaired another section, from a point facing the ascent to the armory as far as the angle. Next to him, Baruch son of Zabbai zealously repaired another section, from the angle to the entrance of the house of Eliashib the high priest. . . .
>
> Next to him, Binnui son of Henadad repaired another section, from Azariah's house to the angle and the corner, and Palal son of Uzai worked opposite the angle and the tower projecting from the upper palace near the court of the guard. Next to him, Pedaiah son of Parosh. . . . Next to them, the men of Tekoa repaired another section, from the great projecting tower to the wall of Ophel. (Nehemiah 3:19-27, NIV)

They worked next to one another. They labored side by side. Is there a big task in your future? Is there a big obstacle to overcome? Is there a challenge that feels insurmountable?

Divide up the project, and work side by side with those who are like-minded until it is completed.

TO READ
Luke 15:3-10

Suppose a woman has ten valuable silver coins and loses one. Won't she light a lamp and look in every corner of the house and sweep every nook and cranny until she finds it? And when she finds it, she will call in her friends and neighbors to rejoice with her because she has found her lost coin. LUKE 15:8-9

 ## *Smallest of Details!*

Does God care? My friend Gail is convinced he cares about the smallest of details:

> My husband and I were working together in my mom's kitchen when I noticed the diamond in my wedding ring was gone. Not knowing when it happened, we both got down on our knees to start the hunt. As I made my way in one direction, I prayed, *God you know where it is, please direct us.* Within two minutes David called out, "Is this it?" I rushed over to see my diamond in his large hand.
>
> God does care even about the smallest of details. He knew how important this diamond was to me as it was placed on my finger over twenty-seven years ago. My wedding ring, a gold circle of love, now holds a diamond that reminds me to pray and expect an answer in God's timing.

Is there a way for you to remind yourself of God's care? It's easy to forget that even the details of our lives might also be important to God just because we are important to God.

Luke 12:6-7 reminds us, "What is the price of five sparrows? A couple of pennies? Yet God does not forget a single one of them. And the very hairs on your head are all numbered. So don't be afraid; you are more valuable to him than a whole flock of sparrows."

Try creating a screen saver that reminds you to pray and trust God; buy a special magnet for your refrigerator or even a charm for a bracelet. Somehow, remind yourself that if it is important to you, it is also important enough to talk to God about.

The king granted these requests, because the gracious hand of God was on me. NEHEMIAH 2:8

 ## *Stamp of Approval*

Sometimes when you feel God leading in a certain way, you may need to get approval or a "go ahead" from someone official, such as a board, a leader, or a government authority.

Nehemiah, a cupbearer to the king, was heartbroken over the state of Jerusalem. He wanted to go back and rebuild the wall. In those days, if the king didn't like your request, you could be killed!

So he prayed, "O Lord, please hear my prayer! Listen to the prayers of those of us who delight in honoring you. Please grant me success now as I go to ask the king for a great favor. Put it into his heart to be kind to me" (Nehemiah 1:11).

Nehemiah was careful to protect his emotions, but the king one day asked him why he was sad. Nehemiah 2:2-12 explains the full story, but in a nutshell: When Nehemiah explained why he was sad, not only did the king release him to go rebuild, he also offered to help!

Our church was in a building program, and we finally located an empty storefront. We wanted to buy it and turn it into a church. The location was great, and the price was right.

But we needed the planning commission's approval. The review committee recommended a rejection; the newspaper printed an article that made our case seem hopeless. The church gathered to pray. The next night at the planning commission, each commissioner listened as community members and leaders shared why our church would benefit the community (and how it already had). Each commissioner, one by one, gave speeches encouraging my husband, the pastor, and our church, and we won unanimous approval!

The next day the front-page headline read, "Church Gets Approval!"

"Praise be to the Lord, the God of my master, Abraham," he said. "The Lord has been so kind and faithful to Abraham, for he has led me straight to my master's relatives." GENESIS 24:27

 ## Success in Heart

Does God care about success in all aspects of our lives, even in our love life? I love the story of Abraham sending his servant to find a suitable wife for his son Isaac. The servant was so sincere that he prayed all along the way for success:

> "O Lord, God of my master Abraham, give me success today, and show kindness to my master Abraham. See, I am standing beside this spring, and the daughters of the townspeople are coming out to draw water. May it be that when I say to a girl, 'Please let down your jar that I may have a drink,' and she says, 'Drink, and I'll water your camels too'—let her be the one you have chosen for your servant Isaac. By this I will know that you have shown kindness to my master."
>
> *Before he had finished praying,* Rebekah came out with her jar on her shoulder. She was the daughter of Bethuel son of Milcah, who was the wife of Abraham's brother Nahor. The girl was very beautiful, a virgin; no man had ever lain with her. She went down to the spring, filled her jar and came up again.
>
> The servant hurried to meet her and said, "Please give me a little water from your jar."
>
> "Drink, my lord," she said, and quickly lowered the jar to her hands and gave him a drink.
>
> After she had given him a drink, she said, "I'll draw water for your camels too, until they have finished drinking." (Genesis 24:12-19, NIV, emphasis added)

The servant prayed specifically, and God answered specifically! God added blessings to the request: Rebekah was beautiful and a virgin.

Make a list of specifics you would like to see happen in your most vital relationships, and watch and see how God answers.

If the Holy Spirit controls your mind, there is life and peace. ROMANS 8:6

 The Fingerprint of the Spirit

Mary was young, very young. An angel appeared unannounced and gave her amazing news that she was to be the mother of the Savior. She couldn't fathom the idea: "How will this be," Mary asked the angel, "since I am a virgin?"

The angel answered, "The Holy Spirit will come upon you, and the power of the Most High will overshadow you. So the baby born to you will be holy, and he will be called the Son of God" (Luke 1:35).

The angel didn't give a lot of details. "The Holy Spirit will come upon you." What exactly does that mean? How did it happen? The Bible doesn't give the details.

God isn't a man, so conception didn't come through intercourse. It may have been a creation much like the first creation. God may have just spoken and then taken on the form of a human.

Although we don't have the details, we can intelligently conjecture about the characteristics of the "overshadowing" because we are told something about the Holy Spirit. Mary's overshadowing created a new life, one that saved the world. When the Holy Spirit creates, he creates with the same style today and every day (Hebrews 13:8).

A few distinctives of the Holy Spirit's creations are:

- They spread the Good News. (Luke 4:18)
- They speak the truth of God. (John 3:34)
- They worship God in truth. (John 4:23-24)
- They have eternal life. (John 6:63)
- They learn spiritual truth. (John 14:26)

If you are wondering if this is your plan, your creation, or the Spirit's leading, look for the Spirit's imprint.

The Lord, your Redeemer, the Holy One of Israel, says: I am the Lord your God, who teaches you what is good and leads you along the paths you should follow. ISAIAH 48:17

 ## *The Flight*

I was on an airplane I wasn't supposed to be on. My flight had been canceled the night before, and I was given a hotel room and a flight out the next day. I wanted to sleep in a bit since we got to our room at 1 A.M., so I took a 10:30 A.M. flight.

Because so many people from the cancelled flight I was to be on were rerouted to an early morning flight, Terri, a mom flying standby, discovered her first flight option was 10:30, too. As we sat next to one another, I learned she was going to a Christian college to see if she could iron out a housing glitch for her son. He was supposed to have a dorm room but had just received notice he did not.

I also had a son moving out to attend college, so my heart went out to her. I offered to pray for her and her son. I asked her to let me know how God answered. I knew in my heart that God would provide something; her son wanted to grow in his walk with God.

A few weeks later I got an e-mail thanking me for my calming prayers and relaying the good news: Her son had a dorm room!

Every day, there are people along our path whom God has called us to encourage. As we do so, we see miracles, and God builds our faith. We see how God puts two women, neither of whom was "supposed" to be on a flight, in seats next to each other and gives encouragement and hope in Christ.

God moves people to places for their good and for his glory.

TO READ
Psalm 69:13-17

Answer my prayers, O Lord, for your unfailing love is wonderful. Turn and take care of me, for your mercy is so plentiful. Don't hide from your servant; answer me quickly, for I am in deep trouble!

PSALM 69:16-17

 ## *The Heart of Creativity*

Desperation is often at the heart of creativity. Moses' mom was desperate. The pharaoh, afraid the people of Israel were growing too strong in number, was commanding all baby boys to be killed at birth.

She'd do anything to save her son. Where could she hide a baby? What if he cried? What if someone came by the house?

You can almost imagine her scouring the house, looking frantically for an answer and praying. Then she eyes a basket! She might have thought, *It looks the right size, but the baby's cries could still be heard in the house. The river! If I could just hide the baby in the reeds, far from human ears.*

But how could she make sure the basket stayed afloat? Tar and pitch! So she coated the basket, placed the baby inside, and asked her daughter to stand guard. God sparked her creativity, and a whole nation was saved by that baby, who grew into the nation's leader and deliverer.

Are you feeling stuck? Do you need a new idea or to be rescued in some situation?

Pray! Then look around—the answer may be sitting right in front of you.

TO READ
Leviticus 19:32-37

Show your fear of God by standing up in the presence of elderly people and showing respect for the aged. I am the Lord. LEVITICUS 19:32

 ## *Honor for Honor*

One family really rallied to launch the church that we pastored. The Bensons helped launch it with no financial help or staff from any other church. They worked full-time all week and worked full-time in ministry. They opened their home, their hearts, and their checkbook. Their family put in long hours—hundreds and thousands of hours.

In the state where I live, the early settlers risked life and limb to traverse the Continental Divide and trek the Oregon Trail. They faced disease and attacks from native peoples, outlaws, and wild animals. Many said good-bye to their families, knowing they would never see them again in their lifetime.

In our nation's history many of those who first arrived on ships and then braved the wilds and the weather that first harsh winter lost their lives. Still others fought for our freedom as a new democracy was formed.

Looking back honors not only those we pay tribute to but also reminds us of God's faithfulness. It brings honor and dignity to our own lives as we remember that there are long-term reasons for our work, sacrifice, and prayers.

When we take the time to honor those who have gone before us and recount the history of those who paid the price to bring us freedom, opportunity, or training, we are strengthened. Honoring those who built our present brings honor to our own lives and motivates and encourages us to continue with our own work.

Take a look back. Who paved the way for you?

TO READ
1 Kings 10:1-13

The Lord your God is great indeed! He delights in you and has placed you on the throne of Israel. Because the Lord loves Israel with an eternal love, he has made you king so you can rule with justice and righteousness. 1 KINGS 10:9

 ## The Queen

Why do some people succeed? Let's see what we can learn from one famous queen: "When the Queen of Sheba heard of Solomon's reputation, which brought honor to the name of the Lord, she came to test him with hard questions. . . . When she met with Solomon, they talked about everything she had on her mind. . . . She exclaimed to the king, 'Everything I heard in my country about your achievements and wisdom is true! I didn't believe it until I arrived here and saw it with my own eyes. Truly I had not heard the half of it! Your wisdom and prosperity are far greater that what I was told'" (1 Kings 10:1-7).

She had heard about Solomon's power and came to check it out for herself. When she saw all Solomon's wisdom, his palace, all his attendants and officials, and the burnt offerings he made to the Lord, she was overwhelmed.

She respected what she saw: "How happy these people must be! What privilege for your officials to stand here day after day, listening to your wisdom! The Lord your God is great indeed! He delights in you and has placed you on the throne of Israel. Because the Lord loves Israel with an eternal love, he has made you king so you can rule with justice and righteousness" (1 Kings 10:8-9).

The results: The queen gave praise to God (giving credit where credit was due).

TO READ
Ezekiel 18:25-32

Put all your rebellion behind you, and get for yourselves a new heart and a new spirit. For why should you die, O people of Israel? Ezekiel 18:31

 ## The Root of It All

My friend Linda grew up in a family with six children. Her home was always pretty hectic as her mom always had lots of babies to take care of.

Linda says, "Needless to say, we rarely got one-on-one attention, unless we were star athletes or sick. Well, I was the one who had the seizures in the family. It seemed like the only time I did get attention was when I was sick, and that wasn't the kind of attention I wanted because I got picked on at school. I felt like a freak of nature, a burden to my family, very insecure and out of control. So I developed a raging temper whenever I felt ignored, unloved, useless, or out of control. I lost my temper all the time, got in trouble all the time, had no friends, and received negative attention from my parents and family."

Then she started seeing anger in her oldest son and picked up a book called *Kids in Danger*. "God has spoken to me through this book. I thought I was reading it for my son, but after I read an entire chapter on anger, I knew God was speaking to me! Then I looked around: My husband was yelling, the kids were yelling. When you see your behavior in others, it is very convicting."

Second Timothy 2:7 encourages us to "reflect on what I am saying, for the Lord will give you insight into all this." When we look into the Word, it is a mirror to our souls, and we see ourselves more clearly.

Linda adds, "I still struggle emotionally when my world seems out of control, but I am learning to bare my heart, soul, and feelings to the Creator of all things. I am finally realizing how much God loves me, how I can love others the way Jesus loves me, and that love changes a whole lot of behaviors."

August

TO READ
Lamentations 3:28-33

Let them sit alone in silence beneath the Lord's demands. LAMENTATIONS 3:28

 ## The Sound of Silence

Sometimes no answer is an answer. When Herod asked Jesus question after question, Jesus said nothing (Luke 23:9). When Pilate asked him where he was from, Jesus gave him no answer (John 19:9).

To some Jesus gave absolutely no response. In Matthew 11:2-6 when John the Baptist was in prison, he sent his disciples to ask Christ if he was the Messiah, and Jesus told them, "Go back to John and tell him about what you have heard and seen—the blind see, the lame walk, the lepers are cured, the deaf hear, the dead are raised to life, and the Good News is being preached to the poor. And tell him, 'God blesses those who are not offended by me.'"

Others received a response but not the one they were after: "Zechariah said to the angel, 'How can I know this will happen? I'm an old man now, and my wife is also well along in years.' Then the angel said, 'I am Gabriel! I stand in the very presence of God. It was he who sent me to bring you this good news! And now, since you didn't believe what I said, you won't be able to speak until the child is born. For my words will certainly come true at the proper time'" (Luke 1:18-20).

Just because God seems silent doesn't mean he isn't working. The silence might be speaking volumes.

TO READ
Psalm 112:1-10

When darkness overtakes the godly, light will come bursting in. . . . They do not fear bad news; they confidently trust the Lord to care for them. They are confident and fearless and can face their foes triumphantly. PSALM 112:4, 7-8

 ## The Thermostat

One of the privileges of being a traveling speaker is meeting women who have deep roots of faith and women who have taken the Word of God to heart to overcome great obstacles and crises. One woman, whom I'll call Faith, shared a story:

Something had been off in their relationship and family for some time. For years she struggled to encourage a spouse who was unmotivated and had a variety of smaller frustrating habits. Faith was the strong cord of hope, godliness, and stability. She kept growing and getting deeper roots into God's Word. She had a vibrant ministry and a huge impact on her community. Her children were honor students and became leaders in all realms of high school life. Then Faith made a startling discovery: drugs in her husband's car. Now she knew the source of her husband's pain and poor living choices.

Faith went to the top for help: She gained counseling for herself and the children, laid out the options to her husband, and expressed healthy boundaries. She did all the steps anyone in the helping profession would encourage her to do. She didn't panic—she prayed. Then God reminded her that she had been encouraged in a quiet time years before by a small illustration in one of the devotionals written by Corrie ten Boom. Faith gathered her children together and said:

"We have a choice to make. We can be a thermometer or a thermostat. Thermometers go up and down depending on the circumstances of the weather. But thermostats set the climate. Instead of riding an emotional roller coaster, I believe God wants us to set a course of stability and be thermostats—choosing faith, not fear. We can let this ruin us and our family, or we can let it make us stronger."

Are you a thermometer or a thermostat?

TO READ
Revelation 17:3-14

Together they will wage war against the Lamb, but the Lamb will defeat them because he is Lord over all lords and King over all kings, and his people are the called and chosen and faithful ones.

REVELATION 17:14

 ## *This Is Hard Work!*

There are times when doing God's will seems like it's too much, too hard, too impossible. John must have heard a few complaints, and believers under his leadership had real issues: The government was against them, taking businesses, separating families, and even killing Christians. It had to have been tempting to pull up short. But John goes beyond a pep talk. He doesn't guilt them into obedience. Rather, John explains *how* to obey: "This is love for God: to obey his commands. And his commands are not burdensome, for everyone born of God overcomes the world. This is the victory that has overcome the world, even our faith. Who is it that overcomes the world? Only he who believes that Jesus is the Son of God" (1 John 5:3-5, NIV).

John acknowledges that obedience seems like a burden, then goes on to explain the key to victory: faith in Jesus. Earlier in the same letter, he reminds them of the power that lies just beneath the surface of their own skin: First John 4:4 explains, "You, dear children, are from God and have overcome them, because the one who is in you is greater than the one who is in the world" (NIV).

Jesus in them. The Christ who rose from the grave gives his resurrection power to all of us who believe. He won at the Cross, and he can win anytime we give him the cross he has asked us to bear. We can be confident in our victory because Jesus *is* victor. His very essence is victory till the end.

"God, I can't, but through your power, I can!"

TO READ
Proverbs 17:1-28

A friend is always loyal. PROVERBS 17:17

 TLC Days

"People just don't take time for each other anymore." It was a simple comment from a friend who was home on furlough from the mission field. "How do you all keep going? Friendships replenish me emotionally, and it seems no one has time here."

When I did research for my book *Woman of Confidence,* I interviewed numerous women who were successful in a variety of fields. I was looking for the common ingredients they all had in their lives that helped produce that success. One of the key factors: successful women take time for significant relationships. *Significant* is a key word. They don't live borderless lives where anyone and everyone has access to them and their time. Rather, they choose which relationships are most valuable and make time for them. They block off time months and weeks in advance for their husbands, children, and extended family. Many have yearly routines: certain holidays are spent with certain family members.

But they also take time for nurturing friendships: a Monday-morning walk with a trusted friend, a tennis date once a week with an accountability partner, a biweekly prayer date. One group has a once-a-month lunch with a circle of friends who had been college roommates. Then the group became a young brides' Bible study, then a moms' play group, and now all have teens. They planned for their friendships to help them weather the seasons of life. One set of friends who live on opposite coasts programmed each other's numbers into cell phones and have reminder alarms on their PDAs to make a once-a-week call to each other.

Which people in your life replenish and stretch you? Put them on your calendar in advance—pencil in some emotional TLC time.

TO READ
Acts 14:21-28

Upon arriving in Antioch, they called the church together and reported about their trip, telling all that God had done and how he had opened the door of faith to the Gentiles, too. ACTS 14:27

 Togetherness

The word *together* is written more than twenty times in the book of Acts. It seems that the early church liked to be together and felt a need to be together. What does such togetherness accomplish?

One positive impact of togetherness is synergy. *The American Heritage Dictionary* defines *synergy* as "the interaction of two or more agents or forces so that their combined effect is greater than the sum of their individual effects."[1]

That's exactly what the book of Acts is all about. A bunch of fishermen, a few tax gatherers, a couple of religious leaders, and a group of women met together. Out of the small band of afraid, mostly undereducated people, an entire belief system based on the truth of the gospel was forged, and the gates of hell have not prevailed against it!

If God has laid a plan or a passion on your heart, hold a get-together. Pray, and then watch the synergy develop!

TO READ
1 Corinthians 12:22-27

All of you together are Christ's body, and each one of you is a separate and necessary part of it.

1 CORINTHIANS 12:27

 The Answer's in the House

One of the most inspirational pastors I have met is Reverend James Meeks from South Chicago. He and his wife, Jamell, lead a megachurch that has risen out of the ashes of the slums to create a growing dynamic church and community.

The church's bookstore and coffee shop are the city's largest business. When you call Salem Baptist, the receptionist answers, "Salem Baptist, the greatest church in the world." And after a few minutes spent with James and Jamell, you can see why their congregation feels this way. James believes God will always provide, and the provision is usually within the circle of influence you already know. The way he puts it is, "The answer's in the house."

So when the church opened a new bookstore, getting someone with a business background to come to South Chicago and work in the low-rent district was a challenge, but James told the congregation, "The answer's in the house!"

He believed a member of his congregation was the right person for the job, and he was right! God placed a woman, currently out of work, on Meeks's heart. God took a woman in a career transition and created a megabookstore from her talents. She had never run a bookstore before, but God gave her all she needed to know in raw talent.

What do you need to go forward in your dream and calling? "The answer's in the house!" Pray that God will give you his eyes to see the people and resources in your world through his perspective.

TO READ
Philippians 3:7-11

I no longer count on my own goodness or my ability to obey God's law, but I trust Christ to save me. For God's way of making us right with himself depends on faith. PHILIPPIANS 3:9

 ## Under the Surface

A prostitute. She was used to the looks, the catcalls. She was even used to the feeling of being used by men. But she was not used to the kindness and the respect she was given one day by some men whom she knew were spies for the people of God.

She had heard much about the strength of their God. He seemed bigger, more real than the gods of stone and wood that sat carved about her city.

She told the men how she and her people reacted to their God and all he had done. But she also asked them to swear to show kindness to her and her family because of the kindness she showed them. Asking for a sign, she was told by the men that it would be their lives for hers, and they promised they would treat her kindly and faithfully when God gave them the land (Joshua 2:11-14).

Smart woman—she could spot a good deal! All she'd seen were bad deals her whole life. So when she saw the opposite, she knew it had to be the *real* deal.

How about you? The best deal ever offered was Jesus' righteousness for your imperfection. Have you claimed your right to this deal?

You won't get a better offer.

TO READ
Colossians 2:1-5

My goal is that they will be encouraged and knit together by strong ties of love. I want them to have full confidence because they have complete understanding of God's secret plan, which is Christ himself. COLOSSIANS 2:2

 Unity

More can be accomplished together than separately. There's a synergy that happens when individuals join their skills, talents, and resources together, focused on a single purpose. Goals are accomplished.

But achieving unity and keeping it is no easy task: "Again I say, don't get involved in foolish, ignorant arguments that only start fights. The Lord's servants must not quarrel but must be kind to everyone. They must be able to teach effectively and be patient with difficult people" (2 Timothy 2:23-24).

If God's Word acknowledges the challenges of working together, we realize how much we have to depend on God to achieve the unity he calls us to. "What is causing the quarrels and fights among you? Isn't it the whole army of evil desires at war within you? You want what you don't have, so you scheme and kill to get it. You are jealous for what others have, and you quarrel to take it away from them. And yet the reason you don't have what you want is that you don't ask God for it" (James 4:1-2).

So what should we ask God for when we desire unity? According to James in the verses we just read, we should pray that we don't give in to the natural desire to react badly if we don't get what we want.

Then there are some key elements that create unity:

- Choosing a bond of peace (Ephesians 4:3)
- Choosing to love above everything else (Colossians 3:14)
- Choosing to keep Christ as the primary focus (Philippians 2:12)

TO READ
Ephesians 5:10-14

Where your light shines, it will expose their evil deeds. This is why it is said, "Awake, O sleeper, rise up from the dead, and Christ will give you light."

EPHESIANS 5:14

 ## Unlikely Celebration

Sometimes we are caught off guard by God's timing. Mary and Elizabeth were pregnant at the same time. Neither "should" have been. Elizabeth was too old by human standards, and Mary was much too young—and unmarried. Yet both women chose to rejoice in spite of the unlikely timing.

God intervenes, and we wonder at his timing. Have you ever wondered, *God, why did you give me this dream now? I feel too young, too old, under trained, or too busy.*

At times we feel the timing is like waking up out of a great dream. When we are having a lovely dream, we might be irritated at the interruption. However, the interruption is often more important, more life-giving than the dream.

One night when I was in my late twenties, I was abruptly awakened with a sense of impending doom. There didn't seem to be a reason for the abrupt awakening, and I was so tired. I had a preschooler and a young baby; however, I dutifully walked from room to room checking on the kids.

When I got to Zach's crib, his fitful sleeping had untied the bumper pads on his crib, and the ties were twisted into a ropelike cord instead of the soft padding they were intended to be. The bumper pad cord was twisted around Zach's neck, and with each of his twists and turns trying to get free, he was tightening the cord around his neck. He could have died if God hadn't suddenly awakened me. How grateful I am that God interrupted my sleep that night!

Wake up—there's a life-giving reason for God's timing and interruptions!

TO READ
Romans 16:17-20

The God of peace will soon crush Satan under your feet. May the grace of our Lord Jesus Christ be with you. ROMANS 16:20

Vulnerable

Satan cannot read your mind or thoughts (he's a fallen angel), but he can read all the nonverbal clues. His demons listen in on conversations, and I believe they know how to read, too. In other words, Satan knows your vulnerabilities. He knows that you fear failure or you easily feel rejected. He knows if you are insecure in your husband's love or if you are trying to overcome an addictive behavior. And we should expect that he *will* exploit those vulnerabilities.

I expect to have a conflict with Bill right before we teach together, so we have agreed ahead of time to stop and pray as soon as any misunderstandings or hurt feelings happen to prevent Satan from getting a foot in the door. I expect that I will feel tempted when I am tired, and I will be vulnerable to my own whims when I have pushed hard or am preparing to speak to leaders (since leaders influence hundreds).

It seems as if Satan has a list of my fears, and he throws obstacles in my life to make me ask the same questions over and over, in spite of valid and substantial evidence that my fears are unfounded. Questions such as: Am I still being a good mom? Does Bill still love me? Does the audience (the group, the friend, etc.) accept me?

So when the same *old* questions appear anew, I tell Satan the same *old* truth: "God loves me. Jesus gained the victory over you when he died on the cross, and through his shed blood, I have the victory—so you have to flee! Get out of here!"

TO READ
Psalm 56:9-13

You have rescued me from death; you have kept my feet from slipping. So now I can walk in your presence, O God, in your life-giving light.

PSALM 56:13

 ## *Walk On!*

One of my friends has experienced the death of two children; another friend has two prodigals. Though both her children were raised with the truth, they are far from living it; one has declared himself an atheist.

With many trials, the pain feels compounded because one crisis often produces a financial crisis; the pressures mount, and you have a marital crisis!

One of my friends going through a crisis gave me a card that she said had helped her. The front said, "When you feel as if you are going through hell," and the inside read, "keep walking!"

There's much to be said for this stark advice. Keep walking. Keep putting one foot in front of the other. Keep holding on to Jesus one moment at a time. Keep standing when you want to sit and quit.

Bathsheba in the Bible did this. The most powerful man in her world saw her in her most private moment (taking a bath), called for her, and then convinced her to sleep with him. Her husband was at war, and when the king called him home to cover up the pregnancy that resulted from the king's night of sin, the loyal man would not sleep with his wife. So the king had him sent to the front lines, where he was killed.

David and Bathsheba's baby died shortly after birth. All that is enough to crush even the strongest woman. But Bathsheba mourned, then she married the king and later gave birth to the next king of Israel, who went on to build the first Temple to God.

Keep walking.

TO READ
Psalm 40:1-8

I take joy in doing your will, my God, for your law is written on my heart. PSALM 40:8

 ## What Brings Success

No one likes to fail. We buy books, listen to tapes, rent videos, attend seminars, or hire personal coaches and trainers. We are looking for a sure thing. We want a formula that ensures success.

God gave the formula a long time ago: "Stay on the path that the Lord your God has commanded you to follow. Then you will live long and prosperous lives in the land you are about to enter and occupy" (Deuteronomy 5:33).

Walk in the way God has told you to walk: "The Lord our God commanded us to obey all these laws and to fear him for our own prosperity and well-being, as is now the case" (6:24).

Obey and fear (respect) God: "Therefore, obey the terms of this covenant so that you will prosper in everything you do" (29:9).

Carefully watch the details of the plan God laid out. The plan for success is simple: Follow God. He loves you. He has a plan for you.

It's in the obedience that people get hung up. We don't want to watch what we say, what we see, what we do, how we spend, or how we live. By nature people—all of us—are selfish and lazy.

Look at your life. What has God *already* asked you to do? Do it. If you have an attitude toward obeying God, repent. Start down the path of success with a simple prayer: *God, I want to follow you. Help me walk your will. Amen.*

TO READ
Philippians 4:19-23

This same God who takes care of me will supply all your needs from his glorious riches, which have been given to us in Christ Jesus. PHILIPPIANS 4:19

What Do You Need?

If you walk children through a toy store, you will hear their mantra: "But, Mom, I neeeeeeeed that!"

What exactly is a need? In my quiet time journal, I was trying to sort out the differences between a want and a need. I looked up *need* in the dictionary and learned that a need is a condition requiring supply or relief.[2]

I had to agree with God that most of the time when I told God I neeeeeeded something, I was a lot like a child in a toy store. I just *thought* I needed it. Now I ask myself: Is this a requirement? Is it pressing? Is it urgent? Is it a means of basic substance?

In the book of Acts, the church rallied to supply each other's needs: "They sold their possessions and shared the proceeds with those in need" (Acts 2:45).

So then I asked myself, What would I sell if someone I loved needed to eat? needed shelter? I had to be honest—most everything would go! I really don't have that many "needs"!

God says he will supply my needs, and he goes beyond that. He meets needs according to his riches, and he owns it all!

TO READ	Don't be surprised, dear brothers and sisters, if the
1 John 3:11-13	world hates you. 1 JOHN 3:13

 ## *Why Do You Hate Me?*

Sometimes in a work or volunteer environment, we can't figure out why a relationship isn't going as smoothly as we'd like.

Retrace your steps and ask, Did I do something to offend this person? Have I accidentally triggered one of her emotional triggers?

If neither of these is true about you in the relationship, a very possible variable is the one described by Jesus:

> When the world hates you, remember it hated me before it hated you. The world would love you if you belonged to it, but you don't. I chose you to come out of the world, and so it hates you. Do you remember what I told you? "A servant is not greater than the master." Since they persecuted me, naturally they will persecute you. And if they had listened to me, they would listen to you! The people of the world will hate you because you belong to me, for they don't know God who sent me. They would not be guilty if I had not come and spoken to them. But now they have no excuse for their sin. Anyone who hates me hates my Father, too. (John 15:18-23)

One example in the life of our family was the time we went swimming in a hotel pool. One man in particular was upset at my husband and three sons even though none of them had done anything different than anyone else in the pool. The next morning we walked to breakfast and noticed a sign: American Atheist Convention. Could it be that the Holy Spirit's strength was just irritating a man walking contrary to God?

At times just your presence as a representative of Christ may tick off someone who is running from God or is hostile toward God. If that's the case, take comfort in the fact that your faith is so real and strong that it is apparent you love God.

I can't stop! If I say I'll never mention the Lord or speak in his name, his word burns in my heart like a fire. It's like a fire in my bones! I am weary of holding it in! JEREMIAH 20:9

The Biggest Fear

The number one fear of the majority of people is speaking in public. But speaking up seems to be one fear God wants us all to get over. So where do we begin?

- *Speak out about what breaks your heart.* "I cannot keep from speaking. I must express my anguish. I must complain in my bitterness." (Job 7:11)
- *Speak about what you know best, and wait to see what bridge God will provide to speak of himself.* "I speak with all sincerity; I speak the truth." (Job 33:3)
- *Speak about God's love.* "I have not kept this good news hidden in my heart; I have talked about your faithfulness and saving power. I have told everyone in the great assembly of your unfailing love and faithfulness." (Psalm 40:10)
- *Speak to give statistics or reasons of logic and faith.* "To whom can I give warning? Who will listen when I speak?" (Jeremiah 6:10)
- *Speak what God tells you, and leave the response and results to God.* "Whenever I give you a message, I will loosen your tongue and let you speak. Then you will say to them, 'This is what the Sovereign Lord says! Some of them will listen, but some will ignore you, for they are rebels." (Ezekiel 3:27)
- *Speak and tell what you've seen God do.* "I assure you, I am telling you what we know and have seen, and yet you won't believe us." (John 3:11)
- *Speak the truth.* "I speak with utter truthfulness? I do not lie." (Romans 9:1)
- *Speak of victories God has given.* "I will not venture to speak of anything except what Christ has accomplished through me." (Romans 15:18, NIV)

Oh, how I long to speak directly to the Almighty.
I want to argue my case with God himself. JOB 13:3

 State Your Case

Like many Americans, I watched the live courtroom coverage of the O. J. Simpson and Danielle van Dam cases. The lawyers presented evidence and arguments. I watched creativity, like Johnny Cochran's "If the gloves don't fit, you must acquit."

I also saw the passionate plea for justice on behalf of a murdered eight-year-old girl who lived just south of the city, where my then eleven-year-old played.

Some days we feel like the defendant, pleading for grace and mercy from a loving God. Other days we feel like the plaintiff, arguing for justice and demanding our pound of flesh.

God wants you to argue your case before him. He wants you to contend for truth and understanding. However, there are a few things to keep in mind as we approach the bench of God:

- He is God. He is all-knowing. He sees the whole story. He sees all the details.
- He is God. He is perfect, holy, and righteous. He does not make mistakes.
- He is God. He is all-powerful, and it is only because of his amazing mercy and patience that you live on the earth.
- He is God. He is sovereign. He has the ability to make all things work together for your good, even when things look pretty bad.
- He is God. You are not. He deserves respect and praise even if you don't feel like giving it.

Go ahead, make your case. Just remember who the Judge is—and how much he really does love you.

TO READ
2 Timothy 2:23-26

The Lord's servants must not quarrel but must be kind to everyone. They must be able to teach effectively and be patient with difficult people.

2 TIMOTHY 2:24

 Unusual Kindness

In the wake of the September 11 terrorist attacks, couples in New York canceled hundreds of divorces. In light of such tragedy, what really matters comes to light: marriage, family, supportive friends, and faith.

Bill and I fly quite a bit, and we noticed a change in the flying public. Flying rage became rare and was replaced by thankfulness, gratefulness, and kindness.

It reminds Bill and me of a verse we have tried to live out in our marriage of twenty-two years. It is a verse that describes the hospitality Paul received on a missionary trip, "The islanders showed us unusual kindness" (Acts 28:2, NIV).

Is that how you treat your spouse—with unusual kindness? Are your words so kind that others notice? Are your actions so kind and gracious that people stop to watch? People are watching how you treat each other. Your spouse is definitely watching, your friends are noticing, but most important, your children are watching. And they are taking notes because they look to you as role models of marital kindness.

Recently, Bill and I saw firsthand the results that play out in the life of a child whose parents have tried to be unusually kind to each other. Our son Brock was interviewed after breaking a passing record. A reporter asked him, "Who are the most influential people in your life?"

This is what Brock said: "My mom [Pam] and dad [Bill]. My dad is a great example of what a real man should be. I can tell he loves my mom very much. My mom tells me to be an upstanding citizen. She keeps me focused in terms of what's important in life."

What's important? To be unusually kind—it pays big dividends!

TO READ
Genesis 5:1-2

He created them male and female. GENESIS 5:2

 ## Who Does What?

Does your husband always have to be the one to mow the lawn? Do you have to be the one to wash the clothes and the dishes? How about those bills—who will pay them? Or the last minute run to the grocery store for tomorrow's science fair project: Who gets to take care of those ever-present children's needs?

In the home I grew up in, it seemed like my dad's domain was the garage, barn, and yard, and Mom's was anything and everything in the house. However, just down the street lived a family where the man loved to cook, and the woman mowed the yard each week.

Do gender stereotypes factor into your decisions of who does what around the house? Check out what the Bible says in Galatians 3:28: "There is no longer Jew or Gentile, slave or free, male or female. For you are all Christians—you are one in Christ Jesus."

What freedom! Remove the expectations and stereotypes, and write out who is best at what and who feels the most emotion about certain jobs. Delegate chores according to gifts, talents, and passion rather than stereotypes. To start the discussion, share the answers to these questions: What unspoken, unwritten expectations are you bringing into your marriage? Of the household chores that need to be done, which ones do you enjoy doing the most? Which ones do you dislike doing? Which ones are you willing to do even though you neither like nor dislike them?

Instead of arguing and instead of living with unspoken expectations, try to begin the conversation of who is responsible for what with everyone in your family.

TO READ
2 Corinthians 3:7-18

All of us have had that veil removed so that we can be mirrors that brightly reflect the glory of the Lord. And as the Spirit of the Lord works within us, we become more and more like him and reflect his glory even more. 2 CORINTHIANS 3:18

 Fruit of Change

If we truly experience God, we should be different. Take Paul, for example:

> As he was nearing Damascus on this mission, a brilliant light from heaven suddenly beamed down upon him! He fell to the ground and heard a voice saying to him, "Saul! Saul! Why are you persecuting me?"
>
> "Who are you, sir?" Saul asked.
>
> And the voice replied, "I am Jesus, the one you are persecuting! Now get up and go into the city, and you will be told what you are to do."
>
> The men with Saul stood speechless with surprise, for they heard the sound of someone's voice, but they saw no one! As Saul picked himself up off the ground, he found that he was blind. So his companions led him by the hand to Damascus. He remained there blind for three days. And all that time he went without food and water. . . .
>
> Ananias went and found Saul. He laid his hands on him and said, "Brother Saul, the Lord Jesus, who appeared to you on the road, has sent me so that you may get your sight back and be filled with the Holy Spirit." Instantly something like scales fell from Saul's eyes, and he regained his sight. Then he got up and was baptized. Afterward he ate some food and was strengthened. Saul stayed with the believers in Damascus for a few days. And immediately he began preaching about Jesus in the synagogues, saying, "He is indeed the Son of God!" (Acts 9:3-9, 17-20)

Saul had three things happen: (1) He was most definitely changed as a person—even his name changed! (2) He immediately obeyed. (3) He wanted others to experience what he had experienced with God.

Do you see these three things in your own life?

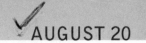

TO READ
Leviticus 11:44-45

I, the Lord, am your God. You must be holy because I am holy. LEVITICUS 11:44

 Holy, Holy

Bing Hunter, author of *The God Who Hears,* describes God's moral purity: "His inherent personal righteousness and holiness—is symbolized in Scripture as light: blinding, unending, undiminishing, dazzling whiteness."[3]

Too often we view justice, righteousness, and holiness by our standards. Hunter brings the issue to our daily life:

> Another reason why holiness is so hard to understand is that *Christians are like fish, living in a fluid medium (society) which has become so morally murky* that "light" seems abnormal. We were born in dirty water and have gotten used to it. Mud and murk are normal; clean and light are threatening. We can see rotten things on the bottom, but assume we cannot get stuck in the muck if we keep moving. And besides, we generally swim (in circles) higher up in the pond. We have learned to live comfortably with unholiness and see lots of others wearing *Ichthus* pins who do too.[4] . . . It is little wonder sin grieves the Holy Spirit who lives in us (Ephesians 5:30). Yet the greater and more astounding wonder is that sin grieves us so little.[5]

What's making your water murky? What used to upset you but makes you yawn today?

Take a good look at God, and then look again; it should help you see things more clearly.

TO READ
Psalm 24:1-6

Who may climb the mountain of the Lord? Who may stand in his holy place? PSALM 24:3

 ## Something We Can't Be Without

The Bible explains, "Everything that does not come from faith is sin" (Romans 14:23, NIV). Or as Bing Hunter says, "Sin is the failure to live congruently with God's holiness."[6]

The late Bill Bright, founder and former president of Campus Crusade for Christ, also acknowledges it is difficult to understand the holiness of God.

"When I think of God's holiness, I am convicted by the sinful nature of my own being. We are all like a man wearing a beautiful white suit who was invited to go down into the depths of a coal mine. In the darkness of the mine, he was not aware that his suit was becoming soiled. But when he resurfaced into the dazzling light of the noonday sun, he was fully aware that his suit had become sooty and dirty. The light of God's holiness reveals the darkness of our sin."[7]

What does God's holiness look like? Nathan Stone, in his book *The Names of God in the Old Testament,* says that the name of God *Jehovah M'Kaddesh* "means dedicate, consecrate, sanctuary, hallow, and holy and . . . it appears [in the Bible] in its various forms some 700 times."[8]

It is this holiness that an old Scottish divine writes: "It [holiness] is the balance . . . of all the attributes of Deity. Power without holiness would degenerate into cruelty; omniscience without holiness would become craft; justice without holiness would degenerate into revenge; and goodness without holiness would [become] passionate and intemperate fondness doing mischief rather than accomplishing good."[9]

TO READ
Romans 4:1-8

Oh, what joy for those whose disobedience is forgiven, whose sins are put out of sight.

ROMANS 4:7

Heart of Darkness

In the classic *Heart of Darkness,* the main character ends the novel with the gripping words "The horror, the horror." At times we sense that same grip of terror and darkness on our hearts. The psalmist says it best, "If I had cherished sin in my heart, the Lord would not have listened" (Psalm 66:18, NIV).

Sometimes what blocks our relationship with God is a sin. Many of us take the first step and confess the sin, but it always seems to be hanging around, haunting us, pointing its ugly, accusing finger of guilt our way. If you have a skeleton in your closet that keeps clanking its noisy chain, get it out.

One way is to write all those nagging sins down; then write the text of 1 John 1:9 over it: "If we confess our sins to him, he is faithful and just to forgive us and to cleanse us from every wrong." After you've written over the sin list with this verse, you can see how God blots out sin. An even better picture is to then destroy the list. A fireplace can come in handy here.

My husband, Bill, bought some flash paper like magicians use and wrote out a list of sins. He then nailed the list to a cross during one Sunday morning sermon, giving an example of Colossians 2:14, which says, "He canceled the record that contained the charges against us. He took it and destroyed it by nailing it to Christ's cross."

Then he took a match, and *whoosh,* in a flash the paper evaporated into thin air! The audience went wild with applause.

That's exactly how I feel when I *know* a sin is forgiven—like cheering!

TO READ
Mark 10:13-16

I assure you, anyone who doesn't have their kind of faith will never get into the Kingdom of God.

MARK 10:15

 ## The Heart of a Child

Try approaching God like a child if you want to keep your relationship fresh and to grow quickly. Lie on your bed in the dark and talk openly and honestly to him about your life. *Now I lay me down to sleep, I pray the Lord my soul to keep. . . .* Then talk to him about how you'd like him to keep your heart and soul.

A few years ago my Sunday evening children's program had many new believers and five pastors' kids. One evening I had the children all lie down on the floor. I dimmed the lights, and I asked the pastors' kids to pray like they do at bedtime. What a refreshing sound! The simple yet great theology of those little children was inspiring. I left that night realizing that I often let the hectic pace of responsibility steal away those simple, peaceful moments.

I made a vow that day to try to recapture some quiet margin in my life. I linger a little longer with the Lord after my husband has started snoozing, I savor the warmth of hot tea, and I pray as I wait and read my Bible in the morning. I walk. I simply walk around the block and talk with God about my life when things get harried in my office or at my house.

Have a quiet time with a child, and ask the child to teach you and explain to you what they think a verse means. Children have a fresh view of God. A mother was teaching her three-year-old daughter the Lord's Prayer. For several evenings at bedtime she repeated it after her mother.

One night she said she was ready to solo. The mother listened with pride as she carefully enunciated each word right up to the end. "And lead us not into temptation," she prayed, "but deliver us some e-mail. Amen."

TO READ
Psalm 119:33-40

Give me an eagerness for your decrees.

PSALM 119:36

 Solitude of Thought

The habit of journaling was easy for me because my journal became a place to write out my thoughts, to think out my life, and to see how my decisions became wiser.

Recently I came across my quiet-time journal from years ago. I noted an entry just days before my wedding was to take place. On the pages before and right after our wedding, I saw pieces of sentences that caught my heart and described the woman I wanted God to make me and the kind of marriage I wanted to have.

"Help me be extra understanding of others. Help me see their needs, not just my own. . . . Please give Bill and me the character qualities we'll need. Make us usable. Give us ideas that glorify you. Let us be an example."

As I continued to read, I realized that God is answering that prayer. He is making me into the woman I long to become, one day at a time. Author Catherine Calvert, a proponent of solitude, says that in solitude we hear our own footsteps walking into the future.

There is a wonderful organization that teaches women how to spend extended times with God. At one of their retreats, I was told to calm my mind, relax my body, and move in faith to receive what Jesus would reveal to me. Then I was to read the passage slowly and gently until I came to a word or phrase that made an impression on my mind or an impact on my heart. Finally, I was to reflect on that thought and invite it to be a guest in my heart.

Whether you take a journaling approach or follow the one I learned at that retreat, solitude can be God's gift to you and help you hear what the Holy Spirit wants to speak to your heart.

TO READ
Psalm 96:1-6

Sing a new song to the Lord! Let the whole earth sing to the Lord! Sing to the Lord; bless his name. Each day proclaim the good news that he saves.

PSALM 96:1-2

 ## Tune Up Your Heart

I think it is unfortunate that music has caused so much controversy in the church. Just as David's harp playing soothed Saul, music is a powerful tool to soothe, inspire, and convict hearts today. Try these musical quiet-time ideas:

- *Pull the lyrical jacket out of a CD or cassette that you don't normally listen to.* See if you can figure out what might have been going through the lyricist's mind or going on in his or her life when it was written.
- *Buy a hymnal, or see if your church has some you might borrow.* Try to sing as many songs as you know. Then try to figure out which are your favorites, which you'd like to be sung at your wedding, your baptism, your funeral, or other significant events in your life.
- *Try to sing a praise chorus until you have it memorized, especially if it is straight from Scripture.*
- *Try to put your favorite verse to a familiar tune.* This is really how some of our favorite hymns were created. Often deep spiritual words were set to familiar tunes because the people knew how they went!
- *Put on a purely instrumental recording.* Have a cup of coffee or tea, take a walk (wear a Walkman), or cook up a treat while you meditate on God's goodness in your life.
- *Try writing a poem or story that could be set to music.* Maybe there is a turning point in your faith you'd like to highlight or a change of heart God wrought in your life.

TO READ
Exodus 16:24-30

Do they not realize that I have given them the
seventh day, the Sabbath, as a day of rest?

EXODUS 16:29

 ## *Super Sundays*

Sunday is a usual day to grow spiritually, but it can be a challenging day to have quiet times. Often in the rush of getting to church, we forget to meet with God!

Try going to church thirty minutes early. Sit quietly in the pew, and pray that God will meet you and the others who come. Or, do as many pastors do: Walk the sanctuary, and pray for each seat and the person who will be in that place seeking to receive from God.

You might also find a quiet spot on your church grounds to sit and read a psalm or sing a favorite hymn or chorus. Ask yourself if you have this atti- tude when you go to a worship service: "The one thing I ask of the Lord— the thing I seek most—is to live in the house of the Lord all the days of my life, delighting in the Lord's perfections and meditating in his Temple" (Psalm 27:4).

Other unique Sunday quiet times can include stopping by your local donut shop and reading your Bible or engaging in conversation to take Jesus to the people. Your faith might be refreshed by being the pastor to people who would never darken the door of a church!

Try walking to church. When I was a child, my walk to and from church was my favorite time spent with God. You might try taking a faith walk in the neighborhood where your church is located. Pray for the neighborhood and the city, and claim the territory for Christ.

Another quiet-time idea that will be guaranteed to cheer up someone else would be to take a small gift (basket of muffins, box of candy, or lunch gift certificates) and go early to a children's Sunday school class or nursery. Leave a gift and thank-you note for the person in charge, then pray for the ministry that will happen in that room.

TO READ
1 Peter 1:13-16

Think clearly and exercise self-control. Look forward to the special blessings that will come to you at the return of Jesus Christ. 1 PETER 1:13

 Anticipate

One of the surest ways to ensure success is to anticipate life. Think through your life transitions: babies, marriage, midlife, teens, or aging parents and how they will impact your life.

Anticipating business growth will help you ensure staffing and supply needs. Anticipating an economic downturn will help you plan for lean times. Anticipating people's responses to change, success, or growth in your organization will help you maintain your relationships.

Anticipating people's questions will help you share your faith. Think of questions people who don't know Jesus might ask. Make a list of those questions and scriptural answers.

I have gotten into the habit of using a quiet time to answer these key questions of skeptics: Why should I wait until marriage for sex? Why should I believe the Bible? What makes Jesus so special? What happens to people who don't accept Jesus? What is heaven like? What is hell like? What does God have to say that will help me be a better parent? a better wife? Why should my family go to church on Easter? How do I know that God created the earth, and when did he do it?

I encourage you to keep these quiet times, file them, or maybe even use a publishing program to add graphics so they'll be ready to give away.

Another positive result of anticipating is that it keeps you looking forward rather than looking over your shoulder, which will always slow you down.

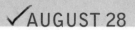

TO READ
Matthew 6:19-21

Wherever your treasure is, there your heart and thoughts will also be. MATTHEW 6:21

 ## *Give Back*

Where does your tithe go? Have you ever actually thought through how much you want to give and where you would like your donations to go? When my husband was a pastor, he told the congregation that your heart follows your money. (Most people think it is the other way around—that your money follows your heart; but I think where your checkbook is, your heart is there also.) Decide where you want your heart to go.

For me, a priority in giving is to give back to the people and ministries that have helped me grow or helped someone in my family. So a part of my giving plan needs to include a thank-you to the Christian radio stations I listen to, the particular ministries I tune into. I also want to make sure that the Christian college I attended sees a piece of the blessing God has given me, as well as the churches that blessed my life during my growing-up years. I also want to remember the Bible-study leaders, pastor, and staff people of parachurch and church ministries that have blessed me or my family.

There are many ways of giving back. For example, I have decided to buy a case of a favorite book to give away as a way of saying thanks, not just to the recipient but to the author! If a sales or service person goes out of his or her way for me, I go out of my way to tell his or her supervisor thanks for the good hire. I e-mail talk shows and recommend Christian authors and speakers. I thank teachers, coaches, and principals as often as I can in as many creative ways as I can think of. Today, take a look back. Who helped mold and shape your walk with God? What resources, institutions, and people do you need to thank this year for building growth into you? Make a list, and decide how and when to encourage those who have so encouraged you.

TO READ
Ephesians 1:15-22

I pray for you constantly, asking God, the glorious Father of our Lord Jesus Christ, to give you spiritual wisdom and understanding, so that you might grow in your knowledge of God. EPHESIANS 1:16-17

Ask Me

What would you like to ask God when you get to heaven? Honestly, if you could ask anything and not be afraid of being zapped, what would you ask?

Write out a list of theological questions for which you'd love to know the answers. Which books of the Bible have you never read or studied? Which theological doctrines do you need to learn more about: eschatology (end times), the person of Christ, the Holy Spirit, baptism, sin, or sanctification?

After you've written a list of questions, go to a Christian bookstore and buy a book that will help you study and learn the answers. You might try asking your pastor what theology books he/she used in seminary or Bible college. You might want to pick up a concordance, Bible dictionary, encyclopedia, church history book, or atlas.

Sometimes these quiet-time journeys of questions can become the basis for entire new ministries if you become a specialist in an area of ministry. Ministries like Christian Financial Concepts, the Institute for Creation Science, and others all began when a person wanted to know what God said about a specific topic.

One of my favorite quiet times was a set of interviews I did with some people who had walked with Jesus for thirty to fifty years. I asked questions like, "Why do you still believe? What has held your faith together all these years?" It was interesting to listen for commonalties. One of them was God's faithfulness to them amidst their questioning.

He's waiting—what do you want to ask?

TO READ
Romans 12:1-3

Don't copy the behavior and customs of this world, but let God transform you into a new person by changing the way you think. Then you will know what God wants you to do, and you will know how good and pleasing and perfect his will really is.

ROMANS 12:2

 ## A Turtle of Change

A woman was walking along the beach when she saw a huge turtle stranded on the sand. She ran to get the ranger, who jumped into his Jeep, drove to the turtle, and hooked one end of a chain around the turtle and the other end to the bumper. Then he gunned the motor and dragged the turtle over the sand. At the edge of the water, the ranger stopped, removed the chain, and heaved the turtle out into the water. She hit the surface with a *splat;* then she shook her head as if she were dazed and dove under the water. As she surfaced, she shook her head once again, swam a few strokes, and then ducked under the waves. She was finally home where she belonged.

Isn't that the way many of us feel when we face change? As we're pulled into new situations and challenges, we're not sure whether the change is going to kill us or be part of God's care for us. Change is uncomfortable— even painful—and we may not be willing to change until the pain of staying where we are (stuck in the sand) becomes greater than the pain it will take to change (the pain of hitting the water).

We may wonder about a woman who stays with a physically abusive spouse year after year, thinking he will eventually change. We may ask why people stay in a job they hate instead of seeking something better. We struggle to understand why some people keep smoking, drinking, or eating the wrong foods long after the doctor has warned them of the health danger. Romans 12:2 tells us not to stay where we are, where the rest of the world is. Instead, we're to be transformed; that is, changed.

Like the turtle, we, too, may feel dazed when we find ourselves in a new environment. But if we keep on swimming, we'll arrive at the place God designed for us. Are you willing to be transformed? Ask God to bring you to the new place he has prepared.

TO READ
Joel 2:12-17

Announce a time of fasting; call the people together for a solemn meeting. JOEL 2:15

 ## Take a Break

Fasting is considered a spiritual discipline. It provides a time to focus on God so he can focus your life. It is a choice to yield your life to God's voice by making a space for him.

"Blessed is the man who does this, the man who holds it fast, who keeps the Sabbath without desecrating it, and keeps his hand from doing any evil" (Isaiah 56:2, NIV).

It isn't just food that can rob our time and our hearts from God. Today's world provides ample opportunity for distractions. Try a unique fast like skipping your favorite TV program, and have a quiet time instead, or take a mental health day and skip the housework and laundry or your normal work routine. Or skip the chocolate, coke, or coffee that seems to have a habitual hold on you.

You might fast from your talk radio or music station in the car as you drive and pray instead. Because I value the discipline that I gain from a fast, I routinely ask myself a few times a year, *Is anything tugging my heart away from God?* or *Is there some action or habit that has taken residence in my life that has a strong command of my time, talent, and thought life?*

Anytime you break the routine and give God the time, he is faithful to meet you there. Which would you like to try: a fast from food, an activity, or a habit?

Use a quiet time this week to try something that will give you a change of discipline.

September

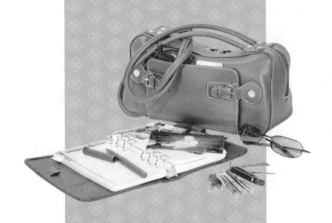

TO READ
John 17:20-26

I have given them the glory you gave me, so that they may be one, as we are—I in them and you in me, all being perfected into one. JOHN 17:22-23

 ## Unity in Heart

Second Chronicles 20:3-4 recounts the story of an invading army. The leader of Israel, Jehoshaphat, was alarmed and went to God for guidance. He also instructed the people to observe a fast, and all the people came together in Jerusalem to pray for help. A serious situation demanded a serious solution.

When Bill and I were looking to move from youth ministry to the senior pastorate, we really had no idea where God wanted us to locate geographically, so we set aside a day to pray and fast.

All day I asked God to simply help me ask the right questions and to help me know what kind of decision-making grid he wanted us to use. As something came to mind, I'd jot it down. By the end of the day I had a list of nearly twenty things we should be looking for in the next ministry location.

When Bill got home from his day, he had his own list, and when we compared them, they were nearly identical! The list helped us greatly because we went from no one really wanting us to many opportunities, and the grid God had impressed upon us became the standard by which we made our choice.

Fasting and praying for unity is a powerful leadership guideline. As you take the time and energy to fast and pray, you are acknowledging a circumstance that is important enough to sacrifice for; thus, it gains seriousness.

Unity is easier to come by when people realize the importance of finding a unified answer.

TO READ
Joel 1:13-15

Announce a time of fasting; call the people together for a solemn meeting. Bring the leaders and all the people into the Temple of the Lord your God, and cry out to him there. JOEL 1:14

 God Gets Your Attention

Fasting is almost a lost discipline. Either people treat it as some legalistic strong-arm technique to get God to grant their petition, or it is connected only to health issues like purifying one's body.

The most encouraging benefit of fasting is sometimes overlooked because it is so simple. Fasting changes my pace, my focus, and my heart so I can have more time and fewer distractions. A fast buys me quality time with God.

In *Greater Health God's Way,* author Stormie Omartian notes that over eighty verses in the Bible refer to fasting. One particularly interesting to me is, "The kind of fasting I want calls you to free those who are wrongly imprisoned and to stop oppressing those who work for you" (Isaiah 58:6).

When Jesus sent out the disciples two by two, they came back frustrated that they couldn't achieve the miracles that people needed in order to set them free. Jesus gently reminded them that "these come with prayer and fasting."

Fasting has a strong side benefit: God gets your attention. Most of the kings of Israel proclaimed a fast for one reason or another:

- He remained faithful to the Lord in everything, and he carefully obeyed all the commands the Lord had given Moses. (2 Kings 18:6)
- Jehoshaphat was alarmed by this news and sought the Lord for guidance. He also gave orders that everyone throughout Judah should observe a fast. (2 Chronicles 20:3)
- And there by the Ahava Canal, I gave orders for all of us to fast and humble ourselves before our God. We prayed that he would give us a safe journey and protect us, our children, and our goods as we traveled. (Ezra 8:21)

If you need more direction or need to repent or draw close to God, try fasting, and God will get your attention.

TO READ
James 1:21-27

Pure and lasting religion in the sight of God our Father means that we must care for orphans and widows in their troubles, and refuse to let the world corrupt us. JAMES 1:27

 It's What's Inside That Counts

There's a section of scripture that is like being thrown into an ice-cold lake on a windy day—it gets your attention. It is so easy to fall into "spiritual" autopilot. Here are some signs from Isaiah 58:2-5:

> For day after day they seek me out; they seem eager to know my ways, as if they were a nation that does what is right and has not forsaken the commands of its God. They ask me for just decisions and seem eager for God to come near them. "Why have we fasted," they say, "and you have not seen it? Why have we humbled ourselves, and you have not noticed?"
>
> Yet on the day of your fasting, you do as you please and exploit all your workers. Your fasting ends in quarreling and strife, and in striking each other with wicked fists. You cannot fast as you do today and expect your voice to be heard on high. . . . Is that what you call a fast, a day acceptable to the Lord? (NIV)

Then God goes on to describe what "real" spirituality looks like: "Is not this the kind of fasting I have chosen: to loose the chains of injustice and untie the cords of the yoke, to set the oppressed free and break every yoke? Is it not to share your food with the hungry and to provide the poor wanderer with shelter—when you see the naked, to clothe him, and not to turn away from your own flesh and blood?" (vv. 6-7, NIV).

Then God shares the impact "real" spirituality will have on your own life: "Your light will break forth like the dawn, and your healing will quickly appear; then your righteousness will go before you, and the glory of the Lord will be your rear guard. Then you will call, and the Lord will answer" (vv. 8-9, NIV).

Are you "real"?

TO READ
Revelation 7:9-12

After this I saw a vast crowd, too great to count, from every nation and tribe and people and language, standing in front of the throne and before the Lamb. They were clothed in white and held palm branches in their hands. REVELATION 7:9

Point of View

Sometimes all we need for a fresh point of view is to look at our Christian faith through the eyes of someone from another language or culture.

I have several friends who serve as Bible translators. I love to hear them explain the process of translation. The missionary will enter a new language area, then ask someone to be a language guide. It is often comical or poignant as the two try to communicate to find the exact translation of a word in the Bible in the new language.

Lon and Leah Knival work in the Interi tribe in Papua, New Guinea. When translating the parable of the sower, they were looking for the best word for good soil. Their language guide took them to a place and showed them deep, rich soil that had been formed through the decay of the best trees. It was "mulchy" soil. In that tribe a heart that was good and ready to grow before God would most closely resemble a compost pile!

My heart has also been renewed when I have visited churches from other cultures. I have been inspired by one friend, a professor who works with international students in the Los Angeles area. He and his wife at one time had to flee a murderous communist regime in their home country of Eritrea, Africa. He began a church for refugees of that area who had fled to the "safety" of Los Angeles. Even though I understood very few words during their worship service, I was lifted to the throne of God by their music and their humble servant attitudes. I have been deeply moved in a Chinese church, an inner-city church, a rescue mission, and a campground church.

If your quiet time is becoming a little stale, step out of your comfort zone to get a new point of view where the language, culture, or worship may be unfamiliar—but the God is very, very familiar!

TO READ
Psalm 119:9-16

I will delight in your principles and not forget your word. PSALM 119:16

✳ *Post It*

Bring God's Word to your world: Design a screen saver that builds your devotional life, or scan in your favorite photo. Then choose a favorite verse, and push Print. You will have a poster to encourage you in your walk with the Lord!

We captured each of our three boys participating in their favorite sport, had them choose a verse to go with the picture, then had the whole thing enlarged. So now they have an inspirational poster in living color on their wall.

In Deuteronomy 11:18-21 God encourages us to "commit yourselves completely to these words of mine. Tie them to your hands as a reminder, and wear them on your forehead. Teach them to your children. Talk about them when you are at home and when you are away on a journey, when you are lying down and when you are getting up again. Write them on the doorposts of your house and on your gates, so that as long as the sky remains above the earth, you and your children may flourish in the land the Lord swore to give your ancestors."

I think personal computers are today's equivalent of writing on the doorposts and gates. There are so many ways to use technology and computers for encouragement and growth from God's Word.

For a fun quiet time, check out a high-tech store, and see what high-tech equipment is available to help you keep connected to God. One of my recent Christmas presents was an electronic Bible. It is handy to tuck into my purse, briefcase, or suitcase so I can have quiet times on the go!

Let the rivers clap their hands in glee! Let the hills sing out their songs of joy. PSALM 98:8

Splurge

Sometimes I feel like splurging on my relationship with God. I escape to a friend's garden, or I bring out the best china and have hand-dipped chocolates or fresh homemade scones with specialty teas as I sit and take in precious gems from God's Word. Or we curl up together, I in a window seat cushioned with pillows, and God enthroned on high.

Since my relationship with God is vital to all the rest of my life, I don't like to shortchange my special times with him. I regularly look for an extra day to spend in solitude at a cozy mountain cabin, prayer in an art gallery, or reading devotional books poolside.

Although always on a budget, I have looked for ways to make my time with God special, out of the ordinary. At times I want my relationship with God to be white linen, crystal, rose petals, and lace. If I have to trim in other areas to splurge with God, I will—that relationship deserves the best.

Find a garden, take your favorite journal, drawing pad, paints, or handwork. Sit quietly and take in just a tiny glimpse of what could have been before Eve ate the forbidden fruit. Try to express back to God your thanks that even though sin entered the world in the Garden, God redeemed humanity.

God is the creator, and since you are made in his image, try some creativity in his presence: Try to create a wonderful poem, photograph, painting, or sculpture.

TO READ
Psalm 51:1-4

Wash me clean from my guilt. Purify me from my sin. PSALM 51:2

 ## *Crystal Clear*

One day I pulled a crystal glass out of my dishwasher and went to fill it with water. I was so thirsty; I had been exercising, and my throat was dry. I filled it to the brim with crystal-clear drinking water from the refrigerator and lifted it to my lips. Just as I was about to take a big refreshing gulp, I spotted food particles crusted on the inside of the glass. I tossed the water down the drain and went for a clean glass.

I had just been reading 2 Timothy in my quiet time, and I immediately remembered this passage: "If you keep yourself pure, you will be a utensil God can use for his purpose. Your life will be clean, and you will be ready for the Master to use you for every good work" (2 Timothy 2:21).

I thought long and hard about that glass. Now years later, when I am tempted to sin and I want to harbor it, keep the sin secret, or justify it, I remember the glass.

Sin is like that. Jesus was so serious about dealing with sin that he said that if part of our body causes us to sin, we should cut it off or gouge it out. A part of our body gone is better than going to hell (Matthew 5:29-30). Sin makes us dirty, and Jesus calls us to get rid of it in no uncertain terms.

If I drink from a glass with debris in it, I am repulsed, sick to my stomach. So I ask myself, *When I see sin in myself, do I feel the same way?*

I'm not trying to live in condemnation, but rather I want to clean the glass and become beautiful crystal again!

TO READ
Psalm 43:1-4

Send out your light and your truth; let them guide me. Psalm 43:3

 Choosing

I was at a *Chosen Women* stadium event where Anne Graham Lotz had been scheduled to speak a year or more ahead. That evening she brought her daughter to the podium and introduced her to the nearly thirty-five thousand women.

Anne and her daughter had had a scheduling dilemma to solve. Mom had been scheduled to speak the same night her daughter was to graduate from Baylor University. As they shared how they had prayed and weighed the decision, the women in the stadium rose to their feet and gave the daughter a standing ovation. Her graduation would have been memorable, no doubt, but not as memorable as a stadium packed with women standing to their feet spontaneously and giving *her* a standing ovation!

There are times when your calling, your family's needs, and many other responsibilities will not fall into perfect order or timing. You will have to make some tough choices. How do you make those choices?

Pray: Ask God to give you a listening heart and observant spirit. Ask God to pull back the curtain of heaven and give your heart and spirit a glimpse of his priorities.

Listen: Talk with your children, your spouse, and your family. Try to listen without lobbying one way or another. Try to read between their emotional lines.

Research: Find out as much detail as you can about all the options. Things that don't seem to be possible sometimes become possible as you gain more information. Or, at other times you will realize that one or the other is more important.

TO READ	He is so rich in kindness that he purchased our freedom through the blood of his Son, and our sins are forgiven. EPHESIANS 1:7
Ephesians 1:3-14	

 ## *Going Back to Move Forward*

As I look back on my life, I can see where the roots of perfectionism were planted. Once when I brought home my seventh-grade report card, it included six 100 percent grades and one 99.9 percent. My dad had been drinking, so "Jack Daniels" said through my dad, "Pam, why isn't that a 100 percent?" I remember wondering if I would ever be good enough to earn his love.

When I was eight, almost nine, the pastor of our small church asked if anyone in my Sunday school class wanted to learn more about Jesus. In the class we learned much about who Jesus was, and we also had an opportunity to gain a place on a quiz team. Now, because I always wanted to achieve, I wanted a place on that team! I could just see myself, like a contestant on *Hollywood Squares,* up on that podium, answering those questions. But to gain a spot on the team, I had to memorize Matthew 5, 6, and 7.

While reading Matthew, I came across the verse "Everyone who asks, receives. Everyone who seeks, finds. And the door is opened to everyone who knocks" (Matthew 7:8).

I thought, *Does this mean that if I ask you to come into my life, Jesus, that you'll do it?* And there, sitting on my bed, I bowed my head and prayed, asking Jesus to come into my life to be my Savior, Lord, and best friend. I believe he met me there that day.

I felt free and loved unconditionally for the first time in my life. The next day was Sunday, and as was tradition, my pastor gave anyone who wanted an opportunity to come forward for prayer. I was crying. I remember my pastor asking me, "What's wrong, Pam?" I answered him, "I am so happy!"

That was the first day I remember crying tears of joy. Up until meeting Christ, my tears had been caused by feelings of failure; now, they were feelings of freedom.

TO READ
Matthew 19:16-24

Jesus told him, "If you want to be perfect, go and sell all you have and give the money to the poor, and you will have treasure in heaven. Then come, follow me." MATTHEW 19:21

 What Can You Let Go Of?

On my mirror is a reminder, a quote by Bernadette Devlin: "To gain that which is worth having, it may be necessary to lose everything else."

To achieve the goals of highest priority, I might need to let go of some things I treasure. Dr. Dean Ornish, a leader in the treatment and prevention of heart disease, was himself struggling with some life choices about career opportunities that were presenting themselves.

A friend said to him, "If you are swimming in the ocean and someone offers you a great big bag of gold—a golden opportunity—and you take that bag and hold on to it, you will drown. Are you going to hold on to something that will keep you from what most nourishes your soul? Either you let go now, or you become a slave to the very thing you created and it tells you how to live."[1]

Reflecting on this conversation, Dr. Ornish writes: "When my self worth was defined by what I did, then I had to take every important opportunity that came along, even if a relationship suffered. Now I understand that real power is measured not by how much you have but by how much *you can walk away from*"[2] (emphasis added).

What do you need to walk away from in order to most obediently walk the path God has for you?

TO READ
1 Timothy 2:1-7

This is good and pleases God our Savior, for he wants everyone to be saved and to understand the truth. 1 TIMOTHY 2:3-4

 ## Saved for Something

Walter and Matilda had an epic love story! He felt called to missions, and his father disowned him when he left the family business to follow God's call. He went to America ahead of his wife and children. He booked passage for his family on the safest vessel of the day, the *Titanic*. However, Matilda missed her husband so desperately that she changed the travel arrangements. The family set sail two weeks earlier than expected on a different ship!

Walter and Matilda's daughter, Helen, just a child herself, couldn't help but notice the providence of God as she heard the newspaper boy shout, "Extra! Extra! *Titanic* Sinks!" Matilda's love for her husband helped save her family. Helen felt God's hand of providence on her life. She was saved for a reason. As a teen she began Vacation Bible Schools in rural communities. Then she went on to marry and founded Christian Business Women's Clubs, which helped fund pastors for rural churches. Then small group Bible studies formed all across the nation.

This ministry, Stonecroft Ministries, has more than sixteen hundred local representatives, and more than fourteen thousand people are involved in various forms of leadership. The work of Stonecroft Ministries reaches all fifty states. In addition, there are sixty-one foreign countries using Friendship Bible Coffees and outreach meetings. In Friendship Bible Coffees alone, there are more than thirty-six hundred involved in leadership.

The hand of providence has been on you, too. Reflect on this question: What have you been saved from? Repeating the pattern of your parents? A tragic accident?

God saved you for a purpose greater than yourself.

TO READ
Proverbs 24:23-27

It is an honor to receive an honest reply.

PROVERBS 24:26

 Get Real

It's hard to be real. We would much prefer that our success be rehearsed, scripted, and airbrushed. I want my sons to say just the right thing when introduced to important people, and I'd love to always sound profound and quotable. No one really likes to look or feel stupid. I wish every day was a good hair day and that I could keep the wisdom I have at forty but have the body I had at twenty. *Get real!*

I force myself to be real. I *do* open the front door when the doorbell rings even if the boys have just walked out with friends and forgotten to pick up the fast-food bags off the living-room table. I go to the grocery store *without* makeup, knowing full well that I might see people I know. I admit mistakes, flaws, foibles, and fears. Why?

It's exhausting to try to be perfect! It's too much work to always wonder what everyone's thinking about me. I love what Patsy Clairmont says: "We'd worry less about what people thought of us if we realized how very little they do!"

In the Old Testament one of the definitions for *honest* is "straightforward." I love that picture because it means I am not going out of my way to present myself as something I am not.

Living straightforwardly saves time, energy, and worry. Once, while working on a writing deadline, I walked out of my home office and into a living room that was a wreck. It was summer, and the guys had everything they owned out! I thought, *What would my readers think if they saw my house right now?* Then I thought, *They'd think I was a real mom with a real deadline and a real life—get over it, Pam!*

TO READ
Luke 15:1-7

Tax collectors and other notorious sinners often came to listen to Jesus teach. LUKE 15:1

All Different? All the Same?

Look around your world. Does everyone look like you? Does everyone not only carry the party line but also hold it? Are you surrounded by yes-men and women? Is everyone in a similar tax bracket? Are your social circles the same year after year? Are all your friends your age and stage of life? There is a danger in this.

Variety in relationships will safeguard your success. Diversity in dialogue will protect your ability to think clearly. Looking at an issue or idea from all angles protects your future.

Of course, your closest friends will likely carry similar backgrounds and beliefs, but it is wise and biblical to expand your relationship circle.

Jesus didn't just hang out with the priests. They weren't his buddies, and their hypocrisy made him angry, but he still engaged them in conversation.

In heaven all types of people will be there. Revelation 5:9 describes the scene: "You are worthy to take the scroll and break its seals and open it. For you were killed, and your blood has ransomed people for God from every tribe and language and people and nation."

Yes, it benefits us to hang out with those who are different than we are. Having a single woman edit my women's books helps me reach a broader audience. Having friends of all races keeps me sensitive to their faith needs or traditions. Having friends in all denominations makes me think through my theology. Having friends of all ages and stages helps better prepare me for life's journey as well as keeps me relevant to a changing culture.

Do you need to make a few more new and unique friends?

TO READ
Colossians 4:2-6

Live wisely among those who are not Christians, and make the most of every opportunity.

COLOSSIANS 4:5

 ## *Rights and Responsibility*

Have you ever wondered why child stars, given every privilege, turn to drugs, alcohol, and sex, often derailing their careers? Have you been shocked when you hear a pop star or pro athlete with outrageous behaviors say, "Don't look at me as a role model!"

Because of their fame, they already are role models—bad ones! After reading and watching celebrity interviews, I have found there seems to be a reoccurring theme: "I have my rights."

However, there is only one right (that I can find) listed in the Bible: "But to all who believed him and accepted him, he gave the right to become children of God" (John 1:12).

With rights there is always responsibility. Servicemen didn't shed their blood and lay down their lives for people's "right" to sin and be selfish. With success comes a challenge from God to be selfless and to focus on the greater good and higher goal.

A friend who is also a pastor said to me in a discussion on this topic, "I was taught the farther up the ladder you go, the fewer options you have." He was saying that we have to think of others, not ourselves, so our options narrow.

Success brings the responsibility to give back to the people and community that helped train and equip you. Success brings a responsibility to be available, especially to those who made themselves available to you all along the way. Success brings the responsibility to be a good role model, rather than a poor one.

TO READ
Isaiah 57:12-14

Rebuild the road! Clear away the rocks and stones so my people can return from captivity. ISAIAH 57:14

 ## *Oh! That's Why!*

There is an observable pattern in those who suffered trauma as children—the death of a parent; physical, sexual, or emotional abuse; or witnessing a horror, etc. These people, as parents, tend to feel excessive stress and anxiety. They may be overprotective or even make irrational, overstated choices and actions as their children, especially their oldest child, approach the age that was most traumatic in their own lives.

For example, Kara was sexually abused by an uncle when she was nine, so when her daughter approached nine, she didn't want to let her out of her sight. She wanted to pull her out of private school and homeschool her. She wouldn't let her visit friends' homes or go on field trips without her. She stayed through every gymnastics lesson—her daughter was never out of her sight. Was her daughter physically safe? Yes. Was she emotionally safe? Not really. Kara's daughter felt controlled and overprotected. She began sneaking out of sight at parks and playgrounds. Her mom's "control" from her own insecurity and pain was actually putting her daughter at a higher risk.

Ephesians 4:27 says, "Do not give the devil a foothold" (NIV). When you do not deal with the issues of your past, you give Satan space to work. If you suffered trauma as a child, seek professional help *before* your oldest child is anywhere close to the age you were when the trauma happened to you. You'll feel better—but so will your children!

The Lord your God is a devouring fire, a jealous God. DEUTERONOMY 4:24

 Caller over the Calling

Os Guinness, in his book *The Call,* says, "We are not primarily called to do something [such as motherhood, politics, or teaching] or go somewhere [such as the inner city or Outer Mongolia]; we are called to Someone [God]."[3] Further, he says, "There is no calling unless there is a Caller."[4]

Romans 1:6-7 clearly supports our call to the *person* of God: "You are among those who have been called to belong to Jesus Christ, dear friends in Rome. God loves you dearly, and he has called you to be his very own people." *You are called!*

In seeking to live out our calling, we can forget that the best way to do so is to stay connected to the Caller—God. How can you know if your perspective is shifting from Caller to calling?

Quiet-time priority: Your personal alone time with God will begin to suffer if your calling takes priority over the Caller. The task will become more important than the relationship.

Revolving-door relationships: If the call is getting top billing, you will begin to be irritated by those calling you back to the Caller, Jesus Christ. You will begin avoiding your most spiritual friends, perhaps replacing people who might point out your pattern of drifting from faith or God. You might spend less time at home, less time with long-time friends, and more time with newer or shallower people.

God is the lover of your soul. He wants time with you. He should be more important than what he called you to do.

> **TO READ**
> Ephesians 5:1-9

Live a life filled with love for others, following the example of Christ, who loved you and gave himself as a sacrifice to take away your sins. EPHESIANS 5:2

 ## *The Five Senses*

Use your five senses to make the sights, sounds, smells, tastes, and textures of the Bible real to you.

Look through the Bible and note the smells, like Jesus being called "the Rose of Sharon."

Gather up a few tasty treats from the Song of Solomon, and then buy a recording of Hebrew music.

Create a night to remember by renting a travel video of the Holy Land, or watch the slide show of a friend who has been there. Create a whole evening using the sights and sounds of Israel.

I have a crown of thorns placed high on my favorite bookshelf as a reminder of the price Christ paid for me. This visual reminder in such a prominent place helps me carry that picture wherever I go.

I have a list going of things I'd love to have that would be similar reminders, like an alabaster vial with perfume in it. The verses that describe the woman who broke her costly vial of perfume, valued at over a year's salary, because of her deep appreciation of Christ's work in her life always moves me to tears because I feel the same.

Ephesians 5:2 reminds me that Jesus was broken and his blood spilled, and it captures my heart. What captures yours?

You are my flock, the sheep of my pasture. You are my people, and I am your God, says the Sovereign Lord. EZEKIEL 34:31

 ## *Your God*

On the flyleaf of the Bibles I gave my children, I wrote a personal inscription that includes a story from the life of Anne Graham Lotz, daughter of world-famous evangelist Billy Graham.

The story tells of a time in Anne's youth when she was struggling with her faith, and a wise youth leader said to her, "You have been looking at God through a prism; your mom's, your dad's, and the church's expectations color your view of God. Look at God for yourself. Go on with God."

Have you been looking at God through someone else's eyes? You may need to get out of your comfort zone so you can own your faith.

Join a Bible-study group that doesn't use any books or guides, just God's Word.

Go on a missions trip, and trust God to use you in a new way.

Pitch a tent in the middle of nowhere, and take some time alone with God in nature. Take food and a map, and your spiritual food and map: a Bible, a journal, and a pen. Matthew 4:1 (NIV) says that "Jesus was led by the Spirit into the desert" before his ministry started. It seems that even the Son of God needed his own alone time with God, not more time with the scribes and Pharisees.

Don't borrow someone else's beliefs and experiences with God—get your own.

TO READ
Psalm 34:8-14

Taste and see that the Lord is good. Oh, the joys of those who trust in him! PSALM 34:8

 Younger Eyes

Read the Bible through the eyes of a teen to refresh your relationship with God. Mark it up to give as a gift to mark a special event.

An appropriate event might be entering high school, graduation from high school, leaving for college, starting a new job, moving into a new apartment, or beginning a marriage. Mark verses that you think would encourage or strengthen your son or daughter.

Try to remember which verses helped you choose a career or a spouse or make a transition in your life. In the flyleaf of my Bible I have headings: *Trust Your Abilities, Keep God's Priorities, Keep Your Word, Have Courage* or *Make Decisions*. Each heading has a set of verses I found helpful in those areas.

Also use this as a time to train the young person in some Bible study skills by writing activities or suggesting studies as you write in the margin.

In the book of Ruth I titled each chapter:

- Chapter 1: Excellent Statement (Underline the key verses in this chapter.)
- Chapter 2: Excellent Woman (Mark each place that shows how and why Ruth was such a great woman.)
- Chapter 3: Excellent Plan (Look up the culture of Israel during this time [I suggested several resources]. How does knowing the background and culture help you understand why Naomi had a good plan in sending Ruth to Boaz at the threshing floor?)
- Chapter 4: Excellent Man (What is Boaz doing here, and how does this show he was a good, trustworthy man ready for the responsibility of marriage?)
- Excellent Ending: (What does this show you about seeking and following God's will?)

As I read and wrote prompts in my son's Bible, I found that totally different verses encouraged me. Do you need a totally new look at God?

TO READ
Luke 2:41-49

He said to them, "Why did you seek Me? Did you not know that I must be about My Father's business?" LUKE 2:49, NKJV

 ## *My Dad's Biz*

I don't attend many home sales parties. It's not because I don't enjoy the products—I do. And it's not because I don't enjoy the company of friends—I do. It's because there's only so much time in the day, and I sometimes have to make hard choices, just like you.

I look for ways to spend time with people who may not know Christ. I try to serve in my community. But when I make hard choices about my schedule, I try to think like twelve-year-old Jesus, who was sitting in the Temple dialoging with the priests for so long that his ride home left! Jesus' parents didn't understand his priorities, and sometimes ours are misunderstood.

His parents and their entire large family had been to the Temple to make a sacrifice. Mary and Joseph thought Jesus was with other family members and were a day's journey away before they realized he was not with them.

Mom and Dad went back, and after he had been missing for three days, they found him in the Temple, conversing with the priests so intensely that the Bible says Jesus was "astonishing" them.

Mom and Dad were not impressed! When they confronted him, Jesus responded, "Why did you seek Me? Did you not know that I must be about my Father's business?" (Luke 2:49, NKJV)

Whose business is coming first? Yours? Someone else's? God's? Will you choose God's priorities for you even if you are misunderstood?

| TO READ | And I, the Son of Man, have come to seek and save those like him who are lost. LUKE 19:10 |
| Luke 19:1-10 | |

On a Mission

We, Bill and Pam Farrel, have a desire to fulfill the great commission through using our skills in professional ministry, with a focus of using the communication gifts God has given us. We are committed to personal discipleship as a lifestyle. We want our home to be an oasis where those who enter can see Christ at work in our marriage and family and where they can find hope. We, the Farrels, are committed to fun and friendships. We value people more than things. We prefer memories over material goods. We are committed to raise our children in such a way that they have the opportunity to know the benefits of personally knowing Jesus and walking with Him. We are committed to helping them discover their talents and equipping them to help fulfill the Great Commission and to have fun and a fulfilling life while doing so.

This mission statement serves as a grid in our decision making.

Dr. Archibald Hart says, "We have to be firm with those who would clutter up our lives with trivia. We must be clear about our own priorities so we can make good decisions about what we will and will not do."[5]

To start writing a mission statement, list the four to six core values that are most important to you. Look at our mission statement again. Notice some priorities? Fun, relationships, and the great commission are some of the obvious ones.

Lillian Dickenson said, "Life is a coin. You can spend it anyway you wish, but you can spend it only once."[6]

A mission statement narrows your scope and gives permission for your passion and purpose.

When you obey me, you remain in my love, just as I obey my Father and remain in his love. JOHN 15:10

 The Slippery Slope

In my twenty-plus years in ministry, I have seen the slippery slope in many a woman's life. She didn't "mean" to have an affair. She didn't think a few glasses of wine would lead her to alcoholism. She didn't think working those few extra minutes would turn into a few extra hours that would turn into her feeling alienated from her husband and children and make her a virtual stranger in her own home. She didn't think buying that purse, that outfit, that makeup was any big deal. She rationalized, *I work hard, I earned it!* Then she found herself with more month than money at the end of the month and headed straight for bankruptcy.

It starts so subtly. A rationalization. An "I can handle it" attitude. *I'll just date the unbeliever once. It's just for coffee.* Then it turns into *Maybe if I go out for dinner, I can talk to him about God.* Then the date turns into a second date, and there is less and less God talk—in fact, less talk at all. Your heart gets hooked, and you start picking and choosing what verses you read in the Bible, definitely avoiding the "Don't team up with those who are unbelievers" sections. Kissing turns into more than kissing, and as time passes, you think, *I am the only one that can reach him. If I don't stay in his life, he will be lonely and forever lost.* You try to replace Jesus as the Savior, and you take on that role, thinking that your love for this man will be his saving grace. You begin to feel that you can't live without him—yet you are now essentially living without Christ. Christ may be "in" your life, but you have tried to guide his hands and do the work that only the Holy Spirit can do.

Are you rationalizing? Are you telling yourself, *I can handle it. It won't affect me!* Is there a still, small voice whispering to you today? *Obey it.*

TO READ
2 Corinthians 9:1-8

You must each make up your own mind as to how much you should give. Don't give reluctantly or in response to pressure. For God loves the person who gives cheerfully. 2 CORINTHIANS 9:7

 ## Promises, Promises

One man committed to God to give a certain percentage of his income for as long as he lived. From his first week's pay he gave one dollar to the Lord. Soon his weekly offering had increased to ten dollars. As time went on, he continued to prosper. Before long he was giving a hundred dollars a week, then two hundred, and in time, five hundred dollars a week.

This process started out as an intense joy because this man felt his hard work was making life better for many people. But after a while he found himself in conflict. He began to think this was his money and that he shouldn't be giving away so much. Finally he called a close friend.

"Please come and see me," he said. "You remember the promise I made to God years ago? How can I get released? When I made the promise, I only had to give a dollar, but now it's five hundred dollars. I can't afford to give away money like that."

His wise friend said, "I'm afraid you cannot get a release from the promise, but there is something we can do. We can kneel down and ask God to shrink your income so that you can afford to give a dollar again."

God deserves the best. First Chronicles 16:29 explains: "Give to the Lord the glory he deserves! Bring your offering and come to worship him. Worship the Lord in all his holy splendor."

Has God blessed you? Have you asked God how he might use you to bless others?

"Lord, you gave me everything. All of what I have is really yours. How do you want me to best use it?"

TO READ
1 Peter 2:18-25

God is pleased with you when, for the sake of your conscience, you patiently endure unfair treatment.

1 PETER 2:19

 ## *Adversity Defines You!*

Mary McLeod Bethune was the fifteenth of seventeen children born to her parents, two freed slaves. Mary worked in the cotton fields as a child, but she received a scholarship to the Moody Institute for Home and Foreign Missions in Chicago (later the Moody Bible Institute), where she was the only black student.

She dreamed of going to Africa to minister to the needs of her ancestors but was told that there were "no openings for Negro missionaries in Africa."

But often it is our response to obstacles and setbacks that most defines us. Instead of being discouraged, Mary became an assistant teacher and then received an appointment to the Haines Institute in Augusta, Georgia. She married, had a son, and continued her mission work by starting a school, where she stayed for five years. Then, with the encouragement of a pastor, she started the Daytona Literary and Industrial Training School for Negro Girls.

For the next twenty years Mary divided her time between making the school a success and stepping into public leadership. She led a drive to register black voters (and was "visited" by members of the Ku Klux Klan for her efforts). She organized a movement against school segregation and served under several U.S. presidents, including Franklin D. Roosevelt.

Over the years the school she had founded grew to include a high school and then a junior college, which finally merged with a men's college to become Bethune-Cookman College, the name by which we know it today.[7]

TO READ
Isaiah 7:1-9

Say to him, "Be careful, keep calm and don't be afraid. Do not lose heart." ISAIAH 7:4, NIV

 ## Changing the Changes

Hormones do impact our lives. Menstruation, PMS, and pregnancy can throw us for a loop. Then we can anticipate another hormonal shift—menopause!

Sally Conway, in her book *Menopause,* encourages women that they are not alone if they feel unstable, out of kilter, or not themselves. She penned the following note about her feelings in a journal: "Lack of concentration/ short attention span. Thoughts come and go; jump in and out. Seem urgent at the time; then quickly forget. Remember again. And seem urgent once more. . . . Paranoia—uncertain and then certain about particular fears and suspicions. Then uncertain again."[8]

I knew Sally during her menopausal years, and even though she may have been feeling uncertain, emotionally unstable, and fearful, she didn't give in to the fears. If you are feeling you are losing your mind (or your memory), or perhaps your mother or sister is struggling with "the change," what helps change the changes for the better?

Get good information: The verse that says, "The truth will set you free" reaches into menopause! Read up on the best medical research, attend seminars, and talk to doctors and specialists in the whole health field (nutrition, psychology, etc.).

Get God in the middle of it: Anytime you are feeling anxious, mindless, fearful, or any other myriads of emotions, ask God to help you.

Get friends and family informed: Don't let biological changes make permanent changes in your relationships. Let them know what's going on and how they can help.

TO READ
Proverbs 17:1-6

A dry crust eaten in peace is better than a great feast with strife. PROVERBS 17:1

 Day 21

Susan Lark, M.D., notes that up to 90 percent of premenopausal women suffer from at least one of the 150 symptoms that define PMS, and up to 10 percent of them have symptoms severe enough to hamper their ability to function normally. "The all-too-familiar symptoms include headaches, depression, moodiness, fatigue, breast tenderness, fluid retention, back-ache, cramps, acne, weight gain, swelling, constipation, allergies and joint pain.[9] So do we use PMS as an excuse to get us out of work, sex, house-work, or pumping our own gas? Well, we can hardly go that far since "at the 1976 Olympics an American swimmer won three gold medals and broke a world record while at the height of her period."[10] I have to admit that I have toyed with the idea that since PMS is followed by menses, maybe I have the right to be pathetic for ten to fourteen days each month. The only problem is, I don't want to be pathetic half my life.

After the birth of our second child, Bill noticed that I seemed to have a pattern of some negative emotions. I regularly became irritable, panicked, bossy, and cynical. On those days Bill could do no right, and the world seemed on the edge of doom. Either I tried to control everything, or I fell into a mild depression. Bill began to mark down the worst days for me, and after a few months he noticed that day twenty-one was my worst day. So I planned a lighter schedule on days twenty, twenty-one, and twenty-two. I tried not to make snap decisions on those days. I set aside time to exercise and rest.

Mark up your calendar for a few months. There may be some days *not* to argue, *not* to get on your children's case, and *not* to react to a friend.

God is more powerful than PMS, and by his grace, we can deal with those difficult days.

TO READ
Psalm 90:1-6, 12-17

Teach us to make the most of our time, so that we may grow in wisdom. Psalm 90:12

 Nothing to Show for It

Nearly 40 percent of people say they *feel* rushed.[11] In a study of time journals, where people wrote down how they actually spent their time, overall leisure time had increased. However, it was usually in smaller increments, so nearly all of the time went into watching TV.[12] Television may be the main reason many of us don't feel like we have any more free time than before because we have nothing tangible to show for it.

One of my seminary professors who had written numerous books was asked one day in class, "Professor, you are so prolific. I know you have a family, you teach here, and you are in the pastorate. How in the world do you find time to write?"

He explained that he used the time most people waste. Most meetings happen between seven and nine, and most family activities are between six and nine. It was the time between nine and midnight that he made use of. Then he added, "And I don't have a TV."

Productive people make use of every spare minute: Time spent waiting for a child can be used for reading a devotional or catching up on phone calls; time not spent playing video games or watching a movie or TV can be used to pray with a child, prepare the grocery list, clean out a drawer, or, as in the professor's case, write a book.

The Bible has more than over twenty references to a "moment," which is just an instant or short piece of time. If a moment is important to God, then it can be important to us.

What can you do to prepare to use those "few minutes" well?

TO READ
Ecclesiastes 12:9-14

Here is my final conclusion: Fear God and obey his commands, for this is the duty of every person. God will judge us for everything we do, including every secret thing, whether good or bad.

ECCLESIASTES 12:13-14

The Middle

After you live life for a while and have time to reflect, it is easy to fall into the "nothing's worth it" syndrome. We see King Solomon at this place. He sums up his disgust at life in Ecclesiastes 2:11: "Then I looked on all the works that my hands had wrought, and on the labour that I had laboured to do: and, behold, all was vanity and vexation of spirit, and there was no profit under the sun" (KJV).

This attitude of giving up hit all areas of his life:

- *Work doesn't feel worth it.* "Therefore I hated life; because the work that is wrought under the sun is grievous unto me: for all is vanity and vexation of spirit" (Ecclesiastes 2:17, KJV).
- *Having people feel you are wise and having them want your counsel and opinion—doesn't feel worth it.* "And who knoweth whether he shall be a wise man or a fool? . . . and wherein I have shewed myself wise under the sun. This is also vanity" (v. 19, KJV).
- *Having wealth doesn't feel worth it.* "He that loveth silver shall not be satisfied with silver; nor he that loveth abundance with increase: this is also vanity" (5:10, KJV).
- *Never wanting for a thing, having everything you want anytime you want, doesn't feel worth it.* "A man to whom God hath given riches, wealth, and honour, so that he wanteth nothing for his soul of all that he desireth . . . this is vanity, and it is an evil disease" (6:2, KJV).
- *Even being young doesn't feel worth it.* "Therefore remove sorrow from thy heart . . . for childhood and youth are vanity" (11:10, KJV).

Is anything "worth it" to Solomon? Can midlife disillusionment turn positive? Actually, yes, Solomon says, "Fearing God," that's the difference.

TO READ
Psalm 26:4-8

I do not spend time with liars or go along with hypocrites. I hate the gatherings of those who do evil, and I refuse to join in with the wicked.

PSALM 26:4-5

 ## What Time Is It?

We spend six years eating, one year searching for our belongings, eight months opening junk mail, and four years doing housework![13] (Only four years?) In total, our personal care and travel (mostly back and forth to work) take up half of our lives![14]

So what do we do with the rest of our time? I know what I don't want to do!

- *Life is too short to carry bitterness.* "I can see that you are full of bitterness and held captive by sin" (Acts 8:23).
- *Life is too short for revenge.* "Dear friends, never avenge yourselves. Leave that to God. For it is written, 'I will take vengeance; I will repay those who deserve it,' says the Lord" (Romans 12:19).
- *Life is too short for needless arguments.* "Again I say, don't get involved in foolish, ignorant arguments that only start fights" (2 Timothy 2:23).
- *Life is too short for sin.* "These evil desires lead to evil actions, and evil actions lead to death" (James 1:15).

Make a list of how you will *not* spend your time, and you might find you gain some time.

All your words are true; all your just laws will stand forever. PSALM 119:160

 It's True!

In recent years there has been an attack on the Bible. One group even gathered together and used colored beads to vote on whether the words of Jesus were actually the words of Jesus. Different colors meant different votes like yes, probably, maybe, and no!

While we need to have relevant and accurate evidence for our faith, when we don't act on the information already given to us, it actually erodes our faith. For example, some schools of thought say that God's Word is truth only as it has meaning for me. This can be dangerous thinking because it becomes easy to ignore whole sections of Scripture. Even worse, you don't want them to have meaning because you don't want to obey them.

God's Word is inerrant. "Inerrancy means that when all the facts are known, the Scriptures in their original autographs, properly interpreted, will be shown to be wholly true in everything they affirm whether it has to do with doctrine or morality or with social, physical or life sciences."[15]

Josh McDowell, in *The New Evidence That Demands a Verdict,* says:

> The Bible is the Word of God . . . and God cannot err (Hebrews 6:18, Titus 1:12). To deny the inerrancy of Scripture is to impugn either the integrity of God or the identity of the Bible as God's Word.
>
> The Character of God demands inerrancy. If every utterance in the Bible is from God and God is truth, as the Bible declares Him to be, then the Bible must be wholly truthful, or inerrant. Jesus said of God's utterances, "Your Word is truth" (John 17:17). The Psalmist wrote, "The entirety of Your Word is truth" (Psalm 119:160). . . . Paul wrote to Titus, "God . . . cannot lie" (Titus 1:2). In the final analysis, then, an attack on the Bible is an attack on the character of God.[16]

How are you acting toward that true book, the Bible? Does it have the final authority in your life? It says it does.

October

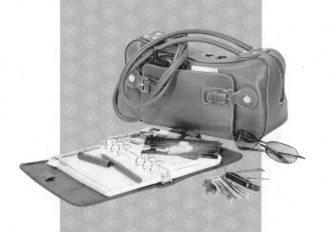

TO READ
Mark 5:1-19

Jesus said, "No, go home to your friends, and tell them what wonderful things the Lord has done for you and how merciful he has been." MARK 5:19

 ## Storm Warning

In Pass Christian, a small tourist town, Police Chief Jerry Peralta drove up and down the highway, stopping at every door. "Evacuate!" he cried. A hurricane was headed their way. Some listened. Others laughed.

At one apartment complex, a large group gathered for a hurricane party. When the storm hit, a wave three stories high crashed into the apartment building. The building was torn apart, and the dead bodies were spread across Pass Christian. The next day one little five-year-old boy was found floating on a mattress—the party's only survivor.

You might have experienced this attitude when talking with someone about his or her need for God: "Well, if I'm going to hell, then that's all right because all my friends will be there and it'll be a party!"

But hell is not a party. Here's a glimpse of the "hurricane" of hell:

- *Hell is like a dungeon, a prison.* "God did not spare even the angels when they sinned; he threw them into hell, in gloomy caves and darkness until the judgment day" (2 Peter 2:4).
- *Hell is like burning sulfur, a night-and-day torment forever.* "Then the Devil, who betrayed them, was thrown into the lake of fire that burns with sulfur, joining the beast and the false prophet. There they will be tormented day and night forever and ever" (Revelation 20:10).
- *Hell is pitch-black darkness so miserable that people cry.* "Now throw this useless servant into outer darkness, where there will be weeping and gnashing of teeth" (Matthew 25:30).
- *Hell is agony so horrible that people grind their teeth.* "Then the fifth angel poured out his bowl on the throne of the beast, and his kingdom was plunged into darkness. And his subjects ground their teeth in anguish" (Revelation 16:10).

You are like the police chief, running to warn people about the coming judgment and to tell them about God's way of escape.

TO READ
John 14:15-21

If you love me, obey my commandments.

JOHN 14:15

 Love in Action

While in college I read Chuck Colson's book *Loving God*. What I took away from that experience is that loving God is an action. Love is a verb.

When you look at the numerous passages that describe loving God, it's easy to see how Colson came to this conclusion:

- You must love the Lord your God with all your heart, all your soul, and all your strength. (Deuteronomy 6:5)
- I have commanded you today to love the Lord your God and to keep his commands, laws, and regulations by walking in his ways. If you do this, you will live and become a great nation, and the Lord your God will bless you and the land you are about to enter and occupy. (30:16)
- Choose to love the Lord your God and to obey him and commit yourself to him, for he is your life. (v. 20)

I don't want to just think about God—I want to obey his commandments. By following his commandments as the guide of my life, I live out his love. This is love, the verb, doing what he calls me to do.

Ready, set, action!

Under his wings you will find refuge.

PSALM 91:4, NIV

 Under His Wings

I hung up the phone. I was exhausted. These conversations with my drunken depressed father were lasting longer and longer, and what he was saying was making less and less sense. And somehow I always left the conversation feeling guilty, depressed, or responsible for the state he was in. It would take me days to recover and get back to a positive place. How could I honor my dad, honor my husband, and care for my children?

My quiet-time verse gave me hope: "He who dwells in the shelter of the Most High will rest in the shadow of the Almighty. I will say of the Lord, 'He is my refuge and my fortress, my God, in whom I trust.' . . . Under his wings you will find refuge; his faithfulness will be your shield and rampart" (Psalm 91:1-4, NIV).

As I prayed through the verses, I decided to pray them whenever I talked with Dad on the phone. I started to see a pattern emerge. I started saying things like:

"Dad, we've gone down this road before, and it hasn't helped you. Let me pray for you, okay?"

"Dad, I love you and I'm going to call you in the morning because you've been drinking. What you have to say is important, and I want you to remember our conversation."

"Dad, God loves you, and he doesn't want you to live in this pain. Would you like some resources to get out of this painful place?"

God sheltered me, and I was able to bring Dad under the Lord's wings, out of the storm of pain—at least when we were talking. God gave me the ability to remain in him as a refuge while giving refuge to my dad.

TO READ
Deuteronomy 32:1-9

Remember the days of long ago; think about the generations past. Ask your father and he will inform you. Inquire of your elders, and they will tell you.

DEUTERONOMY 32:7

 *The Classics*

In English classes students are encouraged to read the classics: Shakespeare, Chaucer, Jane Austin, John Steinbeck, etc. But when was the last time you picked up a classic theology book? Perhaps something by Francis Schaffer, Louis Berkhof, John Calvin, E. M. Bounds, John Stott, A. W. Tozer, or J. Oswald Sanders.

I go back to the classics for new perspective, for encouragement from someone who has already been there. One of the most memorable and freeing passages for me was penned by J. I. Packer in his classic book *Knowing God:*

> There is tremendous relief in knowing that his love to me is utterly realistic, based at every point on prior knowledge of the worst about me, so that no discovery can now disillusion him about me, in a way I am so often disillusioned about myself. . . . There is, certainly, great cause for humility in the thought that he sees all the twisted things about me that my fellow humans do not see (and am I glad!), and that he sees more corruption in me than that which I see in myself (which, in all conscience, is enough). There is, however, equally great incentive to worship and love God in the thought that, for some unfathomable reason, he wants me as his friend, and desires to be my friend, and has given his Son to die for me in order to realize this purpose. We cannot work these thoughts out here, but merely to mention them is enough to show how much it means to know not merely that we know God, but that he knows us.[1]

God knows all about me. He knows every hair on my head and every thought on my mind. He knows that I am utterly imperfect. He knows, yet he still loves me!

Go to the classics section of the bookstore, where you will be challenged in your faith by those who have lived it before you.

God blesses you when you are mocked and persecuted and lied about because you are my followers. Be happy about it! Be very glad! For a great reward awaits you in heaven. And remember, the ancient prophets were persecuted, too.

MATTHEW 5:11-12

 ## *God's Hunting Dog*

Born to a vice-governor in a Chinese province, Christiana Tsai was enrolled in a Christian mission school, vowing to never become a Christian.

Christiana and a friend, Miss Wu, began to write a book denouncing Christianity. However, Christiana began to read the Bible and listen to preaching in English to improve her skills. "God used my love for English to draw me to himself."[2] Soon, Miss Wu also came to faith in Christ.

Christiana shared her new faith with her family. She was bitterly rebuked for disgracing the family name. One brother grabbed her Bible and her hymnbook and tore them to pieces. But Christiana hung in there. She didn't let the immediate failure detour her faith.

One by one her loved ones slowly responded. Her mother came to faith in Christ and quit a lifelong habit of smoking opium. That change sparked interest in other family members. Her mom, two brothers, and their wives were baptized, and her mom opened up her home for Bible studies. At age sixty-two she learned to read so she could read the Bible for herself.

Christiana began teaching in a government school. During class breaks she talked personally with the students, and she opened up her home so interested students could come and talk about Jesus. Seventy-two of her two hundred students came to know Christ.

The school's director, Miss Plum, searched the school and confiscated Bibles and threatened expulsion to students caught attending Bible studies. However, the faith of the students withstood the persecution, and soon Miss Plum herself came to faith in Christ.

Christiana says, "I have never been to college or theological seminary. . . . I have only been God's 'hunting dog.' I simply followed at the heels of my Master, and brought to His feet the quarry He sent me after."[3]

TO READ
2 Corinthians 3:1-6

The only letter of recommendation we need is you yourselves! Your lives are a letter written in our hearts, and everyone can read it and recognize our good work among you. Clearly, you are a letter from Christ prepared by us. It is written not with pen and ink, but with the Spirit of the living God. It is carved not on stone, but on human hearts.

2 CORINTHIANS 3:2-3

The Letter

The apostle Paul explains how God has written a letter on our hearts in 2 Corinthians 3:2-3. Because of what God has done in our lives, others can read his work in our lives through the Holy Spirit. *We are a letter.*

The phrase "written on our hearts" means a past act that has ongoing results. When we decide to surrender our lives to Christ, the Holy Spirit indwells us, sealing us to God (Ephesians 4:30). And the Holy Spirit writes a letter on each of our hearts in permanent, nonerasable ink.

However, even though the letter may have been written in the past (and for many of us who've known Christ for twenty to thirty years, it is a distant past!), this verse explains that our letter is still contemporary, usable, and "with it" because the verbs *known* and *read* are in present tense, which means continual action.[4]

You have been chosen to carry the message of hope. From the moment you received Christ, you became one of his "greeting cards," bringing good news.

God "cares enough to send the very best." Where is he "mailing you" today?

TO READ
1 Peter 4:1-8

Most important of all, continue to show deep love for each other, for love covers a multitude of sins.

1 PETER 4:8

 Pay Tribute

Writing can be freeing. God began to prod me to write a blessing to my dad. I had learned over the years that my father had never heard the words "I love you" from his own alcoholic father. He had grown up dirt poor, so he also had a huge fear of failure that drove him to workaholism. I never made excuses for Dad, but I did seek to understand him and to see him from God's point of view.

At Christmas one year I knew it was time to write the blessing. But where do you start when there are so many painful memories and so few good ones? So I prayed, *God, help me write something to Dad so that he will know I love him, but more important that he will know you love him. Let him see that your love can absorb his pain.*

As I wrote the tribute, I could see how some of my best traits were ones God had redeemed out of darkness into the light. Because I grew up never knowing when Dad would rage, it was as if I lived my life on alert.

Because God redeemed that fear, it turned into an innate ability to read people and sense how they are feeling. Because I grew up mediating between Dad and everyone in our family, I have the ability to mediate now, which is a handy skill for a leader! But my favorite trait that God redeemed' is the ability to see good in a bad situation.

To start writing a tribute to someone who hurt you, look at your own life. What are some positives in your character that resulted from the pain of your growing-up years? They are there; pray and ask God to reveal them. Then pick up a pen, and write your way to freedom.

The tribute may not only free you, but it may free those you love from the bondage of their sin.

TO READ
Proverbs 7:13-27

She seduced him with her pretty speech. With her flattery she enticed him. PROVERBS 7:21

 Pursuing Praise

While spending time with Jim and Sally Conway, our mentors in ministry since seminary, Jim told me, "Pam, people who have been wounded, like us, from homes like ours, often make decisions based on sickness, not health. It is as if you have a tube inside you. You receive a compliment, and it feels so good going down, but the bad thing is it is a bottomless tube, so the positive praise goes right out the bottom. We constantly need more praise. We easily fall into the trap of making our decisions based upon what will bring us the most praise, the most public applause, and the greatest possibility for compliments. But because the tube is bottomless, it is self-defeating. You can't fill the tube."

I responded back to Jim, "Like Solomon says, 'Vanity of vanities, it is all vanity.' No amount of praise will do, so I need a different standard of decision making, right?"

"Right," said Jim. "Because our wounds make us vulnerable to praise, we can also be easily manipulated and sell ourselves to anyone or anything, just to get some praise."

"Like selling our birthright for a pot of stew?" (In Genesis 25:31-34, Esau sold his birthright to his brother because he was hungry and too impatient to cook his own dinner.)

I smiled. I knew exactly what Jim was talking about. I had been aware of this "tube" in me for a while.[5]

Look at your own praise quotient. What lengths do you go to for a little bit of praise?

TO READ
1 Corinthians 1:26-31

God alone made it possible for you to be in Christ Jesus. For our benefit God made Christ to be wisdom itself. He is the one who made us acceptable to God. He made us pure and holy, and he gave himself to purchase our freedom.

1 CORINTHIANS 1:30

 Go to Court!

How does life transformation take place? Romans 3:24 says that we are "justified freely by his grace" (NIV).

Justification is a legal term. It is a picture of all our sins being logged into a portfolio or file. (And each of us has a thick file of imperfections, mistakes, and sins! Think of it as your permanent record or, as those in law enforcement call it, your jacket.) Then God sent his Son, Jesus down to earth to live a sinless life. He had a file folder full of perfect credits; he is righteous. Then on the cross, God took our sins from our file and switched them with Jesus' righteousness. Jesus paid the penalty for our file folders, for our jackets of imperfection! God now looks down on us from heaven and sees Christ's righteousness where our sins once were.

Justification is a onetime act that happens when we meet Christ. Having justified us, God begins a process of sanctification. Second Corinthians 3:17-18 tells us: "Now, the Lord is the Spirit, and wherever the Spirit of the Lord is, he gives freedom. And all of us have had that veil removed so that we can be mirrors that brightly reflect the glory of the Lord. And as the Spirit of the Lord works within us, we become more and more like him and reflect his glory even more."

Jesus is in the process of moving us from the weakness that characterized our lives before conversion toward a position of strength as seen from heaven."[6] It is like going to court to get the legal process moving. When you come to Christ and tell him you want his righteousness for your sin, he makes the trade for your "jacket."

Have you made the trade?

Choose my instruction rather than silver, and knowledge over pure gold. PROVERBS 8:10

 Real Freedom

During my quiet times, I studied the "you are's" that God says about us. I was encouraged by the positive ones, like you are strong, chosen, children of the promise, and standing firm.

But for me personally, the ones that were most freeing first appeared negative. Some of these, I didn't even like. I wished they weren't even there! For example, 1 Corinthians 3:2-4 explains, "You are still not ready. You are still worldly" (NIV). Romans 6:19 says, "You are weak in your natural selves" (NIV). Hebrews 5:11 mentions that we are "slow to learn" (NIV).

I came to realize that freedom isn't the same as denial. I am slow to learn, weak, and still worldly, and if I ever think I have arrived, I will be lying to myself. These things are just as true about me and you as all the other more positive things God says about who we are.

God has done us a favor when he tells us in Matthew 15:19, "For from the heart come evil thoughts, murder, adultery, . . . slander." It is to our advantage to know that we have a selfish bent wanting our way over God's way.

And every time we give in to our selfishness, we prove that "no one is good—not even one. No one has real understanding; no one is seeking God. All have turned away from God; all have gone wrong. No one does good, not even one" (Romans 3:10-12).

God knows that we don't always have it all together. But it is also clear that as we embrace our imperfections and acknowledge we are weak, we gain the ability to become strong. Paul said: "When I am weak, then I am strong" (2 Corinthians 12:10).

First Corinthians seems to say, we have a choice.[7] Choose well today.

TO READ
Psalm 118:22-29

This is the day the Lord has made. We will rejoice and be glad in it. PSALM 118:24

 Don't Have It All Together?

I received some quotations that were said to have been taken from federal employee performance evaluations. Have you ever felt that some of these could be said of you?

- Her women would follow her anywhere, but only out of morbid curiosity.
- Since my last report, she has reached rock bottom and has started to dig.
- When she opens her mouth, it seems that this is only to change whichever foot was previously in there.
- This young lady has delusions of adequacy.
- This employee should go far, and the sooner she starts, the better.
- She's not the sharpest knife in the drawer.
- She's about as bright as Alaska in December.
- One-celled organisms outscore her in IQ tests.
- She has two brains; one is lost, and the other is out looking for it.
- She's so dense, light bends around her.
- If you gave her a penny for her thoughts, you'd get change.
- It takes her an hour and a half to watch *60 Minutes*.
- She has a full six-pack but lacks the plastic thingy to hold it all together. (My personal favorite!)

God knows that we don't always have it all together, yet he still has chosen to work with us! So maybe you weren't perfect yesterday, and you won't be today, but give your day to God, and somehow he'll add himself to the mix.

Say Psalm 118:24 today.

TO READ
Proverbs 1:28-33

All who listen to me will live in peace and safety, unafraid of harm. PROVERBS 1:33

 Undercover, Underground

One year ago I almost left the ministry. I wanted to be a difference maker, but a series of events happened that frightened me. In just a few months nearly every national radio Bible teacher I admired and listened to had to step down.

Three had sexual affairs; two were caught in bold-faced lies where documented evidence showed they weren't really the people they said they were (their résumés were fabricated); two had misappropriated funds; one molested children; and still another was homosexual.

It was such a bad year that at a pastors' conference for couples, the speaker, Howard Hendricks, shared his disillusionment over the same issue. One of his godly friends in ministry, a man full of integrity, had just died, and Howard prayed as he looked at the headlines, *Why did you take my friend, such a good man? Why didn't you leave him and take some of these other men?*

Sam Rima and Gary McIntosh in the book *The Dark Side of Leadership,* explain: "Most often their ambition has been a subtle and dangerous combination of their own dysfunctional personal needs and a certain measure of their altruistic desire to expand the kingdom of God. However, because ambition is so easily disguised in Christian circles and couched in spiritual language (the need to fulfill the great commission and expand the church), the dysfunctions that drive Christian leaders often go undetected and unchallenged until it is too late.[8]

Protect your life and your ministry. Ask a few people to hold your feet to the fire of accountability. The key is you have to listen when they speak up. Then pray God would hound you if you are drifting from him or his principles.

TO READ
Psalm 31:5-13

I entrust my spirit into your hand. Rescue me, Lord, for you are a faithful God. Psalm 31:5

 ## Miss the Crash and Burn

On occasion I watch car racing. It is pretty amazing how someone can go over a hundred miles an hour in the lead, and with one false move, one small mistake, the car crashes and burns, and the driver is out of the race. As leaders, those pursuing our calling, we are susceptible to the crash and burn.

Sam Rima and Gary McIntosh, in their book *Overcoming the Dark Side of Leadership,* describe the importance of allowing God to redeem back the hurts and rebuild our lives with his love: "It was during this research that it became clear that a paradox of sorts existed in the lives of most of the leaders who had experienced significant failures: The personal insecurities, feelings of inferiority, and need for parental approval (among other dysfunctions) that compelled these people to become successful leaders were very often the same issues that precipitated their failure."[9]

God seems to use all our hurts and dysfunctions to motivate us to be difference makers who continue in the race. We have to submit these same motivating factors to him, or they will be the source of our undoing.

List why you want to make a difference. Then pray Psalm 51:2: "Wash me clean from my guilt. Purify me from my sin."

Pray through your motivational factors, and ask God to redeem them.

TO READ
Psalm 69:13-15

I keep right on praying to you, Lord, hoping this is the time you will show me favor. In your unfailing love, O God, answer my prayer with your sure salvation. PSALM 69:13

 ## Put Power in the Prayer

Isaiah 55:11 explains that God's Word has a promise: "It is the same with my word. I send it out, and it always produces fruit. It will accomplish all I want it to, and it will prosper everywhere I send it."

Because of this promise, when I pray, I use God's Word because that's where the power is. For example, here is one prayer I pray over my sons' lives that is simply verses strung together:

> Let those who love the Lord hate evil, for he guards the lives of his faithful ones.[10] My son, if sinners entice you, do not give in to them.[11] May you be as Daniel, who so distinguished himself among the administrators and the satraps by his exceptional qualities that the king planned to set him over the whole kingdom.[12] My prayer is not that you take them out of the world but that you protect them from the evil one.[13] Therefore, I urge you, brothers, in view of God's mercy, to offer your bodies as living sacrifices, holy and pleasing to God—this is your spiritual act of worship. Do not conform any longer to the pattern of this world, but be transformed by the renewing of your mind. Then you will be able to test and approve what God's will is—his good, pleasing and perfect will.[14] Flee from sexual immorality. Do you not know that your body is a temple of the Holy Spirit, who is in you, whom you have received from God?[15] Do not be yoked together with unbelievers. For what do righteousness and wickedness have in common? Or what fellowship can light have with darkness?[16] Submit yourselves, then, to God. Resist the devil, and he will flee from you.[17]

Look up some verses using a few key words in a concordance or on the computer. String them together, and personalize a powerful prayer for someone you love today.

TO READ
Psalm 119:1-20

I will delight in your principles and not forget your word. PSALM 119:16

 ## *Dealing with Doubt*

At times, people wonder why a woman would spend so much time reading the Bible and praying. Maybe in a crunch you have told yourself, "I'm too busy to have a quiet time. Why pray? I need to just work harder and not spend my valuable minutes praying." Perhaps you have forgotten just why so much of the Christian life centers on time in the Word:

- For the word of the Lord is right and true; he is faithful in all he does (Psalm 33:4, NIV). *Do you want to be faithful in all you do?*
- How can a young man keep his way pure? By living according to your word (119:9, NIV). *Do you want a pure life?*
- I have hidden your word in my heart that I might not sin against you (v. 11, NIV). *Do you want to keep from sin?*
- My soul is weary with sorrow; strengthen me according to your word (v. 28, NIV). *Do you need strength for the journey?*
- Turn my eyes away from worthless things; preserve my life according to your word (v. 37, NIV). *Do you need help staying focused on the positive?*
- Your word is a lamp to my feet and a light for my path (v. 105, NIV). *Do you need guidance?*
- You are my refuge and my shield; I have put my hope in your word (v. 114, NIV). *Do you need shelter from a storm?*
- Direct my footsteps according to your word; let no sin rule over me (v. 133, NIV). *Do you want to be in control of your life instead of life controlling you?*

These are just a few of the benefits of reading the Word. I don't have the time *not* to be in the Word!

TO READ
John 9:1-11

"It was not because of his sins or his parents' sins," Jesus answered. "He was born blind so the power of God could be seen in him. JOHN 9:3

 Pain upon Pain

I have the opportunity to hear many people's stories. Sometimes the pain they share is unimaginably difficult. However, at times, friends, family, and spiritual advisers compound the pain with unrighteous theology.

In the Bible, Job was said to be "blameless, a man of complete integrity. He feared God and stayed away from evil" (Job 1:1). So righteous was Job that one day there was a conversation about him in the courts of heaven, and God granted Satan permission to test Job (Job 1:8-12). Satan wiped out all Job's possessions, livestock, and livelihood and took his children. He left Job's wife, who encouraged Job to "curse God and die." Then Job's friends, one by one, came by and said what many might say today to compound pain, "Oh, all this must be because of something you did. Got a secret sin?"

One of our new friends said he and his family had to face this lie themselves when they pulled away from a legalistic church that was filled with guilt and self-righteousness. After being gone just a week, they received news from their doctor that their baby daughter had a terminal illness. The pastor of that church visited them just to say, "It is a judgment from God for leaving our church for another."

But the truths of Scripture, such as John 9:1-11, made this couple say, "No! That's not right!"

Refuse guilt that is not yours. If you are walking with God and tough times come, don't look inward for a secret sin; rather, look upward where you'll find hope!

TO READ
2 Timothy 3:14-17

All Scripture is inspired by God and is useful to teach us what is true and to make us realize what is wrong in our lives. It straightens us out and teaches us to do what is right. 2 TIMOTHY 3:16

Stake the Claim

The Bible is amazing:

- It contains sixty-six books.
- It was written over a fifteen-hundred-year span.
- It covers over forty generations.
- It was written by more than forty authors from every walk of life, including kings, peasants, philosophers, fishermen, poets, statesmen, and scholars.
- It was written in three languages (Hebrew, Aramaic, and Greek).[18]

In *Evidence That Demands a Verdict,* a mountain of irrefutable facts gives credibility to the Bible. For example, "There are now more than 5,686 known Greek manuscripts of the New Testament. Add over 10,000 Latin Vulgate (Latin translations) and at least 9,300 other early versions and we have close to, if not more than, 25,000 manuscript copies of portions of the New Testament in existence today. No other document of antiquity even begins to approach such numbers. . . . In comparison, Homer's *Iliad* is second, with only 643.[19] Manuscripts and copies give credence to the Word you read each day. There are no original manuscripts, but Josh McDowell became a believer when he saw the mountain of evidence, including the fact that "the abundance of manuscript copies makes it possible to reconstruct the original with virtually complete accuracy."[20]

Ours is not a blind faith. Ours is not a faith based on pure feelings or conjecture. No, ours is an intellectually sound faith based on reason and based on evidence.

Have you made the decision to base your life on it?

TO READ
Romans 1:18-25

From the time the world was created, people have seen the earth and sky and all that God made. They can clearly see his invisible qualities—his eternal power and divine nature. So they have no excuse whatsoever for not knowing God. ROMANS 1:20

 ## The Gap

Annie Dillard, in the Pulitzer prize–winning *Pilgrim at Tinker Creek,* writes out of a heart revived after sequestering herself in nature for a year. Solitude was her companion, so she thought, but in the solitude her thoughts turned to God.

Many of us also miss God in the everyday, but when things are still, when we take time in the quietness of nature—or the quietness of our soul—our heart begins to tune into God's thoughts. One can't help but go there. In the quietness, the deeper questions of life arise: Why am I here? Who created all of this? What will happen when this earthly body no longer houses my soul? What is the purpose of life?

Many of us feel that God is silent. I think God isn't silent; rather, he speaks volumes each day. But are we listening?

His presence is obvious if we are looking. Annie Dillard quotes the prophet Ezekiel, who chastises false prophets as those who have "not gone up into the gaps." Those gaps, the times of solitude, lead us to a deeper fellowship and understanding of God.

Dillard says, "The gaps are the thing. The gaps are the spirit's home, the altitude and latitudes so dazzlingly spare and clean that the spirit can discover itself for the first time like a once blind man unbound. . . . Stalk the gaps. Squeak into a gap. . . . This is how you spend this afternoon, and tomorrow morning, and tomorrow afternoon. Spend the afternoon. You can't take it with you."[21] Dillard further reflects, "The secret of seeing is, then, the pearl of great price."[22]

When was the last time you went into the gap—into nature—and looked for the evidences of God's fingerprints?

TO READ
2 Corinthians 13:11-13

Greet each other in Christian love. All the Christians here send you their greetings. 2 CORINTHIANS 13:12

 ## *It's Pretty Simple, Really!*

Relationships can feel so complicated, but really, God created a pretty simple set of relationship principles. If a relationship is feeling complicated, try these simple "one anothers," and see if the relationship improves:

- John 13:34-35 (NIV): A new command I give you: *Love one another.*
- Romans 12:10 (NIV): *Be devoted to one another* in brotherly love. Honor one another above yourselves.
- Romans 12:16 (NIV): *Live in harmony with one another.* Do not be proud, but be willing to associate with people of low position. Do not be conceited.
- Romans 14:13 (NIV): *Let us stop passing judgment on one another.*
- Romans 15:7 (NIV): *Accept one another.*
- Galatians 5:13 (NIV): *Serve one another* in love.
- Ephesians 4:32 (NIV): *Be kind and compassionate to one another, forgiving each other,* just as in Christ God forgave you.
- Ephesians 5:21(NIV): *Submit to one another* out of reverence for Christ.
- Colossians 3:13 (NIV): *Bear with each other* and forgive whatever grievances you may have against one another. Forgive as the Lord forgave you.
- Colossians 3:16 (NIV): *Admonish one another* with all wisdom.
- 1 Thessalonians 5:11 (NIV): Therefore *encourage one another* and build each other up, just as in fact you are doing.
- Hebrews 10:24 (NIV): Let us consider how we may *spur one another on toward love and good deeds.*
- James 4:11 (NIV): Brothers, *do not slander one another.*
- 1 Peter 4:9 (NIV): *Offer hospitality to one another.*

If you practice these principles and the relationship is still difficult, then at least you know it is probably an issue with the other person, not you!

TO READ
Psalm 78:1-4

We will not hide these truths from our children but will tell the next generation about the glorious deeds of the Lord. We will tell of his power and the mighty miracles he did. PSALM 78:4

Make a Moment

My friend Barbara likes to take what God does to make a moment and a memory. Barbara tells this story:

> To my ten-year-old grandson, Zac, it must have seemed like just another ordinary car pool that day. He was sitting in the front seat, chatting away with friends, when suddenly the driver of the car passed out at the wheel! Quick-thinking Zac grabbed the steering wheel and brought the car to safety on the shoulder of the road. This was not an ordinary day at all, but an extraordinary picture to Zac of God's amazing protection.
>
> As grandparents, we started Zac's rock collection when he was around three years old. When I heard the story of Zac's courage, I knew this was a moment God would want Zac to remember! The word *remember* means to "imprint," a great word to describe what we wanted to see happen in Zac's heart regarding this miracle. So many of the Scriptures on remembering were also linked to having one generation pass on the mighty deeds God had done to the next generation. I thought this moment would be a perfect opportunity to carry out the heart of those passages of Scripture.
>
> We gathered our family around Zac, read Joshua 4 together, and explained what we saw as God's teaching from the story. In verses 6-7 an explanation of remembrance stones is given: "To serve as a sign among you. In the future, when your children ask you, 'What do these stones mean?' tell them . . . these stones are to be a memorial to the people of Israel forever" (NIV).
>
> We prayed and gave Zac a stone with the word *courage* etched on it. We wanted this story of Zac's courage and God's protection to be a part of our family's legacy, passed from one generation to another.

<table>
<tr><td>

TO READ
Joshua 4:15-24

</td><td>

He did this so that all the peoples of the earth might know that the hand of the Lord is powerful and so that you might always fear the Lord your God.

JOSHUA 4:24, NIV

</td></tr>
</table>

 Mark It!

As a way to mark growth in your life, you may want to create a tangible remembrance. The book of Joshua tells the story of the Israelites crossing the Jordan into the Promised Land. As a remembrance of all he had done, God told them to choose twelve men, one from each tribe, to take twelve stones from the Jordan River.

Then Joshua called them together and told them, "Joshua set up at Gilgal the twelve stones they had taken out of the Jordan. He said to the Israelites, 'In the future when your descendants ask their fathers, "What do these stones mean?" tell them, "Israel crossed the Jordan on dry ground." For the Lord your God dried up the Jordan before you until you had crossed over'" (Joshua 4:20-23, NIV).

One idea for a tangible marker is to make a memory stone by pouring a small block of cement, like a stepping-stone, and add symbols of God's blessing. Create a path with stepping-stones in a garden. You can add a new one each year, or each family member can create a stone for the year in which you create the garden path.

By creating a tangible marker, a visible legacy is formed. The visible legacy can comfort you during difficult times.

Be joyful in hope, patient in affliction, faithful in prayer. ROMANS 12:12, NIV

 ## *Always Enough Time*

Take care of the needy. Visit the widow. Evangelize the lost. Teach your children and grandchildren to love the Lord. Serve in the church. Serve in the community. Sometimes our to-do list can feel so long. It is easy to be driven by guilt or by need instead of being driven by God.

But look at Romans 12:12. It's all about attitude: Be joyful, patient, faithful. The context helps too. Romans 12:1 says that we are to be "living sacrifices" (NIV). Romans 12:2 says, "Do not conform any longer to the pattern of this world, but be transformed by the renewing of your mind" (NIV). These are attitude adjustments. Romans 12:3: "Do not think of yourself more highly than you ought, but rather think of yourself with sober judgment, in accordance with the measure of faith God has given you" (NIV). *Attitude.* Then Romans 12:4-8 encourages people to be who they are and use the gifts God has given them. No unreal expectations, no harsh criticism, just let people be who God made them. *Attitude again.* God is more concerned with your attitudes than with your actions. Get off the frantic, guilt-driven merry-go-round. Focus less on what you are "doing" and more on who you are "being."

Everyone will share the story of your wonderful goodness; they will sing with joy of your righteousness. PSALM 145:7

 ## *Angel Party!*

God can really throw a party. The angels in heaven rejoice when even one sinner decides to turn to God (Luke 15:10).

Our family has chosen to follow God's example, and we look for ways to celebrate. One of the ways we celebrate is by hosting "angel parties." We first began angel parties when our children made decisions for Christ. And now we also have angel parties to celebrate when anyone in our family introduces someone to Jesus. Early on I had the boys cut out angel pictures and add angel stickers and stamps so they each could make a personal angel placemat for the celebrations. Then we laminated the works of art. We would eat angel food cake, talk about the special moment that was being celebrated, and relive it in conversation.

As the boys have gotten older, they've outgrown the cute placemats, and none of them really loves angel food cake. Now we have the person in charge of the celebration choose the food or the place to eat out, and the celebration continues in a more grown-up form.

The style of the angel party may have evolved over the years, but the principle of celebration is seared into our children's minds. Each child in our family knows: It is important that people know God, and knowing God is a reason to celebrate!

TO READ
Psalm 71:14-17

O God, you have taught me from my earliest childhood, and I have constantly told others about the wonderful things you do. PSALM 71:17

 Signpost

When I was expecting, we chose our child's name, looked up the meaning of the selected name, chose a verse that reflected that name, and had a plaque created that included the name, meaning, spiritual meaning, and a verse. These hang outside our children's bedrooms. This is what hangs outside our oldest son's bedroom:

Brock

English meaning: Badger

Spiritual meaning: Courageous

Joshua 1:9

Have I not commanded you? Be strong and courageous,

do not tremble or be dismayed,

for the Lord your God is with you wherever you go.

Whenever I see the traits of the boys' names displayed in something they say or do, I will point it out to them and compliment them.

For example, Brock was asked to open up our city council's meeting in prayer when he was a sophomore. Afterward, I complimented him. Then I reminded him of his journey to courage.

As a young boy, he would get tousled about in play by older kids. I reminded him that God helped him learn not to whine but to be courageous in both small and big situations.

He smiled and said, "Yeah, it is pretty cool how God works. But, Mom, I've been raised to think courageously, so doesn't it seem natural that I would act courageously?"

I knew it all had started the week he was born when I hung that little sign outside his door.

TO READ
1 Peter 3:13-18

Even if you suffer for doing what is right, God will reward you for it. So don't be afraid and don't worry. 1 PETER 3:14

 The Least Popular

It is easy to peddle a gospel of "happy ever after," but in suffering we discern who we are and what we are made of:

- *Suffering connects our hearts to Christ's.* "But how is it to your credit if you receive a beating for doing wrong and endure it? But if you suffer for doing good and you endure it, this is commendable before God. To this you were called, because Christ suffered for you, leaving you an example, that you should follow in his steps." (1 Peter 2:20-21, NIV)
- *Suffering purifies and forges our faith.* "In this you greatly rejoice, though now for a little while you may have had to suffer grief in all kinds of trials. These have come so that your faith—of greater worth than gold, which perishes even though refined by fire—may be proved genuine and may result in praise, glory and honor when Jesus Christ is revealed." (1 Peter 1:6-7, NIV)
- *Suffering is used by God to put his glory on display.* "Dear friends, do not be surprised at the painful trial you are suffering, as though something strange were happening to you. But rejoice that you participate in the sufferings of Christ, so that you may be overjoyed when his glory is revealed. If you are insulted because of the name of Christ, you are blessed, for the Spirit of glory and of God rests on you." (1 Peter 4:12-14, NIV)
- *Suffering builds intimacy into our relationship with God.* "But those who suffer he delivers in their suffering; he speaks to them in their affliction." (Job 36:15, NIV)

On those "bad days," think of the payoffs: a closer God connection, a more pure faith, a life that puts God on display, and a God who will speak to me in my affliction.

TO READ
Acts 2:32-39

This promise is to you and to your children, and even to the Gentiles—all who have been called by the Lord our God. ACTS 2:39

 ## True to Yourself

Ever feel the pressure to be it all and do it all? We can feel so many expectations from childhood through adulthood:

- Sit up straight.
- Eat your vegetables.
- Study hard.
- Practice the piano.
- Look an adult in the eye.
- Win the science fair.
- Place first in the art exhibit.
- Earn a place on the academic decathlon team.
- Make all-league, all-conference, all everything!
- Go to an Ivy League school.
- Get a prestigious internship.
- Start a record-setting business.
- Give me grandbabies, but don't gain too much weight doing it.
- Be a perfect mom.

John Robinson and Geoffrey Godbey, authors of *A Time for Life,* note that "many Americans have become virtual walking résumés, defining themselves only by what they do."[23] You are more than the sum of your trophies. Success is only one indication of your identity and calling.

Look at your loves, not just your trophy case. What makes you feel excited, full of life, and energized?

Os Guinness calls us all to replace "You are what you do" with "Do what you are."[24]

TO READ
1 Timothy 4:4-10

Since everything God created is good, we should not reject any of it. We may receive it gladly, with thankful hearts. 1 TIMOTHY 4:4

 Wonderfully Made

A psychological study in 1995 found that three minutes spent looking at models in a fashion magazine caused 70 percent of women to feel depressed, guilty, and shameful.

I have had friends put their lives at risk to be a little thinner. The mountains of lawsuits against ephedrine products show how desperate people are to feel better about their bodies. What does God say about the way you were made?

- *God created you, and he saw what he was making!* "I praise you because I am fearfully and wonderfully made; your works are wonderful, I know that full well. My frame was not hidden from you when I was made in the secret place. When I was woven together in the depths of the earth, your eyes saw my unformed body." (Psalm 139:14-16, NIV)
- *God formed you, and he says you bring him glory.* "Bring my sons from afar and my daughters . . . everyone who is called by my name, whom I created for my glory, whom I formed and made." (Isaiah 43:6-7, NIV)
- *God formed you and set you apart.* "Before I formed you in the womb I knew you, before you were born I set you apart." (Jeremiah 1:5, NIV)

What can you do today to help you believe what God has said about you? Do you need to make a three-by-five card and memorize these verses? Do you want to write the truth on your mirror? Want to record the truth on a CD and play it as you walk? Find a way to remind yourself today how very precious you are to God.

TO READ
2 Peter 1:15-21

We were not making up clever stories when we told you about the power of our Lord Jesus Christ and his coming again. We have seen his majestic splendor with our own eyes. 2 PETER 1:16

 ## *I Want out of This Story*

Fables and fairy tales can lure and lull us into false thinking. After all, we women are almost trained to look for significance in the wrong places.

Let's look at some of the common storybook characters many of us grew up with. There is sweet, naive Sleeping Beauty, who has to wait for a prince to come and kiss her to wake up and be free to live.

Little Red Riding Hood, the poor thing, just couldn't follow directions about not going through the forest, and a woodchopper has to kill the wolf and free Red Riding Hood and Granny.

Rapunzel at least took her destiny into her own hands and decided she wasn't going to be locked in a tower anymore, but she had to use her gorgeous good looks (her hair) as the means to gain a new life.

And then there's Goldilocks, a picture of women today, flitting from one thing to another, looking for something that will make her life "just right." Like Goldilocks, we are looking for significance in all the wrong places.[25]

The Bible warns us that we'll be tempted to turn to myths, fables, and men's wisdom rather than God's (2 Timothy 4:4).

Keep moving out of fiction and into real life. Examine the fables you have been told in college, in the home you grew up in, through your cultural network, or by friends. Most things passed on from woman to woman are helpful, but at times, some fiction is thrown in.

Beware of the fairy tales.

TO READ
Matthew 6:9-15

Don't let us yield to temptation, but deliver us from the evil one. MATTHEW 6:13

 ## *Get Me out of Here!*

First John 2:15-16 lays out three ways we fall for false significance: "Do not love the world or anything in the world. If anyone loves the world, the love of the Father is not in him. For everything in the world—[1] the cravings of sinful man, [2] the lust of his eyes and [3] the boasting of what he has and does—comes not from the Father but from the world" (NIV).

Our flesh wants fulfillment; then our eyes want what we see; then we want something to brag about. Eve fell for the same three things. *It feels so good:* Her flesh wanted the fruit. *It looks so good:* Her eyes saw the delicious-looking fruit, and she wanted it. *It sounds so good:* Then she fell for the big one: "You can be like God." Now that would be something to brag about, but it was all lies.[26]

When are you vulnerable to these same three lies? When you are physically tired, do you want something, anything that feels good?

When do you want to toss intellectual thought aside to make sure you get what you want when you want it? What causes you to spend above your ability to pay?

When are you most vulnerable to someone's smooth and persuasive speech? When you feel desperate for money? desperate for love? desperate for attention?

Write down a time you fell for each one of these lies. Then write a personal prayer to give you the strength to walk away.

TO READ
Hebrews 10:19-25

Let us go right into the presence of God, with true hearts fully trusting him. For our evil consciences have been sprinkled with Christ's blood to make us clean, and our bodies have been washed with pure water. HEBREWS 10:22

 ## Low Maintenance

I'm giving my boys some pointers on spotting low-maintenance women because I know that being married to a low-maintenance woman is a lot less complicated and less stressful.

You also can spot a low-maintenance woman (LM). A LM woman:

- Doesn't ask for compliments, but she graciously receives them when they are given.
- Believes winning and whining are spelled differently and are never to be used interchangeably.
- Doesn't try to wear you down; instead she seeks to build you up.
- Follows as well as she leads.
- Is more interested in the team working than the theme working.
- Knows how to use makeup but doesn't hide behind it.
- Believes personal happiness is a benefit, not a goal or right.
- Accepts men's input without needing their attention.
- Appreciates her girlfriend's input but doesn't need her approval.
- Realizes that a bad hair day, a broken nail, a run in the panty hose, or a change in plans are a natural part of the ebb and flow of life, not the makings of a tragic epic made-for-TV miniseries.[27]

Would others call you low maintenance? If you are courageous, ask your friends and family how they'd answer that question.

God can help you be low maintenance.

TO READ
Jeremiah 17:5-10

Blessed are those who trust in the Lord and have made the Lord their hope and confidence.

JEREMIAH 17:7

 ## *Money Can't Buy It*

Oprah Winfrey, who tops the American talk-show circuit and sits at the helm of a $415 million empire, said, "People think because you're on TV you have the world by a string. But I have struggled with my own self value for many, many years."[28]

What! Money, lots and lots of money, doesn't make you feel good about yourself? How about great looks? I personally have counseled many women who are models, beauty queens, and actresses. I can guarantee, it isn't their looks they are counting on to make them feel good about themselves. In their world, any small blemish might wreck your income. To them, beauty is a fleeting tool. So what does give us confidence?

Confidence is gained from an accurate view of God. I know I can be confident that God will fight my battles. In 2 Chronicles 32:8 Hezekiah gave his people reassurance that God would help them and fight their battle.

Here are some other verses about confidence:

- I can be confident because God is my hope, and I know he is the sovereign Lord. (Psalm 71:5)
- God also keeps me from being snared in the traps of this world, and through him I have confidence for every step I take. (Proverbs 3:26)
- God is my helper so that no one can do anything to me. (Hebrews 13:6)

This is the confidence that I can stand on. I don't need money or good looks. All I need is God.

November

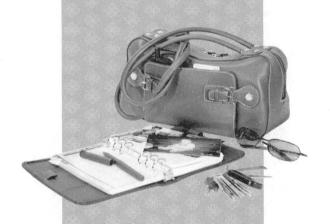

TO READ
John 11:38-44

Jesus responded, "Didn't I tell you that you will see God's glory if you believe?" JOHN 11:40

 ## What Will People Think?

Overall, we have an exaggerated sense of self. We worry about what we will wear, serve, say, give, do, and contribute. We worry because our eyes are on ourselves.

I don't see Jesus calling up Peter and John and asking, "So, what are you going to wear to the wedding today?" I don't see him running around frantically worrying about what he is going to serve for dinner—and he had some big dinner parties. Remember when he fed five thousand men and their families from two fish and some bread?

He didn't even worry when it seems he should have been worried, like when he was on a boat in the middle of a storm. He wasn't worried; he slept!

He wasn't even stressed about not being there when Lazarus, one of his best buddies, died. Everyone was stressed, but when Jesus arrived, he wanted to see the tomb and asked them to remove the stone. Lazarus's sister Martha was concerned and stressed about what the smell would be like, since her brother had been in the tomb four days. But Jesus looked at her and said, "Didn't I tell you that you will see God's glory if you believe?" (John 11:40).

When we worry, all we see is the circumstance, and all others see in us is stress. But when we believe in God despite the circumstances, we see the glory of God.

What do you want to see today?

TO READ
Proverbs 14:15-20

Only simpletons believe everything they are told!
The prudent carefully consider their steps.

PROVERBS 14:15

 Have It All

For my book *10 Best Decisions a Woman Can Make,* I asked women to tell me their description of a woman who "had it all!" These are my favorites:

- *"She is never running late or misplacing anything."* Well, I can never be a woman who has it all then because there are days I hunt for car keys, lost cleats, the pancake spatula, and sometimes my kids or husband!
- *"She's unwrinkled."* This one knocks all of us who are over forty right out of the running.
- *"Perfect figure."* Okay, this one's tough because it keeps changing! Marilyn Monroe wore a size sixteen, and I think the supermodels today shop in the toddler section.
- *"Talented, gorgeous, wealthy, easy life, no job, mother of three well-adjusted kids."* This one is a classic example of what we do to ourselves all the time— contradict our values. If I was talented and gorgeous with an easy life of wealth and I didn't work for the money, would I really have three well-adjusted kids? (And why three kids?) And if I were so wonderfully talented, wouldn't I want to use it in some way?
- *"She's on top of the world. Everything always goes in her favor. Never fails."* Never??? Some of the women I have met, interviewed, or read about in history have had lives filled with failures and setbacks. Often those very failures have become part of the fiber that has formed them into a woman God can use in a significant way.
- *"Someone who has a maid that someone else pays for!"*[1] This is my all-time favorite description of a woman who has it all!

Feeling the pressure to have it all? Reality check: Life is a series of adjustments.

TO READ
Proverbs 16:28-33

A troublemaker plants seeds of strife; gossip separates the best of friends. PROVERBS 16:28

 Space to Recover

I could tell she was upset. She walked straight for me, and her steps were quick, measured, and deliberate. As she began to explain her story, her emotions were obviously packed with anger and frustration. She was mad at her husband, and she was set to tell the world. My answer was perplexing to her.

"Honey, I know you are upset. I know you said you were going to tell his entire family, everyone at his work, and all of his friends, but why don't you hold off on that until you talk with him about this. If he repents and wants to get into counseling, he is going to need a supportive environment to beat this thing. And isn't that what you want? You want him to beat this addiction, don't you?"

"Yes."

"If you tell everyone in his world, he will feel shame around every person in it. That means he has to go outside your circle of friends and family for acceptance and encouragement, and you have just told me that just recently he made a poor choice when he was with someone not in your world, so you don't want to push him out of your world. He needs a safe place to grow with God. First, talk with him, tell him you need two or three friends to support you in prayer as he works on wellness, and be careful to choose women who can encourage you and keep confidences."

Why did I tell her to not air the news of her husband's offense? "Disregarding another person's faults preserves love; telling about them separates close friends" (Proverbs 17:9).

Jesus didn't announce people's sins—except the Pharisees'—and that was because they acted as if they had no sin! Today, don't say something you are just dying to share.

TO READ
1 Timothy 5:3-4, 8, 16

Those who won't care for their own relatives, especially those living in the same household, have denied what we believe. Such people are worse than unbelievers. 1 TIMOTHY 5:8

 ## Family and Finance

Both sets of our in-laws have been very generous, helping us financially with education costs, down payments for homes, etc. We never expected the help, but we were grateful when it came. Our parents are in good health currently, but we have seen families carry huge financial responsibilities for their parents and extended family.

When it comes to family and finances, the opinions seem varied, like these two verses: "Now I am ready to visit you for the third time, and I will not be a burden to you, because what I want is not your possessions but you. After all, children should not have to save up for their parents, but parents for their children" (2 Corinthians 12:14, NIV). "But those who won't care for their own relatives, especially those living in the same household, have denied what we believe. Such people are worse than unbelievers" (1 Timothy 5:8).

What exactly is our responsibility when it comes to using our money to care for relatives? One verse has a principle that children shouldn't have to help parents, a "You're on your own, Mom and Dad" attitude. The second seems to say the opposite, that we'd better take care of our extended family, or we are not only cheapskates but also "worse than unbelievers."

When in doubt, do like God recommends: "Speak up for the poor and helpless, and see that they get justice" (Proverbs 31:9). He doesn't allow people to continue in unhealthy patterns, but if they have tried their best and fall short, his long arm of love reaches out.

God has made everything beautiful for its own time. He has planted eternity in the human heart, but even so, people cannot see the whole scope of God's work from beginning to end. ECCLESIASTES 3:11

 I Don't Get It!

"I don't 'get' God." I have heard that statement from teens, seniors, and everyone in between. There are times when we don't understand why God does what he does; we don't find the logic of his timing; and we don't comprehend some basic tenets of the faith, like the Trinity or free will and God's sovereignty. God is "ungetable."

What we need to get is, we can't "get God." If we could, then he wouldn't be God—he'd be like us. Isaiah 64:4 says that "since the world began, no ear has heard, and no eye has seen a God like you, who works for those who wait for him!" If since the beginning of time, no one else has seen a God who compares with him, how can we think we can?

If we could fully understand him, he wouldn't be God. Solomon, the wisest man who ever lived, acknowledges that he can't understand God either. "No one can discover everything God has created in our world, no matter how hard they work at it. Not even the wisest people know everything, even if they say they do" (Ecclesiastes 8:17).

He is bigger, stronger, wiser, and completely different from us. We need a God we can't get, because then he can give what we so desperately need.

No discipline is enjoyable while it is happening—it is painful! But afterward there will be a quiet harvest of right living for those who are trained in this way.

HEBREWS 12:11

 ## *Braces*

The orthodontist told me that my eleven-year-old son needed braces. The price seemed a lot for our budget, but if the doctor said he needed them, then I was going to find the money for them.

When I shared what had transpired with Bill, his response was, "Pam, that's a lot of money. I don't see it in the budget. Besides, pretty much all of us need dental work, and we've all been putting it off until we see how our books begin to sell. I think we should put off the decision for a few months." Bill had a "wait and see" attitude, and I had a "step out on faith, God will provide" attitude.

I said, "Honey, I just signed my first book contract. I have some speaking engagements coming up over the next few months. I would like to do this."

"There are other things we could use that money for."

"But Bill, the doctor said he needed them." Then I repeated all the horrible things the orthodontist said might happen to Brock if the problem was not corrected.

"Honey, I just couldn't live with myself if I could have prevented it. It's my money."

Bill, sensing it was a losing battle, said, "Okay, Pam, but this bill is 100 percent your responsibility."

I threw the "wives submit" stuff right out, thinking I was more spiritual because I had more faith. Well, God did provide over the next few years as I went *without* all kinds of things to pay that bill. God made sure I kept my word to pay the doctor, but God also made sure I was disciplined by having to give up pretty much *all* of my expendable income.

Today I am not nearly so spiritually arrogant when Bill and I sit and discuss finances.

TO READ
Titus 3:9-11

If anyone is causing divisions among you, give a first and second warning. After that, have nothing more to do with that person. TITUS 3:10

 ## Three Strikes

"Do you know what Teresa said about you at last night's meeting?" This question sounds so like junior high, but unfortunately adult women who aren't mature in Christ can become undermining, insubordinate, and divisive. There's nothing harder on a leader than dealing with this kind of personality.

A good leader works hard to create a place of service and ownership for every person's talent and experience. She looks for ways to build teamwork and a positive work environment. She looks to inspire and encourage team members to move forward and to reach their God-given potential. So when one person joins the team with different motives than the leader's and is consistently spreading strife, discord, or even outright lies, a leader can't allow the person to continue her actions.

For most women, doing something to undermine leadership is usually an innocent mistake, and when a leader lovingly and specifically explains what her action was and how it impacted those around her, a mature woman will own up to the mistake and apologize. In a few cases, even agreeing to disagree and to still love one another is a positive resolution.

But there are some women who are too emotionally needy or have such brokenness that they actually enjoy the strife they cause. A leader cannot allow the behavior to continue, however, or she will be left with a mountain of destruction.

Titus 3:10 gives clear counsel about how to handle these people and situations when they arise. Three strikes and the person is out of leadership, out of fellowship, and perhaps out of the organization if there are not signs of repentance, and the damage he or she caused is severe.

TO READ
Job 33:1-9

You said, "I am pure; I am innocent; I have not sinned." JOB 33:9

It's What's on the Inside

I know I've said it to my kids, and I remember my mother and my grandmother saying it to me. "It's what's on the inside that counts." Money, prestige, beauty are all fleeting; character, integrity, and honesty last. Crisis doesn't just build character—it reveals it.

I think that's why I appreciate David's prayer in Psalm 51. You see, he's just blown it. He tried to run a cover-up scam, and the prophet Nathan blew the whistle on him. David realized that it's what's on the inside that counts! David prayed for God to give him a clean heart and to renew his spirit (v. 10).

How can we keep this type of right standing with God?

- Run away from sin; follow righteousness. (2 Timothy 2:22)
- Ask: Does this thought or action pursue peace, love, and righteousness?
- Walk into God's presence and away from false beliefs. (Psalm 24:4)
- Ask: Does this action or attitude reflect God's Word?
- Walk in the same path as your godly parents and grandparents. (2 Timothy 3:14)
- Ask: What would my God-fearing dad, my pure-hearted mom, or my spiritual mentor do in my situation?

And what are the benefits gained by a clean heart and clear conscience?

We will have quality friendships with people of influence. "He who loves a pure heart and whose speech is gracious will have the king for his friend" (Proverbs 22:11, NIV).

And we will have a stronger life because we have no regrets and no hidden skeletons in the closet (Job 17:9).

Solomon, my son, get to know the God of your ancestors. Worship and serve him with your whole heart and with a willing mind. For the Lord sees every heart and understands and knows every plan and thought. If you seek him, you will find him. But if you forsake him, he will reject you forever.

1 CHRONICLES 28:9

 *Motive*

When you watch a courtroom drama, the district attorney is looking for one thing that will get a solid conviction: *motive*. Motive is the reason why someone does or doesn't do something.

You might have experienced a relationship with someone who has selfish motives; you leave the relationship feeling used. Or you might have been involved in a business or project with someone with ulterior motives, and you leave the relationship feeling betrayed or deceived.

On the flip side, you might have been in a group with people who had selfless motives, and you go away from that experience feeling amazed at the altruistic, kind, and sacrificial nature of people.

How do we know? How can we tell someone's motives? First Corinthians 4:5 gives us a caution to not judge before the Lord comes. He is the One who will expose the motives of each person's heart.

David, too, gave this warning to his own son before Solomon became king in 1 Chronicles 28:9. We are to watch our own motives and pray that we will see people from God's perspective because God says he will bring the motive to light. When God's spotlight gets to me, I just pray my motives are pure.

TO READ
Proverbs 10:20-32

The blessing of the Lord makes a person rich, and he adds no sorrow with it. PROVERBS 10:22

 ## God's Hand of Blessing

When God places his hand on you and trusts you with a calling, why does he do it? Is it to make you happy? Or is it to make you and the world more holy? I think the second leads to the first. As you give, God gives back. See the Proverbs 31 woman's example.

She is an industrious woman, making money, but for what? She underwrites her ministry and family expenses and then she gives to the needy: "Her hands are busy spinning thread, her fingers twisting fiber. She extends a helping hand to the poor and opens her arms to the needy" (vv. 19-20).

With her weaving equipment, she is creating fabric for clothes and goods. And she doesn't just make enough for her own family, but she also makes enough for the poor and needy: "She has no fear of winter for her household because all of them have warm clothes. She quilts her own bedspreads. She dresses like royalty in gowns of finest cloth" (vv. 21-22).

Because she has planned well, her own family is clothed well, and she has enough to even make a bedspread! She has earned enough to clothe herself in fine linen, the color of royalty.

When you treat others as royalty, God sends you a blessing fit for a queen!

TO READ
Isaiah 6:1-8

I heard the Lord asking, "Whom should I send as a messenger to my people? Who will go for us?" And I said, "Lord, I'll go! Send me." ISAIAH 6:8

 ## *Give Me the Ball*

Good bills languish away in Congress when they are "sent to committee." In churches precious time is lost while committees analyze and conjecture about what should be done. There's a measure of safety in this. If you are still talking, you don't have to "do" anything. Anyone can point out the problems; few choose to step in and lead a solution.

I went to three meetings in a row for an organization this year. I heard all about the need to get more members, but even with many good ideas, I never heard anyone say, "I'll run with that idea." At church I hear all about the need to reach the world, but I have wanted to take an exit poll to see how many people actually talked to someone about God during that past week.

First Chronicles 12:38 shows the hearts of a group of fighting men who stepped up to make David king over Israel.

I have also learned about the need to step up from my sons. All athletes must work out, practice, prepare, and gain skills. But a leader sets herself apart when she says to the coach when her team is losing, "Coach, give me the ball, and I will make the play!" Then when the coach gives it to her, she makes the play.

When ideas are "in committee," no one is responsible. But the moment someone says, "Give me the ball, and I'll make the play," then that person has stood out from the pack and said, "It's on my shoulders. I am responsible."

TO READ
1 Samuel 25:1-38

Thank God for your good sense! Bless you for keeping me from murdering the man and carrying out vengeance with my own hands. 1 SAMUEL 25:33

 ## He's a Jerk!

How can you achieve your potential if you are married to a man everyone thinks is a jerk? Abigail's story is told in 1 Samuel 25.

And if you are wondering if her husband was really that bad, here's what 1 Samuel 25:3 says about him: "This man's name was Nabal, and his wife, Abigail, was a sensible and beautiful woman. But Nabal, a descendant of Caleb, was mean and dishonest in all his dealings."

And when Nabal treated David and his men horribly, Abigail intervened and said this to David about Nabal: "I know Nabal is a wicked and ill-tempered man; please don't pay any attention to him. He is a fool, just as his name suggests" (v. 25).

So how did Abigail handle Nabal?

- She did what is right even when Nabal did wrong. Nabal was shortsighted and selfish in his treatment of David and his troops. So Abigail hurried to do the right thing. She took two hundred loaves of bread, wine, dressed sheep, roasted grain, raisins, and figs, and loaded them on donkeys for David. (vv. 18-19)
- She didn't take time to argue. She realized that she couldn't change Nabal (only God could deal with Nabal and his horrible attitudes and actions). In verse 19 she told her servants that she would follow them, but she did not tell her husband, Nabal.

Choose right and do right, regardless of what your spouse chooses, and God will see and so will the people in your world.

TO READ
Ephesians 5:15-20

Be careful how you live, not as fools but as those who are wise. Make the most of every opportunity for doing good in these evil days. EPHESIANS 5:15-16

Strategic Planning

When your back is against the wall and the calendar demands are creating a crunch time on all fronts, what are some principles to use to decide what to do first and fastest?

Life and death: Some issues, especially in people-helping fields are life and death issues. If someone is suicidal, if a person has a terminal illness, if someone is gravely hurt in an accident, or if someone close to you has lost a loved one, you put those people at the top of the list. You may not have to be the one who attends to their needs, but you need to delegate a reliable person who can give them immediate help.

Family over friends: My kids, my mother, and my husband have more right to my time. My family's "A" priority needs are more pressing to me because I have made a higher commitment to them. Take time with your family and define "A" priorities. I don't stop my life to run a forgotten snack to the school, but I will drop off a term paper due that day. Their emotional crisis is my crisis, but their lack of responsibility isn't my crisis.

Heaven or hell: The next set of issues is dealing with helping Christians over helping unbelievers. I always give those unbelievers with a spiritual interest, or those with whom I am developing a relationship, first dibs on my time. I might be the only good news they receive in their life. I need to stay credible with them, and their experience with Christians might have been flawed in the past, so I want to keep my word to them now.

Leader or follower: I choose giving the leader time over the follower. If I can help keep my leaders motivated and holy, they can follow up with the followers.

TO READ
Hebrews 4:6-11

God set another time for entering his place of rest, and that time is today. God announced this through David a long time later in the words already quoted: "Today you must listen to his voice. Don't harden your hearts against him." HEBREWS 4:7

 ## It's Time!

When a person is ready to respond to God, she asks questions and seeks out people who want to talk about God and the deeper issues of life. God draws people to himself for salvation.

It's important that you act when someone you know is seeking God. Assume it is a "God moment" if the person wants to stay after a meeting to talk about God or if she asks you to go to lunch when she has rebuffed prior invitations. Clear your schedule to help someone enter the Kingdom. Most of us pray and pray for our family and friends to respond to God, but when they don't meet our time schedule, we feel inconvenienced. We should feel trusted and chosen instead!

In the same way, when a person is being stirred by God, he or she is excited, animated, or deeply introspective—not bland or benign. When you are sensing God wants you to pull away, study, pray, or listen, do it!

God has a "today" for salvation, a "today" for his leading. He appoints moments; they are not random. Hebrews 4:7 says, "That time is today."

The main point of this Scripture isn't just to mention that God has end-time moments set, but rather God has moments that require our response "now."

To wait is to callous your heart, making it harder for God to get your attention next time.

TO READ
Proverbs 22:4-16

True humility and fear of the Lord lead to riches, honor, and long life. PROVERBS 22:4

 ## *Embarrassed*

You fall on your face in front of a crowd of people, and your dress goes over your head. Your body makes a noise at a dinner party at a moment when all is silent. Your private sin is broadcast in public. You run to the store in your kick-around clothes and a ball cap and see the man of your dreams. You say or do something stupid, and the people you want most to impress are there to witness it. Embarrassed? Sure.

But some choices go beyond embarrassment; they bring shame, dishonor, or hurt to those you love, including God.

To dishonor means to treat in a degrading manner or to bring shame on someone.[2] Dishonor maligns your character, the character of God, or what is true of God because your choice is so contrary to the character of God.

What kinds of things dishonor God?

- Bragging, especially false bravado, brings shame. (Proverbs 13:5)
- Robbing your own parents or acting in a way to drive away your family. (Proverbs 19:26)
- Breaking the law. (Romans 2:23)
- Allowing your hormones to make your choices rather than your intellect, then glorying in the wrongdoing. (Philippians 3:19)
- Losing self-control, not being pure, and not submitting to your husband and the marriage vows you took. (Titus 2:5)

Teach the wise, and they will be wiser. Teach the righteous, and they will learn more. PROVERBS 9:9

 ## *Mentor Me*

When you are looking for someone to mentor you, what should she be teaching you and holding you accountable to? "Teach the older women to be reverent in the way they live, not to be slanderers or addicted to much wine, but to teach what is good. Then they can train the younger women to love their husbands and children, to be self-controlled and pure, to be busy at home, to be kind, and to be subject to their husbands, so that no one will malign the word of God" (Titus 2:3-5, NIV).

Since we are "older" compared to some and "younger" compared to others, let's look at all the traits listed here in Titus 2:3-5:

- Reverent: holy, sacred character that is fitting to a person consecrated to God
- Not a slanderer: not defaming or maligning
- Not addicted: not under bondage or controlled by anything
- Loves husband and children: sacrificing for the good of loved ones
- Self-controlled: self-disciplined
- Pure: discreet and chaste
- Busy at home: working to keep your home a priority of your heart
- Kind: sympathetic and helpful
- Subject to husband: choosing to rank yourself under his leadership

Is the person you are mentoring being trained in these? Are you asking a woman to mentor you so your character matches this list? What trait on this list would you most like to grow in? Ask someone good at that trait to mentor you.

TO READ
Proverbs 13:17-25

An unreliable messenger stumbles into trouble, but a reliable messenger brings healing.

PROVERBS 13:17

 ## Whistle Blowing

You are working away, and you realize someone is undermining the boss. What do you do? Queen Esther ran into this scenario: "One day as Mordecai was on duty at the palace; two of the king's eunuchs . . . became angry at King Xerxes and plotted to assassinate him. But Mordecai heard about the plot and passed the information on to Queen Esther. She then told the king about it and gave Mordecai credit for the report" (Esther 2:21-22).

Esther was laying a foundation of looking out for the king. So when a more twisted, complicated, and manipulative plot came along, formed by someone much closer to the king, he already trusted her.

Haman was a prideful man and thought Mordecai, Esther's uncle, should bow and worship him. When Mordecai wouldn't bow, Haman, knowing Mordecai was a Jew, went to the king with an evil plot: "There is a certain race of people scattered through all the provinces of your empire. Their laws are different from those of any other nation, and they refuse to obey even the laws of the king. So it is not in the king's interest to let them live. If it please Your Majesty, issue a decree that they be destroyed" (3:8-9).

When Esther heard about the plot, she went into action. She invited the king and Haman to a set of dinner parties. She carefully prepared the parties to soften the king's heart. After the first dinner the king couldn't sleep (God can help with these details!), and he read the book of records and found Mordecai had never been honored for saving his life. So the king made Haman honor Mordecai!

Then at dinner the next night the king granted a request to Esther, and she explained Mordecai's evil plot to kill all the people the king loved and trusted.

Whistle blown.

TO READ
John 20:11-18

"Mary!" Jesus said. She turned toward him and exclaimed, "Teacher!" JOHN 20:16

 The Best of Friends

How does Jesus treat the women who love him?

> After the Sabbath, at dawn on the first day of the week, Mary Magdalene and the other Mary went to look at the tomb.
>
> There was a violent earthquake, for an angel of the Lord came down from heaven and, going to the tomb, rolled back the stone and sat on it. His appearance was like lightning, and his clothes were white as snow. The guards were so afraid of him that they shook and became like dead men. (Matthew 28:1-4, NIV)

Jesus came down—to our level. He meets us where we are.

> The angel said to the women, "Do not be afraid, for I know that you are looking for Jesus, who was crucified. He is not here; he has risen, just as he said. Come and see the place where he lay. Then go quickly and tell his disciples: 'He has risen from the dead and is going ahead of you into Galilee. There you will see him.' Now I have told you." (vv. 5-7, NIV)

Jesus rose—and he takes us up a level with him. Knowing Christ elevates our status as women. Christ has a plan to move you up.

> So the women hurried away from the tomb, afraid yet filled with joy, and ran to tell his disciples. Suddenly Jesus met them. "Greetings," he said. They came to him, clasped his feet and worshiped him. Then Jesus said to them, "Do not be afraid. Go and tell my brothers to go to Galilee; there they will see me." (vv. 8-10, NIV)

Jesus entrusts women with ministry. Jesus thinks women have a valuable place in spreading the good news of hope and help found in Christ.

He is reaching you right where you are today, he is lifting you up to maximize your talent and heart to create in you a message. Who is he sending you to tell?

TO READ
Ephesians 5:3-7

But among you there must not be even a hint of sexual immorality, or of any kind of impurity, or of greed, because these are improper for God's holy people. EPHESIANS 5:3, NIV

 ## *Not a Hint*

God asks that we live in such a way that there is not even a hint of sin. *Hint* means: (a) a statement conveying by implication what it is preferred not to say explicitly; (b) an indirect or summary suggestion; (c) a slight indication of the existence, approach, or nature of something: CLUE (d) a very small amount: SUGGESTION.[3]

God asks that we don't leave a clue of sin. We are not to give even a suggestion of wrongdoing.

- Maybe you aren't having sex, but do you spend the night alone at someone's home when you are not married?
- Maybe you don't drink, but do you hang out at parties where they serve drugs and alcohol?
- Maybe you don't cheat, but do you allow someone to cheat off your paper?
- Maybe you don't steal, but do you look the other way when others at the company do?
- Maybe you obey your parents, but do you cover for your siblings who are rebelling?
- Maybe you don't beat your children, but do you ignore a situation where another child might be being abused?
- Maybe you aren't a prostitute, but do you dress like you are?
- Maybe you don't buy porn, but do you read explicit romance literature or watch movies with nudity?

Look at the hints you are leaving in your life. Do they point to the Savior or to sin?

TO READ
Psalm 71:15-23

You will restore me to even greater honor and comfort me once again. PSALM 71:21

 Comfort in Chaos

Have you ever noticed that sometimes the very people you are supposed to be ministering to and blessing end up blessing you? I have a friend who discovered an unusual growth, and during the testing and biopsy process, he and his wife sent us the following verses:

> Praise be to the God and Father of our Lord Jesus Christ, the Father of compassion and the God of all comfort, who comforts us in all our troubles, so that we can comfort those in any trouble with the comfort we ourselves have received from God. . . . We were under great pressure, far beyond our ability to endure, so that we despaired even of life. Indeed, in our hearts we felt the sentence of death. But this happened that we might not rely on ourselves but on God, who raises the dead. He has delivered us from such a deadly peril, and he will deliver us. On him we have set our hope that he will continue to deliver us, *as you help us by your prayers*. Then many will give thanks on our behalf for the gracious favor granted us in answer to the prayers of many. (2 Corinthians 1:3-4, 8-11, NIV, emphasis added)

I had been depressed about some serious issues until I got that letter. The passage changed my perspective completely. I knew that I was on the prayer team for my friend because God encourages us to pray for one another, but the phrase "as you help us by your prayers" gave powerful new significance to the work of prayer. In addition, it gave a new slant on the issues I was struggling with. I was reminded that God doesn't waste our pain; instead, when we go through tough places, God brings purpose to our pain. My time in God's vise grip was preparing me for the role of comforter in a whole new set of circumstances. When life is pressing in on you, look around for purpose, for the lesson, for the way God is training you to serve and encourage others.

TO READ
Hosea 2:2-20

I will betroth you to me forever; I will betroth you in righteousness and justice, in love and compassion. I will betroth you in faithfulness, and you will acknowledge the Lord. HOSEA 2:19-20, NIV

 ## Come Back

When someone is walking away from God, how do you handle it?

God asks Hosea to love unfaithful Gomer, and God uses their relationship as an example of how God deals with us when our own hearts wander (Hosea 2:2-14, NIV). We can use this Scripture as a model for how we should deal with someone who has turned away from God.

- Explain the truth, the standard. "Rebuke your mother, rebuke her."
- Don't bankroll the person's sin. "Otherwise I will strip her naked. . . . I will make her like a desert . . . and slay her with thirst."
- Pray a hedge of protection about her so that anytime she sins, it will be as if she were running into thorn bushes with bare skin—painful! "Therefore I will block her path with thornbushes; I will wall her in so that she cannot find her way."
- Pray she fails at sin. "She will chase after her lovers but not catch them; she will look for them but not find them."
- Allow her to pay the consequences for her poor choices. "Therefore I will take away my grain when it ripens, and my new wine when it is ready. I will take back my wool and my linen, intended to cover her nakedness."
- Don't cover for her lifestyle, decisions, or choices. "So now I will expose her lewdness before the eyes of her lovers."
- Don't keep going along with her ideas and plans as if nothing has happened. "I will stop all her celebrations."
- Take the high road to protect your character, and provide an opportunity to repent. "Therefore I am now going to allure her; I will lead her into the desert and speak tenderly to her."

TO READ
Hosea 2:18-23

"In that day I will respond," declares the Lord. . . . I will show my love to the one I called 'Not my loved one.' I will say to those called 'Not my people,' 'You are my people'; and they will say, 'You are my God.'" HOSEA 2:21-23, NIV

All Fall Down

We can learn much about success by looking at failure. One woman in the Bible who failed and fell was Gomer. Why did she fall?

- *She put sex above God:* "Their mother has been unfaithful. . . . She said, 'I will go after my lovers, who give me my food and my water, my wool and my linen, my oil and my drink.'" (Hosea 2:5, NIV)
- *She became ungrateful:* "She has not acknowledged that I was the one who gave her the grain, the new wine and oil, who lavished on her the silver and gold—which they used for Baal." (v. 8, NIV)
- *She left truth and found a belief system that allowed, even encouraged her lifestyle:* "'I will punish her for the days she burned incense to the Baals; she decked herself with rings and jewelry, and went after her lovers, but me she forgot,' declares the Lord." (v. 13, NIV)

Are you seeing the seeds of any of these failures in yourself or in someone you love? Are you allowing your emotions, your hormones, or your dysfunctions to make your decisions?

Are you allowing resentment, bitterness, or anger to be unaddressed in your life? Are you walking away from truth because it is easier to follow a lie? Maybe you are just sleeping in, missing church today, but what about next week, next year? Maybe you are just thinking that the guy in your class, at work, or at your gym is cute, but how will you respond if he actually talks to you? Maybe you are just angry today, but how do you handle your frustrations day after day?

Most women don't set out to have a hard heart; they just allow the callus to develop because they do nothing to stop it.

TO READ
Joel 2:28-32

I will pour out my Spirit upon all people. Your sons and daughters will prophesy. Your old men will dream dreams. Your young men will see visions.

JOEL 2:28

 Spokeswoman for God

Is there a precedent for women spokespersons for God?

- *A prophetess led the people in celebrating God's deliverance parting the Red Sea.* "Then Miriam the prophetess, Aaron's sister, took a tambourine in her hand, and all the women followed her, with tambourines and dancing." (Exodus 15:20, NIV)
- *A prophetess led the country into war and gained the victory God had promised.* "Deborah, a prophetess . . . was leading Israel at that time." (Judges 4:4, NIV)
- *A prophetess went to a king to bring bad news of God's judgment.* Huldah, the prophetess, said, "Tell the king of Judah, who sent you to inquire of the Lord, 'This is what the Lord, the God of Israel, says concerning the words you heard.'" (2 Kings 22:18, NIV)
- *A prophetess waited for the Messiah to be born and spoke about the redemption of Israel.* "There was also a prophetess, Anna. . . . Coming up to them at that very moment, she gave thanks to God and spoke about the child to all who were looking forward to the redemption of Jerusalem." (Luke 2:36, 38, NIV)

A prophetess is one who speaks the truth. Women, men, children—all people are called to speak the truth. But God specifically gifts and calls some women to do it often and well. If you are called to speak out, God will be there, giving you the words.

TO READ
Acts 4: 1-20

Peter and John replied, "Do you think God wants us to obey you rather than him? We cannot stop telling about the wonderful things we have seen and heard."

ACTS 4:19-20

 ## *Speak Out*

Miss America 2003, Erika Harold, was being pressured to not speak out on abstinence as a spokeswoman for Project Reality, a nonprofit group that pioneered abstinence-centered health-education programs in Illinois public schools since the mid-1980s. Erika had advocated and promoted sexual abstinence for years, but when she became Miss America and told pageant officials that she planned to talk about chastity, they told her not to.[4]

Sandy Rios, former president of Concerned Women for America, shared her opinion on the issue with the press: "In an age where beauty queens are regularly disqualified for inappropriate behavior, who would have thought a virtuous one would be silenced for her virtue?"[5]

Erika, who credits God with giving her the courage to speak out, even before the U.S. Congress, says, "I was fortunate enough to be raised by two loving parents who encouraged me to set high standards, to value myself and to save sex for marriage. But I grew up knowing that I was lucky and that not every young person had the love and support that I did. I saw many of my peers use sex to try to find that love and acceptance. But instead of being able to fill that void, many of them became teen parents, contracted diseases, and had their hearts broken."[6]

Erika is clear and bold in expressing the message God has laid on her heart: "As a role model, I will encourage young people to abstain from drugs, sex, and alcohol, and explain how this commitment helped me to protect, respect, and define myself."[7]

What issue has God asked you to speak on, write about, make phone calls for, or lobby for? Every woman, not just Miss America, should have a platform she cares about!

TO READ
2 Chronicles 30:6-9

If you return to the Lord, your relatives and your children will be treated mercifully by their captors, and they will be able to return to this land. For the Lord your God is gracious and merciful. If you return to him, he will not continue to turn his face from you. 2 CHRONICLES 30:9

 *Hello!*

"Rise up, you women who are at ease, and hear my [Isaiah's] voice; give ear to my word, you complacent daughters" (Isaiah 32:9, NASB).

This verse was written thousands of years ago, but it could have easily been penned on a PC yesterday. Isaiah was trying to get the attention of the women in his world, where things were bad and getting worse. He thought if the female gender joined in, things might get better!

What were the women doing? They were "at ease" and "complacent."

What was going on in their world? Isaiah wrote to move the people back to God. He was especially concerned about the morality of the nation's leadership, both politically and spiritually.

The book's opening gives a picture of the state of the people who claimed God as their own: "Hear, O heavens! Listen, O earth! This is what the Lord says: 'The children I raised and cared for have turned against me. Even the animals—the donkey and the ox—know their owner and appreciate his care, but not my people Israel. No matter what I do for them, they still do not understand'" (1:2-3).

These people were so far from God they didn't even recognize him anymore! What is going on in your world?

TO READ
1 Peter 1:21-25

Now that you have purified yourselves by obeying the truth so that you have sincere love . . . love one another deeply, from the heart. 1 PETER 1:22, NIV

 Nana

I love being around new grandmothers! They have all the joy of a new mother, but without the pain and recovery.

Here's a snapshot of one "Nana" in the Bible:

> The women said to Naomi: "Praise be to the Lord, who this day has not left you without a kinsman-redeemer. May he become famous throughout Israel! He will renew your life and sustain you in your old age. For your daughter-in-law, who loves you and who is better to you than seven sons, has given him birth."
>
> Then Naomi took the child, laid him in her lap and cared for him. The women living there said, "Naomi has a son." And they named him Obed. (Ruth 4:14-17, NIV)

Naomi had a baby? No, Ruth did! But Naomi is just as thrilled as a new mom. She is "renewed," thanks to her beloved daughter-in-law.

How was that relationship between mother-in-law and daughter-in-law established and nurtured?

- *Spiritual talks:* Ruth and Naomi must have had some, because Ruth left the false belief system she was raised with, married a believer, and after her husband died, she followed Naomi home to the Promised Land.
- *Shared memories:* The two women traveled together, back to Israel and around town. They both lost someone they loved: Ruth's husband and Naomi's son.
- *Solved problems:* They were broke, but they came up with a way to earn a living and start a home. They teamed up to triumph.

Mothers and daughters: Build a bridge to your in-laws. You might need them—and you might even enjoy them!

TO READ
Jeremiah 31:1-6

Long ago the Lord said to Israel: "I have loved you, my people, with an everlasting love. With unfailing love I have drawn you to myself." JEREMIAH 31:3

 ## *Whom Can You Trust?*

There's a statement that a young woman makes in the Bible that floors me: "'I will do whatever you say,' Ruth answered" (Ruth 3:5, NIV). She will do whatever Naomi says? *Whatever?* That is amazing trust. They have either a deeply forged relationship or a very dysfunctional, codependent one!

From the context of the book of Ruth, we can see that she isn't some emotionally needy woman. Rather, she is called "noble" and "better than seven sons," and her godly character is noted by everyone around her. So this statement of respect and trust comes from an amazingly trusting relationship. Ruth has come to believe Naomi *always* has her best interests in mind. That's why she can hear a plan and simply say, "That's good, let's go with it!"

Who has your best interests in mind?

- "For I know the plans I have for you," declares the Lord, "plans to prosper you and not to harm you, plans to give you hope and a future." (Jeremiah 29:11, NIV)
- The thief comes only in order that he may steal and may kill and may destroy. I came that they may have and enjoy life, and have it in abundance—to the full, till it overflows. (John 10:10, AMP)
- Greater love has no one than this, that he lay down his life for his friends. (John 15:13, NIV)

To trust God in the next step, remember how he has already expressed his love for you. Make a list of all the times and ways God has been there for you, provided for you, and given you opportunity and blessing. Then, when you are wondering if you should trust a person with your future, check out the person's love level for you (and for the God who loves you).

TO READ
Ruth 2:11-13

May the Lord, the God of Israel, under whose wings you have come to take refuge, reward you fully.

RUTH 2:12

 ## How to Spot a Good Guy

I hear it all the time: "There are no good men left in the world!"

How did Ruth figure out that Boaz was a good guy?

A good man has . . .

- *A good reputation.* Those he trusted, trusted him. "Now Naomi had a relative on her husband's side . . . a man of standing, whose name was Boaz." (Ruth 2:1, NIV)
- *Good manners.* "And Ruth . . . said to Naomi, 'Let me go to the fields and pick up the leftover grain behind anyone in whose eyes I find favor.' . . . Just then Boaz arrived from Bethlehem and greeted the harvesters, 'The Lord be with you!'" (vv. 2, 4, NIV)
- *Women's safety in mind.* "So Boaz said to Ruth, 'My daughter, listen to me. Don't go and glean in another field and don't go away from here. Stay here with my servant girls. Watch the field where the men are harvesting, and follow along after the girls. I have told the men not to touch you.'" (vv. 8-9, NIV)
- *A woman's well-being in mind.* "'And whenever you are thirsty, go and get a drink from the water jars the men have filled.' . . . At mealtime Boaz said to her, 'Come over here. Have some bread and dip it in the wine vinegar.' When she sat down with the harvesters, he offered her some roasted grain. She ate all she wanted and had some left over. As she got up to glean, Boaz gave orders to his men, 'Even if she gathers among the sheaves, don't embarrass her. Rather, pull out some stalks for her from the bundles and leave them for her to pick up, and don't rebuke her.'" (vv. 9, 14-16, NIV)
- *An eye for good character in others.* "Boaz replied, 'I've been told all about what you have done for your mother-in-law since the death of your husband—how you left your father and mother and your homeland and came to live with a people you did not know before.'" (v. 11, NIV)

"The Lord bless you, my daughter!" Boaz exclaimed. "You are showing more family loyalty now than ever by not running after a younger man, whether rich or poor." RUTH 3:10

 ## Building a Track Record

What moved Boaz to want to marry Ruth?

Consider what he knew about her: daughter-in-law of Naomi, a relative, so she had a good character reference. Then he witnessed with his own eyes a beautiful, young woman, gleaning in his fields to make sure her mother-in-law was provided for. He never heard Ruth criticize or complain.

When he asks her to lunch, Ruth is grateful, polite, and respectful. News of her godly character travels through town. This is no ordinary woman who has crossed his path; this is a woman who is building a strong, trustworthy reputation.

Then she shows up at his feet. This is not a sexual advance like a harlot but rather a reaching out, humbling herself to say, "I am interested in you." As if to say, "I will wait, move on, or follow, according to your response."

And he was moved to action by her high character.

Do you need people in positions of power to help you? Our reputation and actions show if we are worthy of others. We must consider how we respond to everyone around us. Is it with respect, courtesy, thankfulness, and honor?

What are you doing to build a track record with all people, powerful and otherwise?

"I will do everything you say," Ruth replied.

Ruth 3:5

 Timing Is Everything

From our Western, twenty-first-century point of view, the scene of Naomi and Ruth pursuing Boaz seems strange. But at this time in history, widows were provided for by a kinsman-redeemer; that is, a man somehow related to the deceased got first dibs on marrying the widow.

But look at this from Ruth's perspective: Everything was new—culture, widowhood, friends, and now a man. Many things prepared Ruth emotionally for the next step of her life. The stair steps of trust looked like this:

Married Naomi's son
  Heard about Naomi's God, the true God
    Believed in God, even after her husband died
      Went with Naomi back to Israel, kept learning about God
        Gleaned the fields to provide, didn't complain
          Attracted Boaz's attention, was asked to lunch
            Received compliments from Boaz, who looked out
              for her
          Told Naomi about Boaz
           Accepted Naomi's plan

Ruth wouldn't have been ready to trust Naomi or Boaz with her future had she not taken the first few steps: believe then act on that belief and keep acting on that belief. Leaving her family, going to Israel, gleaning—none of it was easy, but it was right.

What is the next step God is asking you to take? How has he prepared you for that step?

December

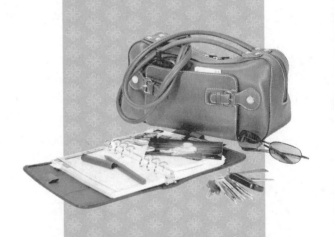

TO READ
1 Timothy 3:1-16

I am writing these things to you now, even though I hope to be with you soon, so that if I can't come for a while, you will know how people must conduct themselves in the household of God. This is the church of the living God, which is the pillar and support of the truth. 1 Timothy 3:14-15

 Moving Others to Health

The apostle Paul was a people mover extraordinaire. He knew how to motivate others.

Level the playing field. Paul shares his fears. Then he gives them an opportunity to fix all of the issues before he even arrives: "I am afraid that when I come I may not find you as I want you to be, and you may not find me as you want me to be. I fear that there may be quarreling, jealousy, outbursts of anger, factions, slander, gossip, arrogance and disorder. I am afraid that when I come again my God will humble me before you, and I will be grieved over many who have sinned earlier and have not repented of the impurity, sexual sin and debauchery in which they have indulged" (2 Corinthians 12:20-21, NIV).

How can you make people feel more comfortable around you? How can you word your requests clearly and compassionately?

Look at the options. Paul shares that there are different approaches to handling problems and getting to the root of the matter. By laying out the worst discipline option (whips), the other looks pretty good. "I will come to you very soon, if the Lord is willing, and then I will find out not only how these arrogant people are talking, but what power they have. For the kingdom of God is not a matter of talk but of power. What do you prefer? Shall I come to you with a whip, or in love and with a gentle spirit?" (1 Corinthians 4:19-21, NIV).

Paul didn't overreact; he acted to get a response that produces fruit.

TO READ
Psalm 84:5-10

A single day in your courts is better than a thousand anywhere else! I would rather be a gatekeeper in the house of my God than live the good life in the homes of the wicked. PSALM 84:10

 ## Have Some Pride

Getting to the top and staying at the top is no small feat. But at what point are your personal pride and principles more important than any power or prestige you have experienced thus far?

One of my favorite examples is from a queen in the Bible. To set the scene, you have to know King Xerxes was the most powerful leader in the then-known world. He gave a banquet lasting 180 days to show off.

Then he gave another banquet that lasted seven days in the garden. He used golden goblets and allowed every man to drink as much as he wanted. His wife, Queen Vashti, also gave a banquet for the women, and on the seventh day, King Xerxes, drunk with wine, commanded her to come into his banquet in her royal robes so all the men could look at her. But Vashti refused to come (Esther 1:2-12).

Good for Vashti! What self-respecting woman wants a bunch of drunken, self-absorbed, lustful men staring at her?

However, she did pay for her choice. The king issued a decree that the queen would never be allowed in his presence and she was to be replaced. Not too bad of a punishment if you consider she didn't have to be treated like a piece of meat anymore.

DECEMBER 3

TO READ
Philippians 1:27-30

Whatever happens to me, you must live in a manner worthy of the Good News about Christ, as citizens of heaven. Then, whether I come and see you again or only hear about you, I will know that you are standing side by side, fighting together for the Good News. PHILIPPIANS 1:27

 Bad News Turned Good

Sometimes we get a phone message, an e-mail, or a secondhand version of negative news or criticism. Immediately our heart sinks. It beats harder and faster. Our head begins to swim with thoughts like, "Oh no! What did I do?" "What if they are mad at me?" "What if I lose this relationship?" or "What if this is just the tip of the iceberg and it gets worse, like a lawsuit, or they leave the church?" The what-ifs can make us crazy!

So when you get a glimpse of bad news, how should you handle it?

- *Focus on God:* Immediately take the concern to God, and plant it in the center of God's loving care. He is in control. He knows all things. None of this is a surprise to God.
- *Focus on getting to the truth:* Get firsthand, accurate information. If possible, quickly return the call, or go to the person. Listen—really listen. Don't try to defend yourself; ask God to be your defense and shield as you seek to listen for the pain or the root of the problem. If you react too quickly or become defensive, you may never really get to the bottom of the issue.
- *Focus on the positive:* Thank the person. Sharing bad news is no easy task. Calm the person with statements that will help everyone involved see how this is an opportunity for God to work or for everyone involved to learn and grow. Ask for time to pray or process the news.

TO READ
Song of Songs 2:10-17

Quick! Catch all the little foxes before they ruin the vineyard of your love, for the grapevines are all in blossom. SONG OF SONGS 2:15

 Catch the Foxes

When little things pile up in a relationship, the weight of all those small things becomes a big thing! Then when the one last "straw" is added, it breaks the back of the relationship just like a camel that can't carry one more thing. The king in Song of Songs wants to make sure that doesn't happen.

The king's wife grew up in the country on a vineyard. And they had small rodents (more like rats than our foxes) that would burrow underground and eat the roots of the vines. Although everything initially seemed lush and green in the vineyard, because the plants had no root system, whole sections of the vineyard would turn brown and die.

The newlyweds didn't want this to happen to their relationship. We all have little foxes that can ruin relationships:

- Holding on to negative attitudes
- Using harsh or critical words
- Taking others for granted
- Not valuing the other person's time, talent, or treasure
- Having unspoken or unrealistic expectations
- Not dealing with your own past baggage
- Never saying, "I'm sorry"

There are a myriad of small things that can pile up. Instead, if you feel hurt or offended, say to that person, "I value our relationship too much to let this come between us. I need to share how I feel."

Are there any piles of unresolved feelings in any of your relationships? Go catch those little foxes.

TO READ
James 3:13-18

Those who are peacemakers will plant seeds of peace and reap a harvest of goodness. JAMES 3:18

 Misplaced Priorities

Achieving success in our personal relationships is vital for healthy living and our future success. So what do you do when you realize you've blown it in an interpersonal relationship?

The king's wife knows what it's like to make a relational faux pas: "I slept but my heart was awake. Listen! My lover is knocking: 'Open to me'" (Song of Songs 5:2, NIV).

Her husband, the king, shows up at her door wanting intimacy (in those days it was customary for them to have separate rooms in the palace). But she has an attitude: "I have taken off my robe—must I put it on again? I have washed my feet—must I soil them again?" (v. 3, NIV).

Even in the palace, they had dirt floors. So to get up would mean she had to rewash her feet, and spending time with him just wasn't worth the hassle. (Talk about having a bad day and a bad attitude. The most handsome, powerful, best catch of a man is your husband, and you don't want to take an extra two minutes to get time with him!)

He then leaves a symbolic calling card of love: myrrh on the door handle (a spice that symbolized romance). So then she begins to realize what a jerk she's been: "My heart began to pound for him. I arose to open for my lover, and my hands dripped with myrrh. . . . I opened for my lover, but my lover had left; he was gone. My heart sank at his departure" (vv. 4-6, NIV).

So she finally does the right thing: "I looked for him but did not find him. I called him but he did not answer. The watchmen found me as they made their rounds in the city. . . . O daughters of Jerusalem, I charge you—if you find my lover, . . . tell him I am faint with love" (vv. 6-8, NIV).

She goes out of her way to find him and make amends. She got it: The bigger the faux pas, the bigger the effort to make things right must be!

TO READ
Song of Songs 2:1-6

Compared to other youths, my lover is like the finest apple tree in the orchard. I am seated in his delightful shade, and his fruit is delicious to eat.

SONG OF SONGS 2:3

 ## An Intimate Awakening

If there is such a thing as a marital sexual awakening, the king's wife had one. We can observe her sexual awakening when she realizes that she is a sexual creature and intimacy is a gift from God to be enjoyed and protected.

She is at first self-conscious, saying to the king, "I am the a rose of Sharon, the lily of the valley" (Song of Songs 2:1). She's fishing for a compliment here, saying she is plain and ordinary like the wild roses and lilies that grew like dandelions in the countryside. But her husband has a great comeback line: "Like a lily among thorns is my darling among the maidens" (v. 2, NIV). Basically the king says, "No way, baby! All the other women are like thorns compared to you!"

Then came her awakening of desire: "Like an apple tree among the trees of the forest is my lover among the young men. I delight to sit in his shade, and his fruit is sweet to my taste. . . . Strengthen me with raisins, refresh me with apples, for I am faint with love. His left arm is under my head, and his right arm embraces me" (vv. 3-6, NIV).

This is a progression of compliments and invitations. When she says you are an apple tree in a forest, she is saying, "You are one in a million!" She wants him near her, near enough to sit in the shade his own body would cast. She comments that his fruit (the intimate part of who he is) is sweet to her "taste," so at this point her lips are on him.

She then transitions to wanting him as much as she needs food, so in a sense she explains to her husband, "I am starving for your love."

If you are married, your husband longs to hear you say these words.

TO READ
Proverbs 31:1-31

There are many virtuous and capable women in the world, but you surpass them all! PROVERBS 31:29

 ## *Worth It All*

For two years I have kept one voice mail message on my phone. It is my oldest son, calling me after the funeral of the mother of one of his friends. The message simply says, "Mom, I'm calling just to say, 'I love you.' Love ya, Mom."

Every few weeks my voice mail service replays that message, and I save it all over again to be heard on another day. My sons tell me, "I love you" almost daily, but the emotion in the voice of a starting quarterback moved spontaneously to bless his mom, that was a unique moment. Those are the moments that make all the work worth it.

The Proverbs 31 woman got her moment too. She was never idle; she worked long, hard days balancing marriage, family, ministry, and industry. The result: her children, now grown, arise (go out of their way) to tell others (and we hope, her) how much they appreciate her and admire her.

And her husband chimes in his glowing compliments as well. He says that she is above and beyond the norm. For the past few Christmases, I told my family I didn't want any gifts except the gift of words—nothing is so sweet as a few words of kindness, thanks, and praise. Not only her family, but also her community said thanks for what she had done.

Keep going—your good work will catch up to you!

TO READ
Proverbs 2:1-8

The Lord grants wisdom! From his mouth come knowledge and understanding. PROVERBS 2:6

 Woman of the Word

The deeper a woman is into the Word of God, the broader her influence and the stronger her life.

People have wondered how Elizabeth Elliot could go back to the Auca Indians, the same tribe that killed her husband. But back she and her baby daughter went, and she reached the entire tribe for Christ. She was a woman of the Word.

In shocked silence we were glued to the television as we watched the twin towers fall and then heard of the amazing bravery of Todd Beamer aboard Flight 93. Lisa Beamer was thrust into the media spotlight at the moment of her worst private pain, and she bore it publicly with such amazing strength that even the jaded media moguls were in awe and wondered at the source of her strength: the Word of God.

The world watched in stunned wonder at the amazing strength of Dayna Curry and Heather Mercer, two young relief workers captured by the Taliban and held for several months during the height of the September 11 aftermath. In a miraculous rescue by American troops, the source of their strength came to light: They were women of the Word.

The Proverbs 31 woman had this same strength: "She is clothed with strength and dignity; she can laugh at the days to come. She speaks with wisdom, and faithful instruction is on her tongue" (Proverbs 31:25-26, NIV).

Want to "laugh at the days to come"? Want to be "clothed in strength and dignity tomorrow"? Then spend time in the Word today!

TO READ
Ecclesiastes 7:10-14

Wisdom or money can get you almost anything, but it's important to know that only wisdom can save your life. ECCLESIASTES 7:12

 Entrepreneurship

Funding a ministry or organization can be one of the first obstacles to overcome. Often a family's budget can't underwrite a whole new ministry, outreach, or business, so another income source has to be found.

One of today's largest churches started its ministry with funds earned by selling vegetables at a Farmers' Market!

Check out the Proverbs 31 plan: "She considers a field and buys it; out of her earnings she plants a vineyard. She sets about her work vigorously; her arms are strong for her tasks. She sees that her trading is profitable, and her lamp does not go out at night. . . . She makes linen garments and sells them, and supplies the merchants with sashes" (Proverbs 31:16-18, 24, NIV).

First, she goes into real estate; the land she buys appreciates in value. Then she plants a vineyard, which is a long-term investment with a yearly yield. She is strong physically (her arms are strong for the task), so most likely she is a part of the labor force as well. Then she goes out trading (bargaining and bartering), and she stays up late at night (probably counting her money!). Then she diversifies and makes clothing, and she expands until she has her own line of clothing that merchants carry (think of it as a franchise).

If you are launching into a ministry or business, go hang out with some women in the workplace. Contact ministries who help women in business, like Workplace Influence. And pray that you will find a mentor who has succeeded in building an economically sound ministry, company, or organization.

Make sure a financial plan is a part of your plan to influence the world, and live out the call.

TO READ
Matthew 5:13-16

In the same way, let your good deeds shine out for all to see, so that everyone will praise your heavenly Father. MATTHEW 5:16

 ## Where's Baby Jesus?

Have you ever thought about what would happen if you took Christ out of Christmas? There would be no gifts because the wise men brought gifts to the babe. There would be no carols; they all talk about Jesus. There would be no tree because it was a saint who first started that tradition. There would be no stars or angels. It pretty much becomes empty.

Think about the impact believers have had throughout history. Many hospitals were started with church affiliation. Most colleges and universities (including the Ivy League schools) were started as seminaries. Missionaries were some of the first people to cross the plains to offer help for weary settlers along the way.

Then take a look at our communities. Christians believe in making a difference, in serving and giving back. We believe in respecting authority—so many of the highest-ranking positions in our communities, states, and nations would not have the light of godly wisdom if believers pulled back. Many believers are in the ranks of doctors, lawyers, military, policemen, and all sectors of the public service.

Then think about the holiday calendar. Without presidents like Washington and Lincoln, who both claimed a faith in God, we wouldn't have President's Day. There would be no Martin Luther King Jr. holiday because he was a pastor before he was a public figure.

People of faith have changed our world through their impact on holidays, health, education, and the leadership of our communities. God uses Christians to shine his light and lead many to praise him.

TO READ
Ephesians 5:25-33

Again I say, each man must love his wife as he loves himself, and the wife must respect her husband.

EPHESIANS 5:33

 ## *Getting Him on Your Team*

If you are married, having a supportive spouse is vital to your ongoing success. If you are going to overcome a habit or your past or step into the future God has designed for you, it is all easier if your spouse is on your team. What kinds of things win your spouse over?

Let's look at the model the Proverbs 31 woman left: "A wife of noble character who can find? She is worth far more than rubies. Her husband has full confidence in her and lacks nothing of value. She brings him good, not harm, all the days of her life. . . . Her husband is respected at the city gate, where he takes his seat among the elders of the land" (Proverbs 31:10-12, 23, NIV).

Her husband feels she is worth much more than rubies because

- he has full confidence in her;
- he isn't lacking anything he needs;
- she brings him good not harm;
- he is respected among the public leadership.

As you reach toward your stars, does your husband still feel like he puts stars in your eyes? Looks like the Proverbs 31 wife made sure her husband had all the basics covered—at least everything that mattered in the public eye.

What he needed was there when he needed it (clean socks and underwear, the kids' needs being met and doing well in school, etc.). This doesn't mean she handles every detail, but she has made sure there is a system in place to get the needs met. You can delegate some to your spouse and the kids, and you can hire some out; but somehow you need to make sure he has confidence in both your dream *and* the dreams you have together.

I led Israel along with my ropes of kindness and love. I lifted the yoke from his neck, and I myself stooped to feed him. HOSEA 11:4

 ## *Home Base*

Stability at home equals success outside the home. When home base is running smoothly, your focus and that of each person in your family can then be turned outward and onward. So what helps home base run more effectively?

Let's look at the Proverbs 31 woman for a few clues: "She finds wool and flax and busily spins it. She is like a merchant's ship; she brings her food from afar. She gets up before dawn to prepare breakfast for her household and plan the day's work for her servant girls" (Proverbs 31:13-15).

She is eager to do what it takes to provide for her family. She starts with the basics—wool and flax, to make clothes. Then she moves on to food. She is willing to go to great lengths to bring home the best food, so much so that she is compared to a merchant ship.

Then she obviously has a smart daily schedule: She gets up before the rest of her family and gets prepared. First, she fixes food for her family; then she feeds all those who work for her. For a passionate woman, the home front can sometimes get neglected. Macaroni and cheese, pizza, and burgers are okay for meals when you are under a deadline, but your family will begin to complain (and eat elsewhere) if you have a consistent pattern of neglecting them. You don't have to be a gourmet, but it helps to have some staples on hand and a little creative energy left over for dinner.

The unwritten benefit of a strong home base is that a mom who rises early is interacting with her family at the start of the day. It's easier to be teammates cheering one another toward success if you see one another!

TO READ
Proverbs 31:1-31

Her children stand and bless her. Her husband praises her: "There are many virtuous and capable women in the world, but you surpass them all!"

PROVERBS 31:28-29

 Action!

Proverbs 31:10 introduces a poem explaining a woman of noble character. I have italicized the verbs in the passage. Notice how many there are:

- She *brings* him good, not harm, all the days of her life.
- She *selects* wool and flax and works with eager hands.
- She is like the merchant ships, *bringing* her food from afar.
- She *gets up* while it is still dark; she *provides* food for her family and portions for her servant girls.
- She *considers* a field and *buys* it; out of her earnings she plants a vineyard.
- She *sets* about her work vigorously; her arms are strong for her tasks.
- She *sees* that her trading is profitable, and her lamp *does not go out* at night.
- She *holds* the distaff and *grasps* the spindle with her fingers.
- She *opens* her arms to the poor and *extends* her hands to the needy. . . .
- She *makes* coverings for her bed; she *is clothed* in fine linen and purple. . . .
- She *makes* linen garments and *sells* them, and *supplies* the merchants with sashes.
- She *is clothed* with strength and dignity; she *can laugh* at the days to come.
- She *speaks* with wisdom, and faithful instruction is on her tongue.
- She *watches* over the affairs of her household and *does not eat* the bread of idleness. (Proverbs 31:12-27, NIV)

Do you notice a common thread? She's in action! Proverbs 31:28-29 is the result, and you're sure to want to be honored and have your kids call you blessed. But remember how she got there—she had an action plan. She's performing multiple tasks at home, at work, and in the community and is combining those with the responsibilities of parenting and character building. It is biblical to make those to-do lists! Are you in neutral gear in one area of life (home, work, service, church, parenting, etc.)? Select the weak link, and write a goal that will move you into action to make progress in that area.

TO READ
Proverbs 11:12-16

A gracious woman attains honor.

PROVERBS 11:16, NASB

 Grace

You'll get further with grace. One compliment a woman loves to hear is, "What a gracious lady" or "She has so much grace." In ballet, grace means a flawless performance that is so beautiful that those in the audience hold their breath. In beauty pageants, grace might mean gliding across the floor or having a witty, articulate answer to a stumping question. But what is a woman of grace from God's point of view?

God's grace is the giving of unconditional love and unmerited favor. God's grace is also the ability to see us as we can be, not as we are. God always sees his children's potential.

What is grace? Romans 3:24 explains that we "are justified freely by his grace through the redemption that came by Christ Jesus" (NIV). We are justified, or rendered free. We are redeemed, or ransomed.

So when we model Christlikeness in our ability to love and in our ability to yield to God so the fruit of the Spirit is seen in us, we are gracious.

Grace is especially noticed when it is in the midst of people of chaos, character flaws, and crudeness. Are you rising above the sea of sinfulness around you? Are you holding out a lifeline of God's love by modeling love?

TO READ	A worthy wife is her husband's joy and crown; a
Proverbs 12:1-5	shameful wife saps his strength. PROVERBS 12:4

 Better Than Houses and Money!

Proverbs 19:14 says, "Parents can provide their sons with an inheritance of houses and wealth, but only the Lord can give an understanding wife." The NIV uses the word *prudent* for *understanding,* and other Bible translations use the word *wise* or *worthy*. If being wise or prudent or worthy is better than inherited wealth of homes and money, how does the Bible define this concept?

- Proverbs 12:16: "A wise person stays calm when insulted."
- Proverbs 12:23: "Wise people don't make a show of their knowledge, but fools broadcast their folly."
- Proverbs 13:16: "Wise people think before they act."
- Proverbs 14:8: "The wise look ahead to see what is coming."
- Proverbs 14:15: "The prudent carefully consider their steps."
- Proverbs 22:3: "A prudent person foresees the danger ahead and takes precautions."

A common thread seems to run through these verses: The prudent person *thinks* it through.

Notice that prudence or wisdom isn't a feeling. How many of your decisions are made out of emotions? Do you buy something because the person selling it is sweet or is your cousin or you owe your aunt some favor? (The favor is now a guilt offering!) Do you spend when you feel depressed or eat treats because you feel entitled?

For a week, track how you make decisions, and see how much emotion might be influencing your thought process.

TO READ
Titus 1:5-9

An elder must be well thought of for his good life. He must be faithful to his wife, and his children must be believers who are not wild or rebellious.

TITUS 1:6

 Those Kids!

Janie's daughter is pregnant and not married. Jim's son just got arrested for drug possession. Mandy's honor-student son was arrested for breaking and entering. Kim's daughter refuses to attend church and says she is becoming a Buddhist. And all these parents are in leadership, so what do they do with Titus 1:6?

How wild is wild? (Purple hair, a nose ring, or a tattoo?) And how disobedient? (Sent to the principal's office, juvenile hall, or jail?) How perfect do our kids have to be to keep us in ministry? At what point should we (if ever?) set our ministry, call, dreams, and leadership aside? What is hard about this part of the character checklist for leaders is this small section that includes the behavior of others (like having children who believe and are under control).

Bill and I have come to see this as a practical guideline: Those over eighteen are adults and under their own responsibility to God for this verse. The heart of the verse is to encourage parents who love God, hold God's standards, and seek to help their children do the same.

Kids aren't perfect; they will make mistakes. The key question as parents is, Are you *dealing with* the mistakes, getting your kids the resources they need, and helping them to grow in grace?

The point at which you may need to set aside your own dreams and plans is when you don't have enough time to help a child keep his or her faith. When that becomes the case, you may need to take time away from a call to leadership and focus your energies on being spiritual leaders to your kids. There will be other opportunities to lead in an official capacity. But first you want to be sure that your children are on the way to the finish line.

A deacon must be faithful to his wife, and he must manage his children and household well. Those who do well as deacons will be rewarded with respect from others and will have increased confidence in their faith in Christ Jesus. 1 TIMOTHY 3:12-13

 ## *A Good Grid*

If we are going to lead others, and if we want people to buy into our dream, we have to live a life worth following. Church elders have a set of prerequisites, and this is a great checklist for anyone in leadership.

Titus 1:6-9: "An elder must be blameless, the husband of but one wife, a man whose children believe and are not open to the charge of being wild and disobedient. Since an overseer is entrusted with God's work, he must be blameless—not overbearing, not quick-tempered, not given to drunkenness, not violent, not pursuing dishonest gain. Rather he must be hospitable, one who loves what is good, who is self-controlled, upright, holy and disciplined. He must hold firmly to the trustworthy message as it has been taught, so that he can encourage others by sound doctrine and refute those who oppose it" (NIV).

Run through the following list and check how your life measures up:

- faithful in marriage
- children that are under control and love God
- not overbearing
- not quick-tempered
- no addictive behaviors

- not violent
- hospitable
- loves good
- self-controlled
- upright, holy, disciplined
- holds to the truth and knows it well enough to counsel or correct

Do you have some areas that need growth? Select one trait that you would like to grow in. Set a few goals. If you are a growing leader, soon others will want to follow your personal growth example. If you are going to be a woman on the go, it is also great to inspire others to get going in their growth as you work on yours. Is there a friend who might also want to work on one of these areas? Invite her to join you in your growth plan.

TO READ
Ruth 3:1-18

While it is true that I [Boaz] am one of your family redeemers, there is another man who is more closely related to you than I am. Stay here tonight, and in the morning I will talk to him. If he is willing to redeem you, then let him marry you. But if he is not willing, then as surely as the Lord lives, I will marry you! RUTH 3:12-13

 ## *A Second Opinion*

Some of the principles in the Old Testament were structured because for the most part, men were in charge. However, behind many of these old rules are wise principles. Here's an example from Numbers 30:3-9:

> If a young woman makes a vow to the Lord or a pledge under oath while she is still living at her father's home, and her father hears of the vow or pledge but says nothing, then all her vows and pledges will stand. But if her father refuses to let her fulfill the vow or pledge on the day he hears of it, then all her vows and pledges will become invalid. The Lord will forgive her because her father would not let her fulfill them. Now suppose a young woman takes a vow or makes an impulsive pledge and later marries. If her husband learns of her vow or pledge and raises no objections on the day he hears of it, her vows and pledges will stand. But if her husband refuses to accept her vow or impulsive pledge on the day he hears of it, he nullifies her commitments, and the Lord will forgive her. If, however, a woman is a widow or is divorced, she must fulfill all her vows and pledges no matter what.

On face value, this seems ridiculous or even demeaning. My father can tell me what I can or can't commit to?

But look again: The divorced or widowed woman makes her own decisions and commitments, but those who have decisions or commitments *that might have an impact on others* have a check-and-balance system.

God places a fail-safe on her relationships so that her vows or commitments don't come between her and her relationships. It's like getting a second opinion or the thirty-day "buyer's remorse" clause.

Discussing big decisions until there is unity and consensus is a safeguard to relationships.

TO READ
Job 2:1-10

[Job's] wife said to him, "Are you still trying to maintain your integrity? Curse God and die." But Job replied, "You talk like a godless woman. Should we accept only good things from the hand of God and never anything bad?" So in all this, Job said nothing wrong. JOB 2:9-10

 Yikes!

It's good to encourage your spouse to succeed, but it's not good to provoke him to win at all costs. Look at this picture of what it looks like to have a wife who pushes achievement without conscience:

> His wife Jezebel came in and asked him, "Why are you so sullen? Why won't you eat?"
>
> He answered her, "Because I said to Naboth the Jezreelite, 'Sell me your vineyard; or if you prefer, I will give you another vineyard in its place.' But he said, 'I will not give you my vineyard.'"
>
> Jezebel his wife said, "Is this how you act as king over Israel? Get up and eat! Cheer up. I'll get you the vineyard of Naboth the Jezreelite."
>
> So she wrote letters in Ahab's name, placed his seal on them, and sent them to the elders and nobles who lived in Naboth's city with him. In those letters she wrote:
>
> "Proclaim a day of fasting and seat Naboth in a prominent place among the people. But seat two scoundrels opposite him and have them testify that he has cursed both God and the king. Then take him out and stone him to death." . . .
>
> As soon as Jezebel heard that Naboth had been stoned to death, she said to Ahab, "Get up and take possession of the vineyard of Naboth the Jezreelite that he refused to sell you. He is no longer alive, but dead." When Ahab heard that Naboth was dead, he got up and went down to take possession of Naboth's vineyard. (1 Kings 21:5-10, 15-16, NIV)

We don't want to think we have anything in common with Jezebel, but she started down this road with small things. Are you tempted to be controlling, pushy, or manipulating? Do you use others to get what you want or shade the truth? No amount of makeup or jewelry can camouflage an evil heart.

TO READ
Proverbs 21:15-21

It is better to live alone in the desert than with a crabby, complaining wife. PROVERBS 21:19

 ## The Roadblock

The number one reason pastors leave ministry is an unhappy pastor's wife. Sometimes an attitude or lack of focus can block God's call.

It's not only in ministry homes. I have seen a husband held back from all kinds of career paths because a wife doesn't want to leave her new home, her family, her ministry, or her current career assignment.

It isn't that his call is more important than hers, for God calls a husband to sacrifice for a wife's call, too. But I don't think God ever honors a bad attitude on a woman's part.

Think of two biblical examples: King Ahab and Michal, King David's wife. King Ahab did so much evil that 1 Kings 16 says it was more than any of those before him. Then he married a woman who enjoyed killing prophets. Ahab was bad, but his wife encouraged him to do more evil. Instead of encouraging him to walk with God, she cheered louder when he was pure evil!

David's wife, the daughter of King Saul, was angry, bitter, embarrassed, or convicted because when David had conquered thousands for God and came in dancing, singing, and praising, she hated him for it! She did not want him to succeed. In 2 Samuel 6:16, it says she "was filled with contempt for him." How's that for supporting your husband?

What is your attitude toward your husband's success? Are you so focused on your own wants and needs that you are forgetting his?

TO READ
Titus 2:3-5

Then they can train the younger women to love
their husbands and children, to be self-controlled
and pure, to be busy at home, to be kind, and to be
subject to their husbands, so that no one will malign
the word of God. TITUS 2:4-5, NIV

Workers at Home

How can we balance work, home, family, marriage, and ministry? Some
people of faith try to balance a woman's life by limiting her call to home and
family, often citing Titus 2:3-5.

What does "busy at home" mean? Word studies define "worker at home"
as "a guard of the home; a keeper of the home; domestically inclined."

I studied this verse and that phrase in depth, I read volumes of commen-
tators and word study books, and in the end, the best synopsis for "worker
at home" is that a woman's heart is home. Her priorities reflect a God- and
family-focused value system. So her feet could be anywhere, but her heart
was at home.

I have operated under this definition for all of my children's lives, and it
seems to be working. My husband feels loved, my children are mostly
grown, and all are strong spiritually. I have helped provide for my family,
and some people have also been helped in ministry along the way.

Your feet can be anywhere, but is your heart at home?

TO READ
2 Corinthians 8:10-15

Now *finish* the work, so that your eager willingness to do it may be matched by your completion of it, according to your means.

2 CORINTHIANS 8:11, NIV (emphasis added)

 ## In Your Court

Tennis is compelling. A serve is volleyed, and there are only two choices: Hit it back, or miss the opportunity and lose control of the ball again. When the ball is in your court, you have to keep control of the ball to win.

"The ball is in your court," a phrase we toss about freely, is a pretty strong challenge said in a nice way. It means "I pass the responsibility to you, so you better follow up and do something." The best option is always to do something quickly and completely, then "pass the ball" to someone who can "take the ball and run with it."

What happens all too often is that the ball gets lobbed into someone's court with no warning and no instruction. A failure to communicate that you are passing the ball into someone else's court is dangerous because that person can assume it is still in your court. Whenever you give responsibility for part of your call or dream to someone else, make sure to write out instructions, the results you hope to see, and when you hope to see them.

Remember, it is still your ball, no matter who is carrying it, and God holds you responsible for that call.

TO READ
Luke 15:8-24

He returned home to his father. And while he was still a long distance away, his father saw him coming. Filled with love and compassion, he ran to his son, embraced him, and kissed him. His son said to him, "Father, I have sinned against both heaven and you, and I am no longer worthy of being called your son."

LUKE 15:20-21

 *Dramatic Action*

For many, a crisis can lead to a dramatic action in a person's life:

- "When my husband held me at gunpoint in front of the children, I knew that if I got out of this alive, the kids and I would not go on living with this man!"
- "When I had a heart attack at forty-five, I knew I needed to change my lifestyle."
- "When I finally realized that spending my days getting high was getting me nowhere, I knew things had to change."

After the Prodigal Son spent his inheritance and found himself with the pigs, he realized that if he went back to his father, he would at least be eating better as his servant. This revelation spurred him to move back to his father's house, apologize, and change his ways (Luke 15:17-20).

So after the drama, what? Take action. The son went to his father with the right attitude—repentant, willing to serve, and humble.

When God gets your attention in a dramatic way, it may be because he expects a dramatic action plan and wants to work a dramatic life change.

However, follow-up is the key. Make a phone call and ask for help. Write a letter to someone who is a leader in the field. Send an e-mail to your friends and family asking for prayer or counsel. God didn't move heaven and earth for you to just sit and ponder—do something!

By taking action, you may see some dramatic positive results, too! Saul was struck to the ground when Jesus appeared and called him, but he didn't stay on the road where Jesus appeared—he got up. And the change in him produced the greatest apostle of Christianity, Paul (Acts 9).

TO READ
Psalm 73:23-28

I still belong to you; you are holding my right hand.

PSALM 73:23

 ## *It's a Simple Thing*

Women carry so much guilt about feeling they don't share Jesus enough. My encouragement is simply to take Jesus with you wherever you go. Take my friend Julie:

> While sitting in the doctor's office, I was reading *Just Give Me Jesus,* and there was an older woman sitting across from me whom I believe was a cancer treatment patient. She asked me what I was reading. I shared some information about the book, and she asked if I was a believer. I said yes. Then she proceeded to tell me that she once had believed until her sister passed away at a young age. She said that her sister had been good and gone to church, but that God struck her down with cancer and she passed away. She said that she gave up then and has since lived a miserable life. She conveyed that she was angry at God, and I just spoke to her with empathy but explained what I had come to realize about God's grace and his love in my own life. By the time our conversation was over, she had made a decision to go back and seek the Lord. It was an incredible moment to see the change in her demeanor in such a short time.

What Julie thought was a doctor's appointment ended up being a divine appointment.

Think of Jesus being with you everywhere you go, like a best friend who is a traveling companion. You'll have opportunities to introduce him naturally.

God has your appointment book already filled.

DECEMBER 25

TO READ
Matthew 6:5-15

Don't be like them, because your Father knows
exactly what you need even before you ask him!

MATTHEW 6:8

 Touched by an Angel

An angelic visitation announced the birth of two very important people:
Jesus and John, the one who prepared the way for Jesus. However, the way
the angelic message was received was very different.

Zechariah was doubtful and asked, "How can I be sure?" The angel picked
up on the unbelief. Zechariah was a priest, an older, mature leader—yet he
had doubts. The angel rebuked him, and Zechariah's unbelief was
silenced—for the entire pregnancy!

Mary was young, very young. She was afraid, like Zechariah. She also had
a question: "How will this be?" But the angel didn't punish her for the question. Why?

Zechariah knew better. He had represented God for years. Zechariah
was asking for proof—and God had given him all kinds of proof in the
Scriptures. Zechariah was another Abraham-and-Sarah story, a story he
knew well.

Mary believed but wanted to know how it was going to happen because
nothing like this had ever happened before.

Has God given you a promise, a promise with proof? Are you still stalling
on carrying out the promise? Are you asking God for more and more proof
so you don't have to walk by faith?

Choose Mary's heart—believe, then ask God, "How?" How do you want
me to react? How do you want me to go forward? How to you want me to
step out in faith?

TO READ
Psalm 23:1-6

You prepare a feast for me in the presence of my enemies. You welcome me as a guest, anointing my head with oil. My cup overflows with blessings.

PSALM 23:5

 ## *Top It Off*

When you allow God to strengthen you and ignite your heart, you gain strength to share. He fills you up, and out of the overflow of your life, other lives are changed.

This thank-you note from Robin to her sister is an example:

Dear Sis:

Wendy, I see God in you. You are the one person who has helped me make the changes I needed. You and your husband delivered me out of a bad situation. You gave me more support—emotional, financial, and spiritual—than I ever expected. You gave me a job, and at that job I met my husband.

Once again, Wendy and Gabe, you are helping us as you are putting a roof over our heads while we build our home. I would not be as good of a mother as I am to Kendall if I hadn't seen a great mom in action! I am grateful for everything you have done for me. I am different because of you. God bless you.

Your sister,

Robin

How many thank-you notes would you like to see in your lifetime? Changed lives are a result of allowing God to continually change you.

My mom used to tell the gas station attendant to "top it off," meaning keep the tank filled to the brim. Fill up on God, and let his light and love overflow to the world around you.

TO READ
Ecclesiastes 3:1-8

There is a time for everything, a season for every activity under heaven. ECCLESIASTES 3:1

 Spending Time

If time were currency, how has yours been spent? If God looked at your checkbook, your PDA, or daily planner, what would he see are your priorities?

How we spend our time reflects our priorities. If you have experienced calling, your daily life should match the passion and plan God gave.

Is that how you are spending your time? If God called you to write, how much time do you spend writing? If God called you to teach, how much time are you teaching, training, and preparing? If God called you to launch a business, how much time are you actually putting into getting it off the ground? Or has your life swung the opposite direction? Or have all your thoughts, day and night, been only business, causing you to forget priorities like loving your husband or talking with your children?

Keep a time log this week. When lawyers or accountants work, they keep a meticulous time log, accounting for each minute of time they spend on a certain case or client. Keep track of how you spend your time for seven days, and see if your life is truly reflecting your passion and priorities.

TO READ
Galatians 6:1-10

Share each other's troubles and problems, and in this way obey the law of Christ. GALATIANS 6:2

 Sistering

There is strength in numbers!

"Those in the building trades use the word *sistering* to describe the process of nailing one board to another in order to strengthen the first. In joining two boards side-by-side, both pieces become stronger. The "sistered" boards now can bear a heavier load because they benefit from each other's strength."[1]

How can you find "sisters?" Search places like Bible studies, committees where you work for common goals and beliefs, or friends who have children or husbands at the same age or stage of life.

What can you do to build a sister bond? Host a girlfriend getaway for a week or just one night. Enjoy common activities: creating scrapbooks, hiking, boating, or reading—just about any activity will work. Or take a trip together to a women's conference, a tourist attraction, or a spa. Hearts open up with time and travel. The best sistering is honest sharing and praying.

"The more friends you have, the healthier you are. However, this effect is due almost exclusively to the degree to which you have talked with your friends about any traumas that you have suffered. But here's the kicker. If you have had trauma that you have not talked about with anyone, the number of friends you have is unrelated to your health. (Social support only protects your health if you use it wisely.)"[2]

Plan a girlfriend getaway. Look for ways to encourage conversations—you'll all go away feeling stronger.

TO READ
John 12:20-28

The truth is, a kernel of wheat must be planted in the soil. Unless it dies it will be alone—a single seed. But its death will produce many new kernels—a plentiful harvest of new lives.

JOHN 12:24

 ## Pretty Good Company

I was worshiping one day at a friend's church. Bill and I were at her church because he had a health issue that made it impossible for him to continue leading both the church ministry and our parachurch writing and speaking ministry. Our own congregation had just completed a new building. Fifteen years of work, sacrifice, and love had gone into those walls and, even more, into those people. I sat in my friend's church that morning, broken. During a worship song, I prayed, *God, Bill is such a good man, such a godly man, such a great teacher and shepherd. This is just so hard. Bill preached on the life of Moses to move the church from temporary facilities, through the building project, and into our "promise land" building. But like Moses, we didn't get to enter it. Lord, I feel like David, who gathered all the goods for the Temple but knew that his son Solomon would build it. I feel like Stephen, who was stoned so early in the book of Acts, that he never saw the church and its power.*

Then the Holy Spirit seemed to whisper to me, *Moses . . . David . . . Stephen . . . That seems like pretty good company, the kind of people you have always prayed I'd make you two.* Moses, a patriarch of Israel, was prepared specifically by God to move his treasured people into freedom. David, a man after God's own heart, was often seen as Israel's greatest king. Stephen was the first Christian martyr.

Then I thought of today's verse: "A kernel of wheat must be planted in the soil. Unless it dies . . ." *Dies. Lord, this does feel like death, the death of a dream.* Then the Holy Spirit reminded me, *But its death will produce many new kernels.* In my mind, I took the dream of the ministry I thought we would have, placed it in the ground like a seed, and prayed, *God give us the new harvest, the new fruit you have for us.* Is God waiting for you to let go of an old dream so that he can give you a new one?

TO READ
Genesis 2:18-24

"She is part of my own flesh and bone! She will be called 'woman,' because she was taken out of a man." This explains why a man leaves his father and mother and is joined to his wife, and the two are united into one. GENESIS 2:23-24

 ## Run Back Home

A wonderfully wise woman shared a story of her own daughter:

> Kathleen didn't like me much that day. I think she thought I'd take her side. I think she assumed I would sit and cry with her and join her in criticizing her new husband—but that's not what I did. He hadn't hit her. He wasn't a drunk. He wasn't addicted to drugs, gambling, or porn. He simply didn't let her have her way, and she felt slighted. She got angry, packed a bag, and came home. I gave her a cup of coffee, heard the story, and then picked up her suitcase and walked back to her car.
>
> "What are you doing?" Kathleen said.
>
> "I am sending you back home."
>
> "I don't want to go."
>
> "Then you can stay at a hotel, but you can't stay here. You made a vow before God to work it out; now go work it out."

Genesis 2:24-25 makes the priorities clear—marriage first, in-laws second. The principle is true for the newlyweds and for the in-laws. We have to let our adult children leave—emotionally, not just physically.

The reason is clear: "They will become one flesh. The man and his wife were both naked, and they felt no shame" (NIV).

Strong emotional and sexual bonds create a strong new family. Paul, in Ephesians 5, teaches that a marriage reflects the relationship between Christ (the bridegroom) and the church (his bride). It is a relationship of purity and complete commitment. Therefore, we must help our children and ourselves take seriously the relationship sanctioned by God.

TO READ
Hebrews 6:11-19

Our great desire is that you will keep right on loving others as long as life lasts, in order to make certain that what you hope for will come true.

HEBREWS 6:11

 Diligence Delivers

Last year my son met a friend on his college football team, Nigel, who had to commute to college from a city over an hour away. Because he had to take public transportation, during the summer practice schedule he had to get up at 3 A.M. and didn't get home until well after 9 P.M.

He never complained. It took until the end of the season for word to spread through the team because Nigel just quietly did what he needed to do. At the end of the season his teammates voted him Most Inspirational, and every person in that room wanted to do whatever they could to help him succeed in the future.

Some verses about diligence illustrate the commitment and follow-through of my son's friend Nigel:

- Work hard and become a leader; be lazy and become a slave. (Proverbs 12:24)
- Good planning and hard work lead to prosperity. (Proverbs 21:5)
- Do you see any truly competent workers? They will serve kings rather than ordinary people. (Proverbs 22:29)

How diligent are you? Are you working hard in the place God has called you?

NOTES

January

1. JoAnn's comments were recorded in a personal interview, August 18, 1998.

February

1. *One to One Discipleship* (Vista, Calif.: Church Dynamics, n.d.), 24.
2. Stephen Arterburn, *Flashpoints: Igniting the Hidden Passions of Your Soul* (Wheaton, Ill.: Tyndale, 2002), 152.
3. Quoted on the Focus on the Family Web site: http://www.family.org/pastor/faq/a0011323.html.
4. Phil Newman, "Go with the Flo-Jo," *Aspire,* June/July 1996, 24.
5. Judith Viorst, *Alexander and the Terrible, Horrible, No Good, Very Bad Day* (New York: Aladdin, 1987).
6. Oswald Chambers, *My Utmost for His Highest* (Uhrichsville, Ohio: Barbour, n.d.), March 17.

April

1. Proverbs 3:25-26 paraphrased.
2. Ephesians 3:12 paraphrased.
3. Philippians 1:6 paraphrased.
4. Hebrews 4:16 paraphrased.
5. 1 John 5:14-15 paraphrased.
6. Hebrews 6:9 paraphrased.

July

1. Author unknown. Quoted from Elizabeth George, *Beautiful in God's Eyes* (Eugene, Ore.: Harvest House, 1988), 210.

August

1. *The American Heritage Dictionary of the English Language,* 4th ed., s.v. "synergy."
2. *Merriam-Webster's Collegiate Dictionary,* 11th ed., s.v. "need."
3. W. Bingham Hunter, *The God Who Hears* (Downers Grove, Ill.: InterVarsity Press, 1986), 18.
4. Hunter, *The God Who Hears,* 20.
5. Hunter, *The God Who Hears,* 26.
6. Hunter, *The God Who Hears,* 23.
7. Bill Bright, *God: Discover His Character* (Orlando, Fla.: New Life Publications, 1999), 131.
8. Nathan Stone, *The Names of God in the Old Testament* (Chicago: Moody Press, 1944), 97.
9. Stone, *The Names of God,* 99.

September

1. Dean Ornish, *Love and Survival: The Scientific Basis for the Healing Power of Intimacy* (New York: HarperCollins, 1998), 94.

2. Ornish, *Love and Survival,* 95.

3. Os Guinness, *The Call: Finding and Fulfilling the Central Purpose of Your Life* (Nashville: W Publishing Group, 1998), 43.

4. Guinness, *The Call,* 20.

5. Archibald Hart, *Adrenaline and Stress* (Dallas: Word, 1995), 138.

6. Pam Farrel and Sandy Clough, *Hats Off to You!* (Eugene, Ore.: Harvest House, 1999), 11.

7. Based on information taken from Sheila Y. Flemming, "Bethune-Cookman College 1904–1994: The Answered Prayer to a Dream," http://www.cookman.edu/Welcome/Founder/Default.html.

8. Sally Conway, *Menopause* (Grand Rapids: Pyranee, 1990), 39.

9. "Vegetarian Times: New Hope for PMS," http://www.findarticles.com/m0820/n247/20380025/p1/article.jhtml.

10. John Nicholson, *Men and Women: How Different Are They?* (Oxford: Oxford University Press, 1984), 39.

11. John Robinson and Geoffrey Godbey, *Time for Life: The Surprising Ways Americans Use Their Time* (University Park, Penn.: PSU Press, 1997), 231.

12. Robinson and Godbey, *Time for Life,* xvii.

13. Patsy Clairmont, ed., et al., *Joy Breaks* (Grand Rapids: Zondervan, 1997), 241.

14. Robinson and Godbey, *Time for Life,* 110.

15. Josh McDowell, *The New Evidence That Demands a Verdict* (Nashville: Nelson, 1999), 338.

16. McDowell, *New Evidence,* 338.

October

1. J. I. Packer, *Knowing God* (Downers Grove, Ill.: InterVarsity, 2002), 42.

2. Packer, *Knowing God,* 337.

3. Packer, *Knowing God,* 338.

4. Excerpt from Pam Farrel, *A Woman God Can Use* (Eugene, Ore.: Harvest House, 1999).

5. Excerpt from Farrel, *A Woman God Can Use,* 70–71.

6. Excerpt from Farrel, *A Woman God Can Use.*

7. Excerpt from Farrel, *A Woman God Can Use.*

8. Excerpt from Farrel, *A Woman God Can Use,* 14.

9. Gary McIntosh & Samuel D. Rima, Sr., *Overcoming the Dark Side of Leadership: The Paradox of Personal Dysfunction* (Grand Rapids: Baker, 1997), 11–12.

10. Psalm 97:10.

11. Proverbs 1:10.

12. Daniel 6:3.

13. John 17:15.

14. Romans 12:1-2.

15. 1 Corinthians 6:18-19.

16. 2 Corinthians 6:14.

17. James 4:7. This paragraph is taken from Pam Farrel, *Celebrate! I Made a Big Decision: Creating A Spiritual Scrapbook with Your Son* (Colorado Springs: Chariot Victor, 2000).

18. Josh McDowell, *Evidence That Demands a Verdict* (San Bernardino, Calif.: Here's Life Publishers, 1979), 16.

19. McDowell, *Evidence,* 34.

20. Norman L. Geisler and William E. Nix, *A General Introduction to the Bible* (Chicago: Moody Press, 1986), 386.

21. Annie Dillard, *Pilgrim at Tinker Creek* (New York: Harper & Row, 1985), 269.

22. Dillard, *Pilgrim at Tinker Creek,* 33.

23. John Robinson and Geoffrey Godbey, *Time for Life: The Surprising Ways Americans Use Their Time* (University Park, Pa.: PSU Press, 1997), 44.

24. Os Guinness, *The Call: Finding and Fulfilling the Central Purpose of Your Life* (Nashville: W Publishing Group, 1998), 46.

25. Excerpt from Pam Farrel, *A Woman God Can Use* (Eugene, Ore.: Harvest House, 1999).

26. Excerpt from Farrel, *A Woman God Can Use.*

27. Excerpt from Farrel, *A Woman God Can Use.*

28. Kevin Markey, *100 Most Important Women of the 20th Century,* ed. Lorraine Glennon (Des Moines, Iowa: Ladies' Home Journal Books, 1998), 113.

November

1. Adapted from Pam Farrel, *A Woman God Can Use* (Eugene, Ore.: Harvest House, 1999), 11(13.

2. *Merriam-Webster's Collegiate Dictionary,* 11th ed., s.v. "dishonor."

3. http://www.m-w.com/cgi-bin/dictionary.

4. http://www.detnews.com/2002/nation/0211/16/nation-12044.htm.

5. http://www.detnews.com/2002/nation/0211/16/nation-12044.htm.

6. http://www.projectreality.org.

7. http://www.atfstandup.com/index.cfm?fuseaction=events.speakers&tac=3.

December

1. Kathleen Laing and Elizabeth Butterfield, "Need a Getaway?" *Today's Christian Woman,* May/June 2002, 45.

2. James W. Pennebaker, *Opening Up: The Healing Power of Confiding in Others* (New York: William Morrow, 1990), 118–119.

REFERENCE INDEX

Isaiah 43:1-4	May 10	Matthew 17:1-9	June 27
Isaiah 43:1-7	February 7	Matthew 17:14-20	July 9
Isaiah 43:18-21	May 8	Matthew 18:2-6	June 24
Isaiah 48:12-19	July 27	Matthew 19:16-24	September 10
Isaiah 57:12-14	February 29, September 15	Matthew 26:36-41	January 19
		Mark 2:1-12	May 13
Jeremiah 17:5-10	October 31	Mark 5:1-19	October 1
Jeremiah 20:7-9	August 15	Mark 6:7-13	July 22
Jeremiah 24:6-7	January 24	Mark 6:30-44	July 17
Jeremiah 29:11-14	March 13	Mark 9:17-29	January 11
Jeremiah 31:1-6	November 27	Mark 10:13-16	August 23
Jeremiah 32:17-20	March 28	Mark 10:35-45	April 17
		Mark 12:28-34	March 24
Lamentations 3:22-27	July 6	Mark 14:3-9	May 18
Lamentations 3:28-33	August 1	Mark 16:15-18	January 12
Ezekiel 18:25-32	July 31	Luke 1:39-45	April 3
Ezekiel 34:11-16	June 2	Luke 2:41-49	September 20
Ezekiel 34:25-31	September 18	Luke 5:17-26	February 13
Ezekiel 36:22-27	April 9	Luke 6:27-36	January 10
		Luke 6:36-42	July 5
Hosea 2:2-20	November 21	Luke 10:25-37	April 13
Hosea 2:18-23	November 22	Luke 12:4-12	March 29
Hosea 11:1-4	December 12	Luke 12:22-34	May 30
		Luke 12:42-48	January 5
Joel 1:13-15	September 2	Luke 13:10-13	June 22
Joel 2:12-17	August 31	Luke 15:1-7	September 13
Joel 2:28-32	November 23	Luke 15:3-10	July 23
		Luke 15:8-24	December 23
Zephaniah 3:14-17	June 30	Luke 17:1-4	January 23
		Luke 19:1-10	September 21
Matthew 5:11-16	October 5	Luke 19:11-26	July 16
Matthew 5:13-16	December 10	Luke 22:1-6	May 22
Matthew 5:21-26	January 22	Luke 22:31-39	July 11
Matthew 5:33-37	January 28	Luke 22:39-46	July 10
Matthew 6:5-15	December 25		
Matthew 6:9-15	October 29	John 4:34-38	April 26
Matthew 6:19-21	August 28	John 8:31-47	April 22
Matthew 6:25-34	January 30	John 9:1-11	October 16
Matthew 7:6	May 21	John 11:38-44	November 1
Matthew 7:7-12	February 21	John 12:20-28	December 29
Matthew 9:18-29	April 25	John 12:23-28	June 26
Matthew 9:27-31	February 4	John 14:15-21	October 2
Matthew 13:44-52	May 7	John 15:1-11	September 22
Matthew 14:22-32	May 19	John 17:20-26	September 1

1 Timothy 3:8-15	December 17
1 Timothy 4:4-10	October 27
1 Timothy 5:3-4, 8, 16	November 4
1 Timothy 5:17-21	July 12
2 Timothy 1:5-7	June 12
2 Timothy 2:1-10	January 17
2 Timothy 2:23-26	August 17
2 Timothy 3:14-17	October 17
Titus 1:5-9	December 16
Titus 2:3-5	March 8, December 21
Titus 3:9-11	November 7
Hebrews 4:6-11	November 14
Hebrews 6:9-12	April 8
Hebrews 6:11-19	December 31
Hebrews 10:19-25	October 30
Hebrews 10:32-36	June 11
Hebrews 11:1-40	April 28
Hebrews 11:1-3	June 14
Hebrews 12:1-4	March 15
Hebrews 12:10-13	November 6
James 1:2-5	April 20
James 1:5-8	April 29
James 1:6-8	May 20
James 1:12-18	March 10
James 1:21-27	September 3
James 2:14-20	July 21
James 3:13-18	December 5
James 4:7-10	January 9
James 5:13-20	January 16
1 Peter 1:13-16	August 27
1 Peter 1:21-25	November 26
1 Peter 2:18-25	September 24
1 Peter 3:8-12	July 8
1 Peter 3:13-18	October 25
1 Peter 4:1-8	October 7
1 Peter 4:7-11	April 6
1 Peter 4:10-13	June 23
1 Peter 5:6-11	January 6
2 Peter 1:3-11	February 2
2 Peter 1:15-21	October 28
2 Peter 3:13-18	January 13
1 John 2:15-17	May 15
1 John 3:11-13	August 14
1 John 5:1-5	April 1
2 John 1:1-13	May 25
Revelation 2:2-5	February 22
Revelation 7:9-12	September 4
Revelation 17:3-14	August 3